The Grammar of Systems
From Order to Chaos & Back

The Grammar of Systems
From Order to Chaos & Back

Patrick Hoverstadt

Cover painting: Norman Stevens RA
Illustrations: Jonathan Rogers & Patrick Hoverstadt

SCiO Publications
Edited by Lucy Loh
© Patrick Hoverstadt 2022
All rights reserved
ISBN 9798414307754

Contents
Introduction   1

Part 1
How to think like a systems thinker (a systemist's grimoire)

1. Emergence   13
2. Holism   25
3. Modelling   37
4. Boundaries   50
5. Difference   61
6. Relating   73
7. Dynamics and loops   83
8. Complexity   93
9. Uncertainty   107

Part 2
The Grammar of Systems

10. The Laws as a Whole – Order to Chaos to Order   125
11. 33 Systems Laws and Principles   130
12. How to use Systems Laws – splicing   194
13. The Laws and Methodologies   208
14. A Miscellany of Systems ideas   214

The Grammar of Systems
33 Systems Laws and Principles

Law of Calling — 130
Difference creates boundaries and boundaries create difference

Viability Principle — 132
A system's viability depends on how well it can balance autonomy with cohesion and stability with change over time

Homeostasis Principle — 134
A system will be stable if all its key variables remain within their physiological limits

System Stability Principle — 136
Systems are patterns that are recognisable over several observations

Law of Requisite Variety — 138
How well any system manages depends on how well it matches the variety it faces

1st Circular Causality Principle — 140
Positive feedback drives state change

2nd Circular Causality Principle — 142
Negative feedback drives stability

The Law of Crossing — 144
Crossing a boundary is a change of state

Network Power Law — 146
Structural complexity goes up exponentially with the number of elements

System Survival Theorem — 148
Systems fail if their environment changes more than the system

System Resonance Principle — 150
Resonance occurs because of similarities in systems

Power Structuration Theorem — 152
A system has optimal agency when its needs for agency are balanced with those of its sub-systems

Conservation of Adaptation Principle — 154
Change is the only constant in the relationship between a system and its environment

Darkness Principle — 156
There is always something about a system you can't know.

Adams 3rd Law — 158
A system's overall risk depends on balancing the risk across levels of the system

Self-organised Criticality   160
Systems whose dynamics drive the system to collapse
Complexity Instability Principle   162
Systems with too many changing parts tend to become unstable
Order Osmosis Principle   164
Sub-systems migrate from less ordered to more ordered systems
The Two Black Box Principles   166
The outputs of a black box are predictable
Self-Organising Principle   168
Parts generate wholes
Law of Reciprocity of Connections   170
If 'A' connects to 'B', then 'B' also connects to 'A'
Redundancy of Potential Command Principle   172
Your ability to be effective in a complex situation depends on bringing together the right mix of information.
Root Structuration Theorem   174
Structuring a system to have the same number of sub-systems at each level reduces its complexity
Structural Viability Theorem   176
A system has optimal viability when its change rate / environmental change rate is similar to that of its sub-systems
Steady State Principle   178
Stability of the system depends on the level of stability of its sub-systems and vice versa
Law of Sufficient Complexity   180
The system does what it does because it is what it is
Fractal Principle   182
Systems replicate their own form
Relaxation Time Principle   184
A system that is repeatedly shocked at shorter intervals than its recovery time may never stabilize
Scaling Stasis Principle   186
The more complex a system is, the more constraints it has
Conant-Ashby Theorem   188
The ability to deal with any situation depends on how good your model of it is
Feedback Dominance Theorem   190
Loops with strong feedback will take you where they take you, irrespective of the size of the input
Principle of Emergence   192
The whole is more than the sum of its parts

Acknowledgements

This book has been a long time in the making and thanks are due firstly to those who have been actively involved in helping in it: Lucy Loh and Jonathan Rogers; my thanks to them, not just for their hard work, but also for their patience. For advice on the publishing process, thanks are also due to Steve Hales and Jan de Visch of SCiO and Steve Morlidge.

Part of the reason this has been such a long process is that it's the fruit of quite a lot of archaeological excavation – many of the Laws and Principles that make up the second half of the book have had to be disinterred and that has taken quite some time.

The real authors of much of the thinking in the Grammar are of course the pioneers of Systems Thinking. First, from the 'pre-history of systems' in the 19th & early 20th centuries there's James Clerk Maxwell (father of modern physics), G.H. Lewes and Jan Smuts (founder of the League of Nations and the UN and the only person to have signed the peace treaties of both world wars). Next from the era of the Macey Conferences: Norbert Weiner (father of Cybernetics), Warren McCulloch (father of neural networks), John von Neumann (father of Game Theory, Cellular Automata and much else), Ross Ashby – a great developer and codifier of theory, Gregory Bateson who seemed to create breakthroughs in every field he entered – of which there were too many to list here, and Margaret Mead who was first to talk about second order cybernetics. Then came the practical methodologists: Jay Forrester, Stafford Beer, Peter Checkland. Russ Ackoff and William Powers. Finally, another generation of theorists: Spencer-Brown and the Chileans Humberto Maturana, Francisco Varela and Roger Harnden.

I am indebted to them all and if I have distorted, misrepresented their ideas, then the fault is mine. But this is not just a dry archive of dusty and forgotten ideas. Both parts of this book are about how I use the ideas in the field, so some licence is due, and I hope acceptable.

Finally, thanks to all the practitioners out there, who have been asking *"so when will the laws book be ready?"* Well, here you are, and I hope you find it as useful as I have.

Introduction

Once upon a time, everyone knew that the earth was flat. Well, almost everyone. And that was fine. Even in the 21st century, you can go through your entire life without ever having to deal with the fact that it's round. Intellectually of course people 'know' the world is round, but that's just an idea, it has almost nothing to do with how they live their lives. In their everyday existence, the world is flat and in our embodied consciousness it's flat – we behave as if it's flat. For what most of us do most of the time, it really doesn't matter whether you believe the world is flat or round, it doesn't create any navigational problems that would stop you getting to the shops.

Systems Thinking is a bit like believing that the world is round rather than flat. And just like flat-earthism, lots of people try to take on systems thinking whilst still really living in a non-systemic paradigm. For a time, that works for them, so they can pay lip-service to systems ideas, but actually think non-systemically, but sooner or later, there is a clash. For flat-earthers, it comes when you try to sail round the world – which wouldn't work so well if the world was flat – and so you have to start to live round-earthness. For systems thinkers, it tends to spring up unexpectedly and trip you up.

So, part of the reason for writing this book is to help people who are interested in systems to walk through some of the differences in thinking, to become more familiar with this as a way of thought, to learn what living on a round earth is actually like and how it differs from living on a flat earth and to be able to recognise systems thinking in themselves and others when they see and hear it.

The need for clarity or The Hunting of the Snark?
I can't remember how often I have seen people who claim to be systems thinkers debating what systems thinking is. And to a novice, the sight of people who count themselves as experts in the field arguing about what the field is must be bewildering – surely it speaks of incompetence of the individuals or of the immaturity of the field. If the people in it don't know what Systems Thinking is, then maybe it isn't anything at all, they

Introduction

could (and do) argue. And, of course, there is some justification for that. The natural tendency then is to define the field and here we hit our first snag. Because the way that those striving for clarity generally try to go about the task of defining Systems Thinking is by doing a definition. Which would be fine, except that Systems Thinking isn't one thing, and so isn't susceptible to definition in that way. As soon as you try to define it as one thing, someone will pop up and point out that your definition excludes something else that has an equal right to be called Systems Thinking. It isn't even like the old story of the six blind men and the elephant where one describes the elephant with reference to the trunk, one with reference to the ear, another by describing the tail and so on, because you can't really have an elephant without a trunk – which is kind of the point of the story. Systems Thinking isn't like that because it isn't a single thought pattern. There is no single way of thinking that is 'Systems Thinking'. There are several aspects to it.

And so to this book, which is a personal view of the thinking habits or patterns of thinking that systems thinkers use. And it is personal because, others may - and undoubtedly will – disagree. That's fine, let's have the debate.

The way I have set out in this book to define the field is not by doing a dictionary definition, for two reasons. First, that would work if and only if we were talking about a single thing rather than a collection of different thinking patterns and second, because in systems thinking that's not how we go about things. Etymologically, the word 'define' means 'of the edge' so 'setting the limit of'. Setting the edge – the boundary – of a system is a classic Systems Thinking exercise. Boundary setting is important in Systems because it tells us what is inside and what is outside the system we're interested in. What is inside is a set of elements or components of the system, and critically the relationships between them, and outside the boundary is the environment of the system. In Systems Thinking the word 'environment' has a technical meaning and refers to what is outside the boundary of the system, which acts on the system and is acted on by it. The approach I have taken in this book is to define Systems Thinking not using a definition, but by seeking to sketch out what I see as the boundary of the territory and doing that by reference to some of the principal thinking elements within the boundary, how these connect

Introduction

together and how they are different to other ways of thinking that sit outside of the boundary. In other words, I am going to try to describe Systems Thinking as a system of thinking and I'm going to try to do it by using systems thinking.

To some extent, there is some justification to the claim of immaturity of the field since different people genuinely do take very different views on what is and what isn't Systems Thinking. The 'problem' of differences of view comes about partly because the field *is* immature – it is still growing albeit in a different way than at the beginning. At the beginning, there was what I think can best be characterised as an explosion of thinking and most if not all of the thinking approaches in this book came from that initial period. As time went on, a second generation of systems thinkers started to formalise this into a set of approaches and methodologies and people concentrated on what their particular tool set allowed them to do.

And so the field spread out as systems approaches got taken into more and more areas of application – from organisation to neuro-science to biology to sociology to ecology, to computing to psychotherapy and so on and so on. With this spread, three things happened.

First, people applying systems approaches tended to lose sight of Systems Thinking principles as the methodology overtook and became a substitute for the concepts and laws generated in the early thinking. If the relevant ideas were encapsulated in a methodology, then there was apparently no need to go back to the raw concept, we could just follow the method. Second, people working in these fields forgot that what they were doing was systems thinking; the success of a field almost inevitably meant the attribution to the source of the thinking became lost, so it wasn't just that people working in these fields stopped thinking using core Systems Thinking disciplines, they also lost sight of the fact that their very domain had in some cases been built from Systems Thinking. The goose that had been so prolific at laying eggs got forgotten. The third thing that happened was that different fields of study and practice lost sight of one another. For example, in the US where Jay Forrester had developed System Dynamics at MIT, Systems Dynamics became synonymous with Systems Thinking and people started to assume that they were the same

Introduction

thing, in ignorance of both the roots of Systems Thinking and the rich diversity of other approaches that had been developed elsewhere.

As the field spread, the coherence of the field was lost and it seemed that the more successful an approach, the faster it lost its roots in the core thinking. I think it is worth asking 'does it matter?', does it matter if the basis of Systems Thinking is lost? After all, it's a natural process for concepts to be supplanted by methodologies to be supplanted by methods as approaches become more widely available. Well, I think it really does matter, so for me this isn't an academic issue about what we do or don't think Systems Thinking is. It matters for three reasons.

First of all, it matters because if we lose the source of systems thinking, we have no way to tap into it to do new things. The systems approaches that we have got have been developed for particular uses, so if we want to develop new approaches for new uses then we need to go back to the core of systems thinking as an approach. We need to be able to get to the taproot.

In 2008, the financial system crashed. I have lost count of the number of supposedly informed and influential people who have told me that this was an unprecedented and totally unpredictable event. This is nonsense. This crisis was but the latest in a long series of financial collapses and it was predicted not just by conspiracy theorists, but by respected commentators who talked freely about the imminent bursting of credit bubbles and the toxicity of sub-prime mortgages. The crash was predictable and was predicted and was just one more data point in a repeating pattern. After the crash, Queen Elizabeth asked economists in the UK why they had not seen this coming and they had no answer and still have not come up with an answer – probably they've forgotten the question was ever asked, or at least hope the rest of us have forgotten. The reason how and why the financial system crashed is easily explained using Systems Thinking and is predictable. But the real point is this: the economic models that we use to run our economies and our societies are fundamentally flawed and drive us to collapse repeatedly. And we stick with them because – well, because there is no credible alternative. If we wanted to build an alternative that was systemically sound, then you don't get there using systems methodologies that were designed for other

Introduction

purposes, you have to go back to first principles. And that is why first principles are important, that is what they are for.

The second reason that keeping sight of the core of Systems Thinking matters is because this way of thinking can be extremely powerful. One of the highest leverage things you can do in any problem situation is to change the paradigm you use to understand the situation and within which the problem exists. In many, many cases, Systems Thinking provides you with a completely different way of seeing the situation which – once you understand it – you can tap into whenever you need it. It will almost always provide fresh insights and usually fresh options for changing things. Systems Thinking is a mental toolkit for doing really heavy lifting.

The third reason relates to the second. In building systems methodologies, some aspects of core concepts have been incorporated, but these are hidden from view. They tend to get wrapped into procedure – you model a situation in this way or in this order rather than some other way. But the reason why you do it in that order gets lost. Procedurally, practitioners may or may not go through the prescribed procedure that says 'now think of this', but they may not – because they've lost sight of why that was important. But even if they do continue to follow a thinking procedure that they don't quite understand, they may not actually do the thinking. It's the difference between blindly using a systems methodology that was designed by a systems thinker, and actually being a systems thinker. And these are not the same thing. Following methodology, no matter how good, can only get you so far. Systems Thinking requires you to actually think in a different way.

Recently this problem has got a bit more acute. Some people coming new to systems have adopted the 'Great Model Collider' approach. This involves taking the easy bits of a number of systems approaches and smashing them together in the hope that they will somehow work as a coherent approach. Typically, this might use the easy bits of Soft Systems Methodology such as a rich picture, but ignore the hard bits of SSM, take the easy bits of System Dynamics – a causal loop diagram and a casual dusting of archetypes, but missing out the hard bits like actually having to build a stocks and flows model, chuck in a stakeholder model (but not a

Introduction

difficult one like CATWOE or TASCOI) and whisk those together with some facilitation and voila! Without a strong grounding in the roots of Systems Thinking, it's easy to miss the point of the whole exercise.

A way of thinking

I've talked about this as a set of concepts, and for sure there are concepts in there, but really, Systems Thinking is a way of thinking. It involves thinking in a different way to the conventional and if you've been trained in conventional thinking then it means learning different thinking skills. And here is a real problem, because most of us are not conscious of our thinking patterns. We think as we breathe. It's automatic, the neurons fire in repeating patterns and follow familiar trackways through the brain (and we know this thanks to the work of veteran systems pioneers: Warren McCulloch, Walter Pitts and Lorente de Nó – the people who first mapped and named neural networks). The emotions respond in waves to stimuli that are familiar or not and can overwhelm the thinking patterns. And all this goes on for the most part without us being aware of why we think what we do, what the pattern of thought was, why we used that thought pattern or how we got to the conclusions or indecision we did.

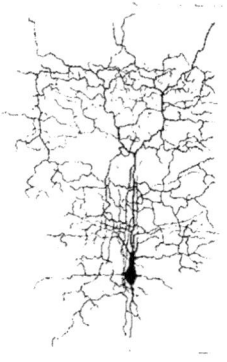

Lorente de Nó drawing of a neural network in the cerebral cortex.

For the most part, the patterns we follow when we say we are thinking are patterns that have been used repeatedly, patterns we have learnt and used again and again. The sad truth is that most of us most of the time don't actually think at all, we just run learnt response patterns. Mostly these have come from people long dead – we mostly think the thought of dead people. As Keynes said: *"Practical men, who believe themselves to be quite exempt from any intellectual influence, are usually the slaves of some defunct economist"*.

And so for the purposes of this book, the problem of learning to think like a systems thinker starts with recognition, with awareness of what is

Introduction

going on inside us and then starting to consciously experiment with alternatives.

The structure of the book - thinking patterns & systems laws

The book is split into two parts — a 'grimoire' and a 'grammar'. The grimoire is, if you like, a personal notebook about nine thinking patterns with a short chapter on each.

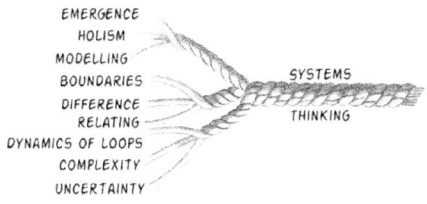

EMERGENCE
HOLISM
MODELLING
BOUNDARIES
DIFFERENCE
RELATING
DYNAMICS OF LOOPS
COMPLEXITY
UNCERTAINTY

SYSTEMS
THINKING

Each can be learned and practiced as a thinking discipline in its own right. Putting these together in combinations when looking at situations, moves us towards doing Systems Thinking. The grimoire is about the thinking processes and patterns of Systems Thinking – it's about the properties of the thinker, whereas the Grammar is about the properties of systems that the systems thinker is thinking about.

As well as being a way of thinking about the world, Systems is a discipline in its own right and has a number of laws and theorems. Many of these have proofs in maths or logic and they form a hard structure for the discipline and a hard skeleton of linked concepts around which the more flexible thinking disciplines can act. The Grammar lists 33 of these laws, principles and theorems. I've also taken some of these laws and applied them to a couple of problem situations to show how quickly and easily they can be used to unlock new insights. Although some of them do have mathematical proofs, you don't need maths to understand them or in most cases to apply them.

This book is an attempt to see systems as a self-referencing system of thought. All true disciplines, from physics to the law, are built as self-referencing systems with the same characteristics. There is a set of underlying principles that are derived from a knowledge-building loop between theory and practice. At the start, every situation encountered is different and has to be treated as unique, but gradually patterns emerge and first the recognition of repeating patterns and then capturing those and encoding them as theory and practices forms the basis for a body of

Introduction

knowledge and of professional competence. By testing theory in practice – in a range of different situations – the theory is developed to the point where it can be used across different areas of application. Knowledge and experience become transportable and sharable, it's no longer an individual's insight about a particular situation, it's a group's insight about a generic type of situation that we can observe repeatedly playing out. And that means that we don't always have to re-invent the wheel, we can reuse and build on prior learning. Practice encapsulates aspects of theory and theory is tested by practice and as that loop is run, both the practice and the theory on which it relies get reinforced and what we end up with is a coherent body of thought and practice.

So far, so easy. Except that, in systems, a lot of the underlying theory has become disconnected from the practice – embodied as that has been in methodologies. Practitioners and academics alike have tended to focus on talking about methodologies such as Soft Systems Methodology, System Dynamics etc. rather than on the underpinning ideas. The theory-practice-theory-practice loop has been broken. This is in part a small step to restoring that.

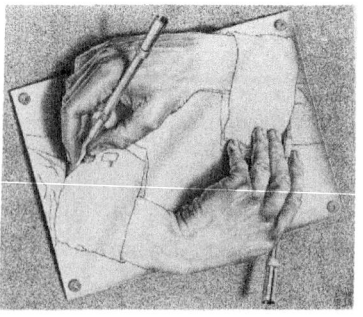

When you get an intact theory-practice loop running, then as that runs, it starts to encapsulate a space and that space has a boundary, an edge. Now you have a boundary for the body of thinking and that boundary has been built by self-reference – we recognise physics as a discipline because it's the domain of things done by physicists using the laws, theories and practices of physics. The 'doing' (practice) and 'thinking' (theory) of physicists defines physics and physics in turn defines what is a physicist. The people define the discipline and the discipline defines the people within it.

Having an intact and functioning theory-practice learning loop is the mechanism that defines the boundary of the discipline. Having a boundary for the discipline is what enables us to distinguish between

Introduction

what is systems thinking and/or practice and what isn't. To distinguish the actual gold from the fool's gold.

Once the theory-practice loop is running and that has established a boundary, you're left with the problem of ossification – how do you stop the body of knowledge becoming so tight, so fixed and constraining, that no new theory and practice can emerge? Managing that is a combination of openness and referencing. Openness to new ideas, to cross-fertilisation and to challenge when either theory or practice fails to deal with situations encountered and then referencing to core ideas to see whether the new is genuinely a part of this body of thought or a different one. And that process is only possible if you have on tap what the core ideas are.

The 'Grammar' part of the book lists a set of laws and principles that were developed in Systems Thinking by Systems Thinkers, and which formed the foundation on which methodologies like System Dynamics were built. They form an underlying body of knowledge and of thinking that can be, and largely has been, invisible to practitioners. Working with them leads you into thinking systemically. Naturally, they all have a different focus, but taken together as a body of thought, they form a very clear, coherent and simple picture of the discipline. Together they talk about how, when and why it is that systems remain stable and change at the same time, or when and how they don't, how and why they collapse into new forms or disintegrate, and they talk about our process of knowing and the limitations of our knowing.

The two parts of the book, the grimoire and the grammar, offer two different routes through the world of thinking systemically. One – the grammar – is formal in the sense that it's rooted in the history of the field and provides a route back to some of that underlying thought. The laws are abstractions, very powerful, but you can pick them up and put them down and play with them in different contexts and they may have a lasting effect on how you see the world, or not. The other – the grimoire – is more of a personal take on what is going on inside the Systems Thinker, what it means to think and feel like this. If you use these patterns of thinking, you cannot not be changed by them. Within each of these two parts there are a lot of cross references and the two parts also

Introduction

cross reference. That means that there isn't a linear route through, and some readers may interpret the cross referencing as repetition. The cross referencing is the overall pattern of this as a way of thinking - it is a map of the territory with its network of interlinking pathways.

Lost and found ...

All of which does rather beg the question of whether there is actually anything in here that isn't already well known. This is an attempt to assemble what I consider the ways of thinking like a Systems Thinker, those that are most important. These are patterns of thinking that I look for in others and look for in myself if I want to assess whether Systems Thinking is actually happening. Despite the fact that none of these is new, many may be unfamiliar to people who call themselves Systems Thinkers. In particular, I think it may be new to many to think about these as patterns of thoughts that you actually use, thinking pathways that you can learn independently of any systems methodology and that you can train your brain and instincts to use.

Many of the books that are ostensibly about systems thinking are actually about systems – about how systems are dynamic or how they are complex, or how systems are deeply mysterious or whatever; and about how you can deal with that. This book is different in that Part 1 is primarily concerned with the actual process of thinking and thinking in the way a systems thinker does. So the focus of this is not just on something that has been lost – some core, seminal ideas and approaches – but on something that I believe has been largely neglected, the actual way of thinking.

# Part 1

How to think like a Systems Thinker

Emergence

In the beginning...

Emergence may be a slightly controversial place to start, but I'm starting here because emergence really is the start of the story, both in terms of chronology and in terms of what it is that systems thinking as an endeavour seeks to get a handle on. Emergence is the point. The quintessentially systems statement is that *"the whole is more than the sum of its parts"* and that difference, that 'more than' is at the heart of emergence.

There have been a number of commentators who have claimed that the idea was developed in the last quarter of the 20th century, but they're out by almost exactly 100 years. Emergence, both the term and the concept, was developed by

"The emergent is unlike its components insofar as these are incommensurable, and it cannot be reduced to their sum or their difference."
Lewes

G.H. Lewes in 1875. Lewes was a bit of a renaissance man: philosopher and art critic, but he's probably best known as the live-in lover of George Eliot, the author of Middlemarch and half a dozen other novels. I don't know if Lewes got to the idea of emergence through a philosophical route, or through art criticism, or a combination of the two, but either route is possible. Certainly, if you think about it in terms of art then the connection is obvious – all art is about the overall effect the work of art has, not the individual brushstrokes of the painting or the individual notes of the music. What matters in art is the ability art has to transport us, to convey meaning, to elicit emotions in us and to do that in ways that are not mechanistic, but nevertheless real. And in a very systemic way, no art is independent of the artist or of the audience or observer.

Curiouser and curiouser

Part of the appeal of the *"whole is more than the sum..."* statement is that it has an almost Zen Koan quality to it. Conversely, that same quality of inbuilt paradox is what infuriates some, perplexes many and leads to the whole idea being dismissed as flummery. I once had the somewhat disconcerting experience of talking about systems thinking to around a

Emergence

dozen professors of systems engineering who to a man declared themselves confused by the 'mystery of emergence'.

One of the nice things about this is that there is some mystery to emergence, yet it is also utterly commonplace and something those professors worked with and towards every day. But like a lot of systems thinking, and a lot of what we're going through in this book, the commonplace and common-sense nature of emergence can suddenly give way to reveal its elusiveness. So we'll start the discussion of emergence, and what it means in terms of thinking like a systems thinker, with the more mechanistic end, move to some of its more fugitive qualities and then talk about how emergence relates to topics of the rest of the chapters in the book, or rather, since emergence is the point, how they relate to emergence and specifically, the role each plays in understanding emergence.

The most basic definition of emergence is that it is *"a property of a system that is not a property of any of the parts of the system and which could not be predicted from understanding each of the parts on its own"*. For a systems engineering professor then, a really commonplace example of emergence that they didn't merely experience, but actively worked for, would be speed in a vehicle like a motorbike or a plane. The motorbike as a whole has the property of speed, but take it to pieces and not only do none of the components have the property of speed on their own, if you hunt through the components, you will not find any 'speed component'. It isn't a component, isn't a thing in its own right and it isn't a property of any of the bits. The bike only has the property of speed once it is integrated into a system. Now, not only was this no mystery to our professors, it's exactly the sort of thing they and their discipline exist to create. Systems engineering as a discipline is all about what's involved in designing parts so they do integrate so you get the emergent properties – like speed – that you want.

So far so commonplace, why then the mystery? I think partly because of the disconnect between a commonplace tangible measurable and, in the case of engineers, planned-for property like speed and the intangible nature of where it comes from. You can measure the speed of a motorbike, you can feel it and yet you can't see 'it' because 'it' isn't a tangible thing. Take the bike apart and there's nothing but a pile of bits, there is no speed. There is an undeniably weird aspect to emergence; it's there, it's normal, it's tangible and in the case of a motorbike, for many bikers, speed is *everything* and at the same time it is in a literal sense nothing. Emergence nearly always can play that trick of the mind on you – a strange shapeshifting, harlequin that despite its elusiveness is the point of everything.

For the systems engineering professors, their discipline is that integration to produce emergence and at a mechanistic level, this is the explanation of emergence. As Smuts put it: *"A whole, which is more than the sum of its parts, has something internal, some inwardness of structure and function...some internality of nature that constitutes that 'more'."* The *"inwardness of structure and function"* is exactly what the systems engineers work with. It's about how the bike's engine connects to the gearbox connects to the back wheel connects to the road. Connect all that up differently or in a different order and the parts may stay the same, but the emergent will be totally different.

That's the case for pretty much all engineered systems, but the same applies to biological systems. Take a human being and they have emergent behaviours – for example singing or laughing. Take the human being apart and the emergent properties disappear. All life forms have the emergent property of life, but for most, if you deconstruct them into individual components, life goes. Some of the components will continue to have life for a time, which is how blood transfusions and organ transplants are possible, but the life that was an emergent property of the person as a whole, laughing, singing, running around, is gone and the life of the organs and cells is generally not far behind. As with all emergence, there is that disconcerting jump from obvious and commonplace – we experience people, dogs and butterflies on an everyday basis and take their life for granted and yet biologists, philosophers and theologians have argued the nature of life for centuries and still it's hotly contested. We know it when we see it.

As with the motorbike, Smuts' observation holds for biological systems. It's the *"inwardness of structure and function"* between organelles within cells,

Emergence

between cells within an organ and between organs within my body that allows me to walk, talk, think and laugh. As with the bike it's their integration that matters – connect the heart, liver and lungs up in a different way and you get a very different result, and you might get an emergent property, but it certainly won't be the same emergent.

The same is true for many human endeavours – a musical performance, for example. The emergent property, that ability to change how you feel within seconds depends on the "*inwardness of structure and function*" of the notes. Change the relationships between the notes and you have a completely different effect, a different emergent. Emergence is not only all around us, from gang violence to economic prosperity, from climate change to the level of efficiency of a factory, the most important things we experience and that affect our lives are emergent properties. Emergence is not just the point of systems thinking, it is The Point.

Five thinking paths
In thinking about emergence, there are typically five main aspects to bear in mind: looking for the emergent properties of a system; looking for the system of an emergent property; looking for the effect emergence has on the system, looking for emergence through time and looking for the work of the invisible hand.

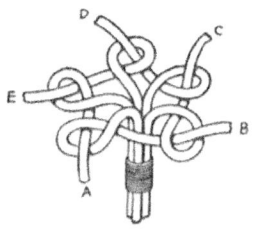

A   What's the Emergent of this System?
Once you've got the basic idea of emergence, you might think that looking for the emergent properties of a system would be the most natural thing for any systems thinker to do, but for lots of practitioners, it appears to be at best an afterthought and for many, emergence can be little more than an arm waving exercise. You can see this in several systems approaches where there is no standard way to translate from a model of the system to what the emergent properties are likely to be. Fortunately, that isn't true of all approaches. But formal approaches aside, the basic thinking pattern here is to look at the pattern of boundaries, relationships and dynamics, the effects these have on one another and

Emergence

what that creates. As a thinking discipline, going from system to emergent is important for systems design for two reasons: firstly because you design systems precisely to get an emergent effect, and secondly because, as Beer put it: *"Instead of trying to specify it in full detail, you specify it only somewhat. You then ride on the dynamics of the system in the direction you want to go."* If you understand 'system to emergent' then not only is the design and creation process easier, it's much more likely to be successful. This working from system to emergent is much less common in problem solving and the relative scarcity of 'system to emergent' as a thought pattern amongst practitioners reflects the emphasis in a lot of systems practice on problem solving. But that scarcity is not a reflection of its importance even for problem solving and one of the most common mistakes in problem focused systems practice is the POSIWID error. POSIWID is 'Purpose Of a System Is What It Does' and as Beer pointed out, *"There is after all, no point in claiming that the purpose of a system is to do what it constantly fails to do."* The error is to blithely assume that the purpose of a system is what the designer, owner, or person paying the bills wants it to be. If you don't actually and actively look for the emergents, it's ridiculously easy to assume that they are what you'd like them to be.

B What's the System of this Emergent?

Going the other way, starting with an emergent property and looking for the system that creates it, is much more common, partly because it's a natural flow in problem solving. Most problems that a systems practitioner is likely to have to deal with are emergent properties and whatever the systems approach used, the basic direction of travel is to recognise the problem as an emergent property and then seek to understand what the nature of the system is that creates it and how it does that. That in turn takes us to looking at the structure of boundaries and relationships and the dynamics of the system and what the effect of those is and whether that provides an adequate explanation of the emergent property we're interested in. Once you understand the relationship between system and emergent, then you can intervene in the system to change the emergent.

Emergence

C   How does Emergence change the System?

Because of that 'properties of the whole that are not properties of the part on their own' definition, the temptation is to think of emergence as something that is only exhibited at the level of the whole and not at the level of the parts, as something 'on top'. But emergence is not limited to just the behaviour of the whole. Everything within a system is changed by being a part of that system, every element, every relationship is changed. It's not just emergent behaviours that happen at the level of the whole system, it's also emergent behaviours that happen at the level of its sub-systems. In biological systems, the bacteria that were the building blocks of cells back down the evolutionary chain are constrained by being part of a cell in a higher-level system. The emergence to which parts of an organism contribute also binds and constrains those parts. The integration into a system changes the parts and whilst they are a part of the system, they are no longer apart and no longer have the freedom afforded by separation.

Exactly the same is true for us as people within a social or organisational system. The system I am part of has emergent properties that I find beneficial, but those also constrain me. I benefit from being part of society, but I am subject and subjected to not only its laws, rules and regulations, but also by social norms. Being part of a system changes you. Some people see organisational systems as 'just the people' and assume that the will of individuals drive the direction of the system (the evidence is that isn't the case, which is one of the reasons why strategy fails quite so often). Others look at the effect the system has on driving behaviours of people in them against their will, where a sort of mechanistic causation view and the effect of reward systems is a common example. Fewer see that people become less individuated the more tightly coupled they become and turn into 'parts of the system'. A common example is 'being a mum' which is life giving and for many life affirming but changes your ability to act, think and feel independently. If you have to look after a child, pulling all-nighters suddenly isn't as easy.

The effect emergence has on the system is not intrinsically good or bad, it just is. You see as a part of the system, feel as a part of the system, think as a part of the system, whether the system in question is a family, a team, a gang, or a corporation. You cannot really understand a part of a system without understanding the system of which it is a part and the thinking pattern here is to look for the constraints the system places on its parts in creating the emergence. Those constraints come in all sorts of flavours, but for those of us working in social or organisational systems, the hardest to envisage is how much, and in what ways, being part of a system constrains what people are able to see, think and feel. It's hard not because it's technically difficult, but because the realisation is so uncomfortable and so antithetical to the prevailing occupational psychology paradigm.

D   Emergence through time

The 'property of a system that is not a property of any of the parts' definition of emergence leads us naturally to think of phenomena at the level of the systems and between the system and its environment. Most of what we need to look for there is covered in points A & B but there is a further factor to take into consideration which is the formation of a system as an emergent property. It's so easy to slip into a way of thinking that 'you have a system x and that has emergent properties y & z' and whether you start with y & z and seek to uncover x or start with x and seek to uncover y & z, both these views assume a static situation where the system and its emergent properties exist. However, the system ↔ emergence relationship is a dynamic. Half of that dynamic is in C – how the emergence changes the system elements, but the other half of the dynamic is that the emergent can itself be a system at a higher level. As Smuts once again put it: *"the tendency in nature to form wholes, that are greater than the sum of its parts, through creative evolution"*. In one sense, this is a more colloquial use of the term emergence, since what we are looking for is to see what stable order emerges from the interaction of the parts of a proto-system that then creates the system. None of these – the parts, the system and the emergent properties – is fixed, all are mutually dependent.

E   The Invisible Hand or *"outrageous fortune"*

The post enlightenment world view has at its heart a belief that understanding of the world gives us a degree of control over it. And that has been phenomenally successful to the point where we can now envisage our power to destroy the world as we know it. This paradigm of

Emergence

knowledge and control stands in stark contrast to the views of the ancients. Two bastions of logical thinking stem from the 5th century in Greek and Confucian philosophy. But even those rationalist traditions both held to a belief in the overwhelming power of non-rational forces that limit the power of us mere humans. In Confucian philosophy, this was encapsulated in the power of the cycle of change, and for the Greeks and most civilisations before and since right up to the enlightenment, it was personified in myths about the power of gods. This was a set of views explaining the limits to the power of mortals. As a world view this fell out of favour in the enlightenment and the scientific revolution, as science and the evident power of human  agency replaced superstition, myth and to a large extent religion. Working with systems approaches, there is a place for a 'higher power' view but instead of capricious gods or fates we have the power of the system. Systems thinking is partly a new take on an age-old theme. The common systems trope of 'unintended consequences' is very like the capriciousness of an ancient god albeit with a rational and scientific explanation. More commonly though, much of political and media discussion is based on what Harold Macmillan famously described as *"Events, dear boy, events"*, those *"events"* are almost invariably emergent properties. Moving beyond seeing them as merely events or Hamlet's *"outrageous fortune"* is largely what systems thinking is about.

From mass migration to global warming, these are emergent properties that can be understood using systems approaches. A dilemma for the systems thinker then is to balance off the evident agency of the individual with the power and complexity of the system they are engaging with. At least the laws and principles in the Grammar together with the methodologies give us a better handle on the workings of the 'higher power' than sacrificing a chicken and gazing at its entrails did for the ancients. Emergence marks our limits.

Last word on this goes to Einstein: *"For the most part we humans live with the false impression of security and a feeling of being at home in a seemingly trustworthy physical and human environment. But when the expected course of everyday life is interrupted, we are like shipwrecked people on a miserable plank in the open sea, having forgotten where they came from and not knowing whither they are drifting."*

Emergence – the central concept
As well as being central in terms of the genesis of Systems Thinking, or rather because of its centrality, all the other aspects of thinking systemically that are in the next eight chapters are part of and depend on emergence, so briefly....

Holism
Of the rest of the thought patterns, holism is the one most obviously directed at emergence. Holism is a pattern of thinking that is designed to direct your attention up to where emergent properties can be most easily seen – at the level of the system rather than at the level of the parts. It stands in contrast to reductionism which takes your focus directly onto the parts and it does it specifically to get the thinker to consider emergence. That reductionist tendency has the allure of the certainty of the tangible components and away from the intangible nature of emergence.

Modelling
Part of the purpose of building models in systems practice is precisely to understand and explain how a system creates the emergent properties it does or to design or change it to be able to produce the emergent properties we want. That *"something internal, some inwardness of structure and function...some internality of nature that constitutes that 'more'"* translates into mapping out the pattern of elements, boundaries, structures, relationships dynamics and variables that are relevant to producing a particular set of emergent properties. That can be starting with an emergent property and modelling which elements, relationships, dynamics etc. produce that or working the other way from system design to emergent, or to understand the effects of the system producing emergent x has on the parts, or to understand what emergent behaviours this system could produce.

Boundaries
Boundaries define the identity of the system that you think produces a given set of emergent properties, so boundaries are key in both modelling and in the creation of emergent properties in reality. In modelling, boundary setting defines what you consider to be the limits of the system creating the emergent properties. Less obviously from the boundaries in

models, when boundaries are created in real world systems, that creates emergent properties both within, across and outwith the boundary.

Difference

Exploring and understanding the 'difference that makes a difference' is fundamental to getting to grips with emergence in systems work. The world is full of emergent properties, so the 'why pick this one?' question is both non-trivial and usually not totally obvious, bearing in mind that the people insisting that this is *the* emergent property of concern are almost always wrapped up in it and therefore their views, thoughts and emotions are being conditioned by it. There are rarely any independent islands on which to stand and view things dispassionately, so critical appraisal of which differences make a difference and why, is essential both for doing good work and for relatively uncontaminated thinking.

Relating

Peter Drucker echoed Smuts when he said: *"And one thing characterizes all genuine systems, whether they be mechanical like the control of a missile, biological like a tree or social like the business enterprise: it is interdependence."* And that 'interdependence' is about the dynamics and complexity of how parts of a system relate to one another. Emergent properties are largely driven by the nature of that relating, mediated as it is by a structure of boundaries and differences. Change the relating and you change the emergent properties even when the parts may stay the same, as Eric Clapton pointed out in an interview about his apparent change of style when he moved from the Yardbirds to John Mayall's Bluesbreakers.

Interviewer: *"Now from the time that you left the Yardbirds and joined up with John Mayall and company, your head seemed to change tremendously as far as your music was concerned. What kind of things were happening to your head then?"*

Clapton: *"Well, I really didn't change as much as you probably think because it's not really, you know, an individual change. I was just put into a different context, so I mean the things that I was doing reflected differently, you know. The context of the Yardbirds as opposed to John Mayall, one is pop and one is, you know, and was then, even earthier blues than it is now, the stuff he played then and you know, I just played the same things, but they just sounded different."*

Dynamics and loops
It's tempting to think of all of the rest of these thinking patterns: dynamics, complexity, boundaries and differences as essentially the same as relating, they are all part of the nature of the system and shape the emergent properties of that system, and to some extent that's true, but dynamics have a particular role in driving emergence. It's the relative power of the dynamics that provides the basic energy of the emergent property, and whether that is highly dynamic or stuck, both will have an effect.

Complexity
Complexity is the stuff of systems and is a major factor in that *"something internal, some inwardness of structure and function...some internality of nature that constitutes that 'more'"*. Complexity derives from the *"structure and function"* and is a defining characteristic of the *"internality of nature"*. Complexity, both structural complexity and dynamic complexity, directly generate emergent properties. Specifically, the relative complexity of the system drives its level of stability through to chaos and that will have a significant effect on emergence.

Uncertainty
Uncertainty takes us back to the element of 'mystery' in emergence and that underpins the necessity of having good thinking approaches to help handle the inevitable uncertainty of emergence itself, the uncertainty of perception of emergence itself given that it is slippery stuff, and the uncertainty about the validity of our models of the system driving emergence.

The difference in thinking about emergence is equivalent to the Copernican shift from a belief that the earth (and by association we, and by association 'I') is at the centre of the solar system to the helio-centric one, where we are merely satellite players. We like to believe that, however imperfectly, someone controls events – this fuels the blame culture that permeates the media and the whole of the political viewpoint.

Emergence

We certainly like to believe that even if we can't control events, we are at least in control of ourselves and what we think and feel, but the emergence view tells a rather different story. We are parts of systems and whilst we do have free will, for the most part what we see think, feel and do is to some extent constrained and channelled by the systems we are part of. To paraphrase Churchill, *"We shape our systems, thereafter they shape us"*.

Holistic Thinking

"Pay it extra"

As Lewis Carrol's character Humpty Dumpty said: *"When I make a word do a lot of work like that," said Humpty Dumpty, "I always pay it extra."* We're in an area where new terms have had to be created to describe new ideas and where words have lost their meanings and because Holism is a word that has been used to mean very different things I need to start with a bit of unscrambling of terminology and 'pay it extra'. The word Holism and holistic have gone into common usage and get used in a wide range of fields, sometime appropriately, sometimes not.

The word was first coined by Jan Smuts, and what he meant by it was something different to what is typically meant today. Smuts defined Holism as *"the tendency in nature to form wholes, that are greater than the sum of its parts, through creative evolution"* so the focus is on the spontaneous self-generation of higher levels of order, and of course this is one aspect of emergence.

Through time and usage, the meaning of the term has come to mean something related, but quite different, so it's now generally used to mean something like *"viewing something as a whole rather than just as parts"* and that's how I'm going to use the term here. Before we completely leave the Smuts definition, though, it's worth reflecting that his definition was echoed in the term 'self-organisation', meaning the spontaneous self-creation of order, and this is also a term that has lost its meaning through common usage, so self-organisation is now commonly used to mean 'self-managing'. These original meanings are about something really important in systems thinking and the degrading of terms to mean something more commonplace is just one sign of how hard it is to hang onto these ideas and how easily they can be watered down.

I'm using the word Holism in line with its more common usage, not the Smuts original and I've already said that there is a close relationship both linguistically and in terms of thought between Holism and Emergence. The importance of holism as a way of thinking is because it's one of the main ways to help see emergence and emergent properties.

Holism

Ups and Downs

One of the clearest expressions of this as a thinking approach came from Russ Ackoff. Now just to confuse even more, Ackoff used the term 'synthetic thinking' rather than holism, but what he's describing here is the thinking technique for seeing wholes rather than parts and this description by Ackoff takes you through the approach step by step:
"We had to develop a new way of thinking, and it's exactly the opposite of analysis.

In the first step of analysis, you take the thing that you want to understand apart. In the first step of synthesis, you take the thing you want to understand as a part of a larger whole.

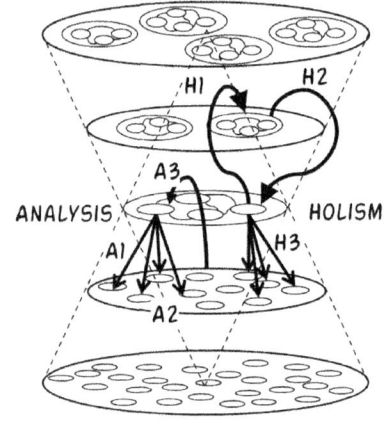

In the second step of analysis, you explain the behavior of each part taken separately. In the second step of synthesis, you explain the behavior of the containing whole. So if we're trying to explain a university, we have to first explain the education system of which the university is a part.

In the third step of analysis, you aggregate your explanation of the parts into an understanding of the whole. In the third step of synthesis, you dis-aggregate the understanding of the whole into an understanding of the parts, so that we explain by identifying their role or function of a system in the larger system of which it's a part.
Within his distinction between analysis and synthesis clearly if the whole is not much more than the parts then you get the same answer whichever route you choose. If the whole is much more than the parts you cannot. Think of a live performance or landmark event – the people are all the parts but the event is a special one off. You can bring the same team along but the result will not be the same."

One of the things I really like about this short description is its clarity on the architecture of the two different thought processes and the direct contrast between them. As Ackoff describes it, this is to take one step up

Holism

from looking at the system you are interested in to the system it's embedded in and ask: of what is this a part? And to understand your system of interest by reference to the part it plays in the system it is part of. More broadly, it's about being able to navigate the vertical dimension of thought with some precision, moving up and down levels of system and levels of abstraction. And critically as a technique and as Ackoff describes, climbing up before dropping down brings you to completely different conclusions to going down and then up. It's the sequence of thinking that matters – this is not simply about 'seeing the big picture' in some vague arm waving way. It's about understanding what you are looking at as part of something bigger *before* you look at what its parts are. The reason why it gives you different answers is that the 'of what is this a part?' question determines what the parts are. If I look at a pub as part of my personal social context, the 'pub system' will have a different set of elements, a different set of parts to if I view the same pub as part of an economic system.

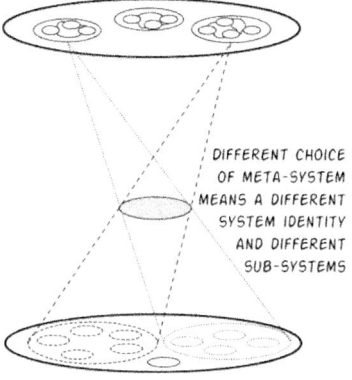

DIFFERENT CHOICE OF META-SYSTEM MEANS A DIFFERENT SYSTEM IDENTITY AND DIFFERENT SUB-SYSTEMS

There are two things I've found repeatedly about this as a thinking discipline: one is that many people who have only ever learned to think analytically or reductively find it very hard even to see holistic thinking as thinking and the other is a common refusal to accept that there could be any difference, or that there could be any benefit to holism.

"Logic can often be reversed, but the effect does not precede the cause."
Bateson

In a way, this is odd because responding to the world holistically is natural to us and normal. If we walk into a cathedral, the normal and immediate reaction is not to look at it as just a pile of stones, even though it is a pile of stones, it is to see the stones as part of the whole and to let the whole soaring grandeur, the light and the space of it affect us. But despite this being a natural way to experience the world, that isn't how we're trained to think and as a result the thinking takes away the

Holism

'immediate reaction' and mediates that through thought. If you walked into a cathedral with someone who reacted to it as if was just a pile of stones then you would think they were a bit of a philistine and with justification because they would have missed the point of the whole thing. Wells cathedral took nearly three centuries to build and I don't think 'pile of stones' was quite the effect they were after. Getting at 'the point of the whole thing' is what holistic thinking is about, what is the meaning of the pile of stones, because it's that that matters. Reductionism or analysis can tell us how the cathedral was built by piling one stone on top of another, but not why it was built, or what it means or why it matters. The effect the cathedral has on us is an emergent property, so there is a direct link between thinking holistically and thinking about emergence. Holistic thinking directs your attention towards emergence, reductionism directs your attention away from it.

Since 'thinking about how to think' is a bit abstract and a bit tricky, let's take a couple of practical examples of using holistic and reductionist thinking and contrast the two.

The first example involves a project around moving a large multi-national manufacturing group over to using a new ERP system (Enterprise Resource Planning software program). The background to this was that the company had grown extremely fast by acquisition to become one of the biggest in the world in their industry. Each acquired company served its own local national market with locally developed products that suited local needs and a proportion of those products were taken up by the group and produced, promoted, and sold internationally as their flagship global brands. As the company grew and with it the number of countries it operated in, the decision was taken to restructure the group into several regions and just after this the decision was taken to put in the ERP system.

If we look at this project in a reductionist or analytic way, then we get one set of answers. Reductionism takes you towards working out what the various elements would be of introducing such a system: the data, process, information and technology architectures for example, then take you down again into investigating the elements of each of those. And the assumption in the reductionist approach is that if you sort out all of those, then everything will go well.

The holistic perspective takes you in the other direction and asks: 'what role does this play within the organisation as a whole and what effect will it have?' and gives you very different answers. The project had been initiated by the new regional structure that sat between the nationally based companies and the global brands, and the effect of centralising financial control at a regional level (where there were no regional products and no regional market) was to reduce the autonomy of national companies and with that, their ability to control their own affairs. It represented a major power shift away from market facing units to administrative regional units with no market contact. Looking at this analytically or holistically gives you very different perspectives and is likely to lead to quite different conclusions and outcomes.

Another example is a local authority planning department. The main operational activity of the planning department is to process planning applications. They take a resident's planning application, often prepared by an architect, check it against the local and national planning regulations, put it out for consultation and send it with a recommendation to the planning committee made up of elected councillors. If you look at this in a reductionist way, this is straightforwardly a process. It's linear, it starts with the application being submitted, goes through a series of process steps and ends with the applicant getting permission or having it denied. Tackling this reductively would typically lead you towards doing some process analysis and if you wanted to improve it, improving each of the steps in the process, or getting rid of the ones that don't add value to the customer. The customer is of course the recipient of the output of the process – the applicant. Quite straightforward.

If you look at this holistically, the picture is very different. We start by asking 'of what is our planning process a part?' and the answer is that it's a part of the system for developing the built environment of the community. This means that it has a much wider remit than just the desires of a single resident to build an extension to their house. It must take into account a range of other concerns: road use, land use,

Holism

demographic pressure on schools and other facilities, wider impact on the natural environment including drainage.

Looked at holistically, there isn't a single customer for the planning process, instead, the planner has to hold a tension between the applicant's desire for their house extension, the preferences of the current neighbours who would rather not have something an architect dreamt up to impress other architects built next door to them and the future needs of the wider community.

Improving this using a reductionist approach leads you to optimising the process for the applicant. Improving this holistically would lead you towards ensuring the balance of interests was maintained. An example of that comes from the work of architect Chris Alexander whose judging criteria for a design prize was if a design was good in its own right, *and* improved what around it, *and* made it possible for other future developments to improve on it in turn. That is very different to just speeding up how long plans take to process.

The lack of awareness of the two approaches means that people tend to find it more difficult to navigate their way up and down levels of the system, or indeed to even understand that there are different levels. Kurt Lewin was the father of much of the thinking that now underpins change management theory: resistance to change, group dynamics, the 'freezing, unfreezing, refreezing' model, force-field analysis, socio-dynamics and action research were some of his major contributions. When Lewin talked about resistance in organisational change, he was talking about the system resisting change (which systems have to do otherwise they'd shake themselves to pieces if they reacted to all the stimuli for change hitting them). He was not primarily talking about resistance by the individual – although the two are linked in Lewin's theory and he even had an equation to describe the link: $B = f(P, E)$. But if you look at this in a reductionist way, then you imagine that the system is just the people in it, so if there is resistance then it must be a characteristic of the individuals not the system. And so a whole field is born based on an assumption – which quickly becomes gospel – that individuals are inherently resistant to change. Now you only have to take a casual look around to see just how fast individuals change their habits, or how fast they adopt new

Holism

technologies in their private lives to know that this is very far from a universal rule. If you look at the same problem holistically, you start where Lewin did and look for the drivers for and against change in the system as a whole – and that is a very different question with some very different answers.

Navigating the vertical dimension: the Gyre

When you are trying to identify or understand any system, the meaning of the system can only be found in its context, so what you discern as 'context' is inextricably a part of what you discern as 'system'. The reductionist approach leads you to see the system in its most immediate and prominent context as that appears to you coming from the direction you did. And that in turn makes you more susceptible to taking things at face value, to believing that what happens to be obvious to you is the whole truth. To discern a wider set of potential meanings we have to see a wider context, a wider set of relationships. As Beer put it: *"We select, from an infinite number of relations between things, a set which, because of coherence and pattern and purpose, permits an interpretation of what otherwise might be a meaningless cavalcade of arbitrary events."* If you have a network of relationships from which you are trying to distinguish and understand a system, a key question is 'how much / how many contexts do I look at?' Theoretically as Beer says, the choice is infinite,

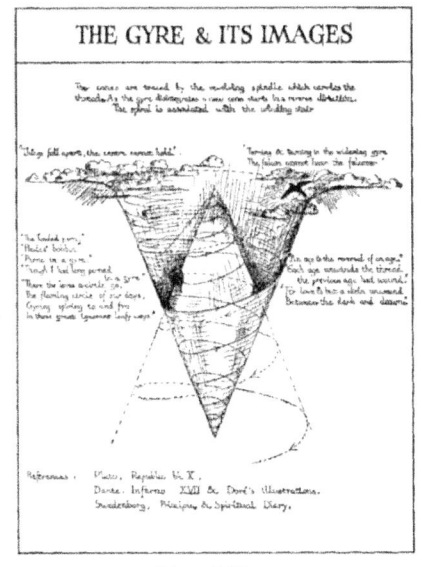

Yeats' Gyre

but unless you want to take the approach used by Douglas Adams's holistic detective Dirk Gently, then practically we have to limit the search area. This is fine, because within a network of relationships, the further

Holism

out you go from the centre of your focus, the more diffuse the effect becomes and the less important relationships become.

Russ Ackoff's description is linear – a vertical ladder that you ascend and then descend, one step up and then two steps down.
In reality, it's more like W.B Yeat's 'Gyre' – two cones interpenetrating. Often, rather than simply climbing straight up, the thinker and the thinking follows a spiral path upward or, as Yeats described, the falcon *"turning and turning in the widening gyre"*. As the falcon spirals upward, it can see a wider area on the ground much more easily. The downward cone is the arc of vision, and from a higher arc of flight, the falcon can see a larger area on the ground. The trick is to rise only as high such that the circles of your vision of the ground still touch at the centre.

Once they become disjointed, you've lost your reference point, you've lost touch with the ground: *"turning and turning in the widening gyre the falcon cannot see the falconer"*. And at that point, when your point of focus on the ground, the territory, is lost, you become detached, the link of relevance to the system you are, or rather were, interested in is lost and it becomes irrelevant to you and you to it. If you have climbed too high to distinguish a 'difference that makes a difference' back on the ground, if you can no longer differentiate the vole scurrying through grass from the clod of earth next to it, then you are too high. That loss of the relevance of the system to you, of your ability to make useful distinctions is immediately recognisable – if you bother to check in on it – and that is the tell-tale sign that you have climbed too high or arced too wide. Pull back in.

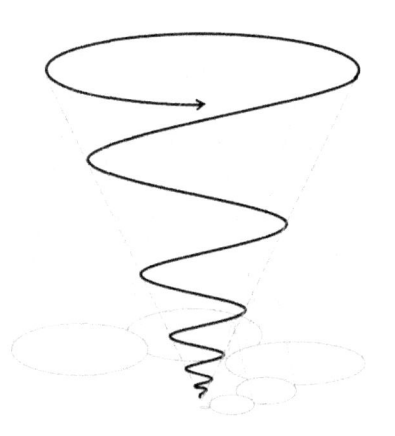

The higher you go in terms of level of system, and levels of abstraction, the wider the set of embedding systems you can see and that extends both the scale and also the timeframe within which you can spot a pattern that will give you the meaning of the system you're interested in. The **Systems Stability Principle** says that a system is a pattern of relationships that is stable enough for long enough to be recognised as a pattern. Obviously, one variable in that is how long a timeframe the observation covers and some systems take a very long time to repeat themselves thereby revealing a deep pattern. To spot that, you have to climb a long way up. What may appear as a random event at one level can appear as just one point in a regular pattern at a different level: this financial crash isn't a random event, it's just one more in a series, not the first, and it won't be the last. What may appear as chaos – and may well actually be chaos – may when viewed from further up be just a transformation. A caterpillar dissolves into gloop to turn into a butterfly, but then it also dissolves into gloop in the digestive tract of a bird. Both involve transformations from structure to chaos back to structure, but you need to reach a higher perspective to know whether this transformation involves becoming a butterfly or becoming part of the bird. This puts a nuance into the heuristic that Systems Thinking is about the realm between stasis and chaos, since both stasis and chaos may just be phase states within a longer, deeper pattern.

As described by Russ Ackoff, this is a 3-step process: a step upwards, then down, then down again. For the systems thinker, though, it needs to go beyond that simple 3 step formulation. It's about how to manage your thinking in the vertical dimension: not just a progression from premise to conclusion, but at the same time up and down levels of structure and abstraction – even when, perhaps particularly when, this is invisible.

When people say 'x is not a strategic thinker' or 'x doesn't have a strategic mind', this is generally what they mean, a lack in the ability to navigate up to see and comprehend the bigger picture and to dive down into the detail when appropriate.

It's extremely difficult to describe the controlled navigation of the vertical dimension: knowing how and when to climb, when to rest at a certain level, when, how far and how fast to drop. Which I suppose is why Russ Ackoff resorted to the simplistic three steps. But the best description of the *feel of it* that I know is from the sublime pen of J.A Baker's The Peregrine.

Holism

> "An abrupt and narrow turn, and he was suddenly still, head to wind, a thousand feet up.
>
> For five minutes he hung motionless, tensing and flexing his swept back wings, dark anchor mooring white cloud. He looked down at the orchard beneath him, twisting and turning his head, mobile, menacing like the head of a snake looking out of a rock. The wind could not move him, the sun could not lift him. He was fixed and safe in a crevice of sky.
>
> Loosened suddenly out into air, he straightened his wings and circled slowly higher. He slowed, steadied, balanced and again was still. He was a small speck now, like the pupil of a distant eye. Serenely he floated. Then like music breaking he began to descend.
>
> He slid forward and down to his left for two hundred feet, and then stopped. After a long still pause he came down two hundred feet to his right, then stopped. In this vertical zigzag, from wing-hold to wing-hold, he slowly descended the sheer face of sky. There was not hesitation or checking. He simply dropped, and then stopped, as a spider drops on a thread, or a man on a rope."

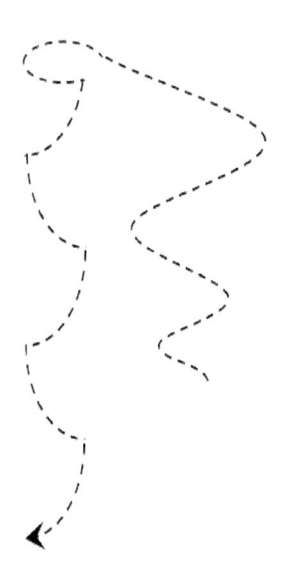

Baker's peregrine perceives and utilises a structure in a medium that is invisible to us. Similarly, systems thinking involves being able to navigate the vertical domain easily and with some precision, even though for many people that vertical structure is as invisible as the structure of the air currents the peregrine uses. That vertical domain can be marked in terms of structural levels, levels of logic, or time (and those are all systemically linked and will often be congruent). This is about knowing when to climb up levels of abstraction and when to drop down into detail and critically, the ability to climb as easily and quickly as to stoop.

In their nature people vary enormously in their ability to climb and drop. Some naturally soar but are incapable of grounding their thinking into reality – and you absolutely need to be able to do both. What's far less easy to get a handle on is your level of control and precision.

Holism

I once timed a group on their relative rate of ascent vs descent. They were people from an IT background but ones who prided themselves on being big picture thinkers and we were supposed to be looking at the usefulness of a modelling approach.

They went from considering the utility of this type of model, i.e. why you might use it and in what context – a question that requires you to look upwards to possible contexts. Instead, they plummeted down several levels, from where the class of model might be used to the class of model itself to this example of the class, to a part of the model, to an element in that part, to a type of artefact that could be in that element, to an actual specific example of the artefact, to an experience one of them had once had with such an artefact. In less than five minutes, they dropped eight levels of abstraction, from a question that had relevance to the profession as a whole in a lot of situations down to something that had been once been experienced by one individual.

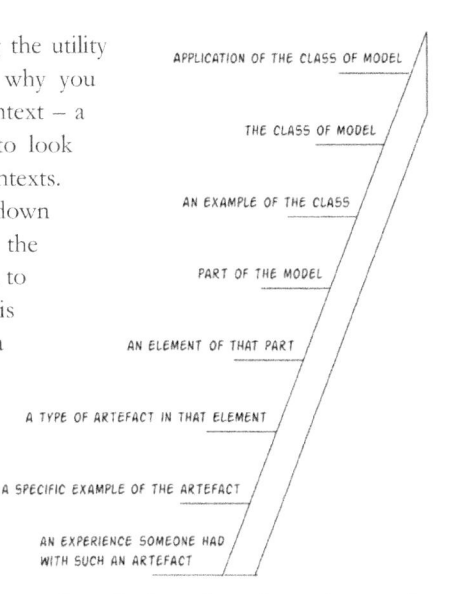

It took them less than five minutes to drop down those levels and after almost two hours of hard work they had climbed halfway back up, but could go no further. Each step on the ascent was followed by a drop which then had to be painfully reversed. If you think about that as relative rate of descending to ascending this was roughly 50:1. When climbing mountains where going up involves fighting gravity and descending is gravity assisted, I come down pretty fast, but I still only manage a descent/climb ratio of about 3:1. 50:1 is uncontrolled mental freefalling.

35

Holism

You can measure your own and other's relative rates of ascent and descent and natural predilection. Some people – like our IT group find climbing extremely difficult and they tend to get wrapped into the detail and some never get out of that level. Some people are natural climbers, but rarely drop down to 'ground' their high-level perceptions in reality. Some people can do both, but lack control – ascending or descending arbitrarily. The Baker passage about the peregrine is about precision and control in the vertical domain.

Assuming you have the ability to both climb and drop, you have a choice, but is the exercise of that choice guided by anything more than habit? The ascent and descent is the search for and the creation of meaning of the system you're interested in. 'How does this work?' is a descent question, 'why does this happen?' and 'what does it mean?' are ascent questions. How high you need to ascend and how wide you need to arc are gauged by the search for meaning. Learning when enough context is enough is a skill acquired by disciplined practice. The Ackoff recipe is a training for that.

Modelling

Conant-Ashby

Back in 1970, one of the cornerstones of management science was being laid by Roger Conant and Ross Ashby in the form of the **Conant-Ashby Theorem**, also known as the 'good regulator theorem'. Conant-Ashby theorem states that every good regulator of a system must have a model of the system being regulated. The word 'regulate' here may be deceptive since they weren't just thinking about regulators like the Financial Services Authority or the Health and Safety Executive. What they meant was any activity that was intending to either ensure a system was doing what it was supposed to be doing, or to decide it should do something different. In other words, Conant-Ashby theorem applies to everything that management does and beyond that to what anyone needs in order to be effective in the world. Translated from 'management science speak' into normal English, what Conant-Ashby says is that your ability to engage with any situation effectively depends on how relevant your mental models of that situation are. In some ways this is obvious, if you have no model of how an internal combustion engine works and try and fix one, then it's vanishingly unlikely that randomly doing things to it will work. Similarly, if you have no model of how a family's dynamics work then intervening in that to try to heal rifts may just make things worse. The point the theorem makes is that model building isn't a luxury or a nice to have, it's essential, you can't manage effectively without it. Of course, as systems practitioners we build formal models for a living, but Conant-Ashby works just fine when the models are tacit – as long as they are appropriate, as long as they cover the things that need covering.

For systems practitioners then, modelling is core to the discipline – if you're not modelling you're not doing systems. And because systems is about understanding the underlying structure or pattern of relationships that drive emergent behaviours, generally what we're modelling is those underlying patterns and how they drive behaviours. And that's true whether we're looking at an existing situation or trying to design a system to do X.

Modelling

A lot of systems practice involves building models of the real world, then experimenting with those models to understand how we might most usefully intervene in the real-world situation. We can identify both points to intervene and also what the nature of the intervention might be. If the type of model we're using is quantitative, then we can work out how much to intervene to get the best effect. Typically, we can use models to understand how particular emergent behaviours emerge and are maintained and this understanding is fundamental in systems, since what we're after is precisely that understanding of emergent behaviours. Following Conant-Ashby theorem, there is also a subset of systems practice that involves building and maintaining a model of the system to be managed, simply so that managers can understand it better and take better decisions. Not necessarily as an exercise to do with any specific problem or issue, but just modelling to support ongoing management of the organisation and its environment.

In this, systems approaches are different to many other approaches. A lot of management approaches do their experimenting with the real world and this has several risks attached to it, both in terms of the damage that can be caused by misguided or random interventions and also in terms of the lack of learning. Once you've done an intervention, you can't always take it back and if you didn't have a model of the situation pre-intervention it's incredibly difficult to dispassionately assess the consequences of your actions. Experimenting on live situations is fraught with learning pitfalls and the tendency to believe what you want to believe. Having a model is intrinsic to a natural learning process which looks something like this: 'given the model of the situation we have, we would expect that if we change factor X, we'll see a change in factor Y and Z in terms of emergent behaviours' and if that all looks plausible then we can go ahead and then check the model against reality and alter the model where there's a discrepancy. With a good model, you can try out a range of options against a range of scenarios without going anywhere near the real world. You get learning safely, quickly and cheaply. And as a useful by-product, you can use the learning to improve the quality of your model for the next time you have a decision to make.

It's easy to interpret Conant-Ashby as an instruction, the systems equivalent of a 'thou shalt…' and to some extent it is. But it's actually a lot more insidious than that. What Conant-Ashby means is that to be effective in the world, we must have a model of that world and that need didn't start in 1970, it's always been there. Even in earliest evolution of animals the problem existed and was literally a matter of life and death. The model might have been as simple as dividing the world into 'food / not food / predator' but it's still a model. For us, most models we have and that we use are tacit, they are models we've inherited, or absorbed through cultural norms or ones we've built ourselves through trial and error. And the problem this creates is that in trying to do more conscious, more formal modelling, we're not starting with a clean slate. We already have a huge amount of conceptual baggage that we carry around, most of it the ideas of long dead people whose situations were in some ways very similar to ours, otherwise we wouldn't still read Shakespeare, and in some ways very different. Shakespeare has pertinent models for lots of things, but not micro-plastic pollution, for example. But separating the tacit from the explicit is a challenge because in formulating an explicit model, you have to become aware of the tacit models that are currently (but inadequately) filling that space for you.

In many situations, managers rely on the tacit models that they have built up themselves over a lifetime. This is particularly true for management teams that have worked in the same organisation or sector for a long time. In these situations, managers' tacit models can very accurately reflect reality, providing the management team with a good basis for dealing with the sort of day-to-day problems that typically beset their organisation. However, tacit models do have a number of potential weaknesses.
1. The fact that they are tacit means they can hide big differences in perception between managers.
2. Being based on experience, they can sometimes fail to give a good handle on new problems.
3. Being personal, they tend to reinforce individuals' strengths and biases rather than supporting their weaknesses or blindspots.
4. Informal models tend to be too simple to cope with the complexity of large organisations.
5. They can restrict the capacity and willingness to initiate and deal with radical change as opposed to incremental change.

Modelling

As organisations become larger and more complex, so the need for the use of explicit formal models that managers can use to share their understanding and to communicate about the situation, tends to increase. Organisations operating in fast changing environments also require the use of explicit formal models.

Box & Korzybski

So far, I've argued that models are essential and ubiquitous and the first thinking challenge is to surface our tacit models in use, lest those undermine or overwhelm our ability to formulate more explicit models.

The next problems are those posed by Box and Korzybski.

George Box observed that *"all models are wrong, but some are useful"*. Box's wasn't an offhand or dismissive comment. All models have to be 'wrong' precisely because they are simplifications. The only way to have a model as complex as the real-world situation is to use the real-world situation itself, with all its extraneous noise and confusion. It's the simplification that makes models usable and useful in that essential aspects of the world are retained and noise is dispensed with. If a model wasn't wrong it couldn't be useful. So if, in model building, we're in the game of simplifying, then the critical question becomes: what do we choose to include and what do we choose to leave out? What do we class as essential and what do we class as irrelevant? And it's this that determines whether a simplification is an over-simplification or not. Picking the right elements, relationships, dynamics and variables to include in your model is one of the key skills in modelling – and if you are a systems person who is not enslaved by a single approach this should largely determine which approach you choose to use.

"*We think we're in control but all that we're controlling is the projection of the model in our heads. If that isn't a good fit to whatever is out there, we're useless."*
Stafford Beer

Deciding which elements to choose to include in a model, or how to model, takes us to Korzybski's *"A map is not the territory it represents, but, if correct, it has a similar structure to the territory, which accounts for its usefulness."* There are two critical aspects to this single sentence: first the distinction

Modelling

between map (model) and territory (reality) and secondly the correspondence (or not) between the map and the territory and there are really commonly encountered problems with both these aspects.

We'll start with the second bit – the choice for inclusion. To use the map – territory metaphor, then if the real world has a river that I would need to cross, it helps if that's represented on the map, preferably with suitable crossing places also marked. It doesn't help if the map maker missed out the river, but had instead taken the trouble to mark the position of sheep or clouds, because those are unlikely to be the same on the day I want to use the map as they were on the day the mapmaker drew it, so reasonably stable features are more helpful. By contrast, for Polynesian navigators the apparently transient form of waves and the ocean currents were the only features they could use to navigate, so that's what was in their 'stick charts'. What goes in a model is totally dependent on the context and use.

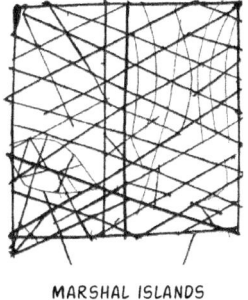

MARSHAL ISLANDS STICK CHART

Deciding what to include and what to ignore relates closely to three other chapters: boundaries, the difference that makes the difference and holistic thinking. It's on the basis of difference that we distinguish the boundary between what is inside a system from what is outside. It's the nature of that differentiation, the basis of that distinguishing, on which the essence of the system depends and the elements, variables and relationships that constitute that difference that we need to include. And anything not relevant to that can be simplified out of the model. How we define those differences and the boundary should be by reference to the system(s) of which our system of interest is a part. The process of modelling is about capturing the elements, relationships and dynamics that are essential for the system to do what it does and be what it is, within the wider system it's a part of. 'What its constituents are' is determined by 'what it is' which is determined by 'what it is part of' which is determined by 'what it is' which is determined by 'what its parts are'. If that seems like a bit of a circular argument, that's because it is and the structure of thinking is necessarily also circular. Unless you are just in clean sheet design mode,

Modelling

you cannot reliably nail any piece of this down first and build everything from there, you have to start holistically and then work it iteratively.

The other part of the *'map is not the territory'* seems much easier but is actually more slippery for a lot of people. The thinking trap here is to mix up the map and the territory, the model and the reality. Distinguishing the two sounds a lot easier, because the model is a formal 'thing' that we have created, a drawing or a computer model or whatever, whereas the reality is 'out there' and observable. But it's not that straightforward – to quote Einstein: *"Whether you can observe a thing or not depends on the theory which you use. It is the theory which decides what can be observed."* Substitute 'model' for 'theory' and it is the models we use that determines what we can see, and critically what we will fail to spot, what we can understand and what we can learn – and indeed whether we can learn at all. Seeing the real world depends on our models and the validity or usefulness of our models depends on the correspondence to the real world and again we're in a loop. This is a thought loop that a lot of people get lost in and when they do, they fail to distinguish map and territory. There are two diametrically opposed traps. Trap one is to lose sight of reality, to assume that our model is right and fail to adjust to match reality. Trap two is to lose sight of the created, overt model and simply be overwhelmed by our tacit models. (And with no model at all, the noise from the actual territory can be too confusing to interpret with any accuracy).

The world of management is full of approaches that have fallen into trap one. Change managers will often reference that change programmes have a success rate of around 30% yet in one longitudinal research study I did, the success rate of changes as planned was 0%. Conventional approaches to strategy have a similarly dismal record and Russ Ackoff reported a failure rate of 98% from one research study. The statistics about the mismatch between the model and the results show that the models for how to do change and how to do strategy clearly do not match reality. Whatever the rivers barring progress in the real world, they aren't shown on the map and yet, whole professions resolutely ignore the reality, stick to the map and fail to get where they wanted.

A critical thinking discipline here is to be very conscious about stepping between model and reality, to consciously and very deliberately step out

Modelling

of seeing the world through the model and use reality as an alternative. Part of this is addressed in the chapter on managing uncertainty. It sounds relatively easy to do, but to some extent both our ability to function in the world and our sanity depends on making useful rough approximations of reality rather than actually seeing the world as it is, so we are all past masters at self-deception. When it comes to raising the modelling game from the tacit models we use every day to more formal and explicit models we use to understand systems, those same self–deceptive behaviours also come into play. It's as if we're engaged in a 'shell game' where we switch the cup covering the pea with the ones that are empty – we practice a sleight of mind on ourselves. This relates to the Cartesian fallacy – the belief that the mind is separate from the body. Managing the relationship between a mental construct (the map / model) and the experience in the real world is critical if we are not to continually practice a sleight of mind on ourselves and others.

Because the relationship between model and observing reality is a self-referencing system of thought, another part of the trick of dealing with the slipperiness of it is to constantly check the validity of the models you are using. That involves periodically standing outside your presuppositions and checking them, checking the conclusions of the model against observed reality and specifically looking for evidence of where your model is wrong, not just where it's right. This is part of C^2 or 'second order cybernetics' – the cybernetics of the observer, the modelling of your own modelling, the act of becoming self-aware of what you actually think and why you think what you do.

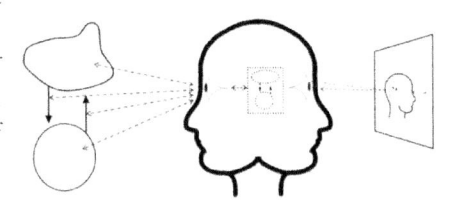

The territory is a system or a system of systems with an internal structure (set of dynamic relationships) and behaviours. The internal structure produces the system which produces the internal structure to form a self-referencing identity. The map is the model and can be of the behaviour set (using **Black Box Principles**) or of the internal structure of the system, or both. The model is wrong by definition and as per Box, it has to be wrong – a simplification in order to be useful, but the validity and

43

Modelling

utility of the model is whether it corresponds well enough to the reality, so that if you intervene in the model or use it to understand how the system behaves, does the reality match what the model says? As the chapters on uncertainty and differences discuss, a critically important thought pattern is to always actively look for mismatches, between what the model says and what the reality tells you. And then to apply Bayes theorem (covered in the chapter on uncertainty): is the model more right than wrong, or more wrong than right? Recalibrate the model based on comparison between what the model says and what reality says. But since the model conditions what you are able to observe, consciously step outside of the model and its constraints periodically.

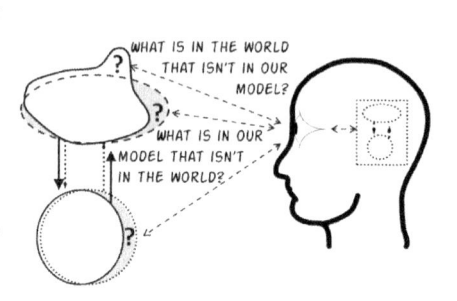

Two Heuristics

I thought I'd finish this section with a couple of heuristics that I find useful in thinking about the standard of models and of modelling. The first is a C^1 observation about the sorts of models used and their sophistication and the second is really a C^2 observation about your level of consciousness about yourself in the modelling process.

Heuristic 1

I'll call this the four paradigms framework and it looks at how people are thinking about managing systems.

Paradigm 1 – Gut feel and the 'garbage can'

In **P1**, people engage directly with the situation as it appears to them and there is no conscious use of mental models or theory to mediate either their perceptions or their actions. In a social or domestic context, this is how infants act, directly in response to their urges and stimuli in the world: when hungry, cry for food, when they see an interesting object they reach for it.

Modelling

Naturally in an organisational context, **P1** managers *are* informed by mental models and management theory, but these operate at a subconscious level, so are essentially out of their control. As Keynes said: *"Practical men, who believe themselves to be quite exempt from any intellectual influence, are usually the slaves of some defunct economist."* Given that what we are able to perceive is conditioned by the mental models we use, then what **P1** managers see in a situation can be quite random, as can their actions. They tend to be based on lessons learnt about social relations in childhood. In other words, **P1** managers typically treat organisations as if they were family or social relationships, based on personal relationships, allegiances of tribe or friendships, positional power (the parent-child relationship transferred into the workplace) and basing their actions and choices on personal likes and dislikes.

The strengths of **P1** are that most people understand the rules of family, although they may not adhere to them or may rebel against them. The weaknesses of **P1** are: 1) the limitation of social relationships – most people can't have personal relationships with more than around 150 people, 2) it fosters tribalism and political strife, 3) it's not capable of dealing with complex tasks. **P1** managers often exhibit as a kind of neo-feudalism: *"I trust subordinates who owe me allegiance and as long as I show allegiance to my boss I'm safe"*.

Back in 1972, 2 years after Conant-Ashby, three academics, Cohen, March & Olsen, did a piece of research on how managers took decisions. Their observations were that, often, decision making was far from the rationalist assumptions of most academics: they described situations in organisations where there are *"a collection of choices looking for problems, issues and feelings looking for decision situations in which they might be aired, solutions looking for issues to which they might be the answer, and decision makers looking for work"*.

Cohen, March and Olsen found that when taking business decisions, managers typically used what they nicknamed the 'garbage can model'. Essentially this involved managers having two mental garbage cans, one filled with problems and one filled with solutions. The garbage can decision-making process involves putting a hand in each can, rummaging about, randomly pulling out one thing from each can and announcing

Modelling

with a flourish that these are a matched pair. The manager, like a magician pulling a rabbit from a top hat, has just found both the most pressing problem and its solution. Simple, easy, quick, dramatic. If you look around in most organisations you can see garbage can decision making alive and well and it is classic **P1** behaviour. In **P1** models are not explicit, often subconscious and managers look for approaches like the garbage can that allow them to function without having to build or consciously work with models.

Paradigm 2 – Silver bullets

P2 is management based on explicit theory or models. That makes it a step up from **P1** in that now the mental models underpinning perception are at least conscious rather than subconscious. However, they are in a sense 'off the shelf', so they are not specific to the situation and are not constructed to suit the particular situation. This means that although **P2** uses models it doesn't involve actual modelling, the models are imported, not built. Because they are off the shelf they tend to be applied indiscriminately and universally. **P2** managers are trapped in Kaplan's law of the instrument: *"Give a small boy a hammer, and he will find that everything he encounters needs pounding."* **P2** managers believe in silver bullets, in cure-alls, but most models are limited in their application, and all need checking for suitability before use. Silver bullets are designed for werewolves – there's no reason to suppose they're going to work on vampires.

At the time of writing, there's a vogue amongst the Agile (software development) community for using the 'Spotify model' for designing tech organisations, but as a director of Spotify wisely pointed out: *"when people ask me about adopting the Spotify Model, I always ask them – so, are you a tech company in the music business based in Stockholm with unlimited start-up funding? If the answer to any of those questions is 'no' then you better think again."* And copying Spotify is **P2** thinking, but it's actually **P2** inside some other **P2** thinking because the wholesale and indiscriminate adoption of 'Agile' is itself **P2** thinking. It's a philosophy and approach that works in one context, so surely it will work everywhere, won't it?

There are two huge attractions to **P2**. The first is that it looks – both to you and onlookers – as though you are actually thinking, but intellectually it's the equivalent of picking over other peoples' thoughts. **P2** managers

Modelling

convince themselves that they are thinking and typically, the more they are pressed, the harder they defend their hammer. To be fair, it genuinely is an improvement on **P1** since there is now a consciousness of the model you are using. The second advantage is that when you are using an off-the-shelf model, it usually comes shrink wrapped with everything you need to know, think and do. It's usually a complete package and not only does this save you a lot of work, it also reinforces the impression and self-impression that you have actually got all the answers. **P2** is a really comfortable place to be – enough of an improvement over **P1** to feel comfortably superior, but without having to work too hard for that, and because it's a single right answer – a silver bullet – it eliminates uncertainty. It's very comfortable. And that level of comfort and certainty makes **P2** relatively easy to spot in others and in yourself.

Paradigm 3 – Modelling

Where **P2** relied on using off the shelf models without having to engage in the hard work of actually doing any modelling, then in **P3** we get to actually build models of *this* situation rather than hoping that someone else's model of a different situation will be good enough. Now we're into systems practice and operations research and similar disciplines. Models are specific, so less generalised than in **P2**, and part of the job of management is to do the modelling, not just take a shrink-wrapped theory off the shelf. There's a set of disciplines around this, how you check the validity of your model against the reality on the ground. Whilst techniques may be replicable, every case is different and assessed as potentially unique. The level of skill you need for **P3** is significantly higher, both because you need to be able to build models and because you need to be able to choose amongst a range of possible approaches one that is appropriate for each specific case.

Paradigm 4 – Closing the loop

In **P4** you hook your model of the world into the real world, so the model's elements, relationships, structure and dynamics are driven by data captured in the world and affirmed or denied by the evidence from the world. Ideally this is where work on building digital twins would sit, but unfortunately many such initiatives are stuck in **P2** thinking and are not built on well-founded systems models.

Modelling

Heuristic 2

This is a C² heuristic which is more about your relationship to the models and has three levels. At level 1 you have a model – let's say of a car. The model either does or doesn't reflect an actual reality and you know if it's accurate because if it is, then you can use the model to fix the car when it goes wrong. There is an objective reality that the observer observes which is not affected by the model or the modeller.

At level 2, the model is one or more partial perspectives of reality and, to the extent that it's accurate, you can intervene appropriately. If we take a model of a social system, there is a reality and there may be multiple different models that could be effective in helping to craft an intervention, but the observer is seen as outside the system; as Maturana put it *"every observation is made by an observer."*

At level 3, the model affects the observer's interaction with the system which responds to the intervention (and therefore responds to the model), so the process of modelling affects both the observer and the system that is observed.

"if men define situations as real, they are real in their consequences."
Thomas' theorem

The observer observes themselves as both inside and outside the system at the same time and manages their modelling for the effect it has on themselves and the effect the model is likely to have on the system. At level 3 you have to ask yourself: if we choose to see it this way, how will that lead us to act and the system to react? As Spencer-Brown puts it, perception is generative, we create the reality we observe. An example of this is 'Theory X and theory Y' two models of human motivation at work. Both theory X managers and theory Y managers receive feedback from observing the system that their theory is correct and the other theory is wrong. They both receive confirmation because holding each theory changes the manager, their interaction with the system and the system's interaction with them. Which model you use has an effect outside yourself.

All of these are valid and useful. Which level you choose to operate at depends partly on you and partly on the situation. Faced with a broken-down car, slipping into level 2 and choosing to use any model other than

Modelling

the workshop manual is unlikely to get you back on the road and a level 3 assumption that the simple act of choosing a different model will have any effect on the problem is delusional. Level 1 works for a 'natural system', where the observer is separate from the system being observed. Conversely, when faced with a complex and intractable organisational problem that is locked by its own internal logic, using the organisation's 'workshop manual' will just reinforce the problem, whereas simply holding and speaking from a different model can effect change. In a social system it's different, because simply having the model will affect how you are as an actor within the system and that will affect the system itself. The act of modelling or possessing a model produces a state change in the system, it isn't neutral. In a social system, you don't always have to actually act, the nature of your observing is itself an act, something Quakers have long understood with their concept of 'witness'. However non-interventionist it may appear to be, the act of witness, of seeing, of listening is an act that changes both the observer and the observed. Models are not neutral.

Boundaries

Ouroboros

The Ouroboros – a serpent or dragon eating its own tail – is simultaneously a symbol of: wholeness, closure, identity, death, rebirth, the emergence of order from chaos and boundary. Which is quite a lot to pack into one relatively simple symbol. All of those ideas are also tightly linked in exactly the same way in Systems Thinking. How, you might ask, can it mean all those things at once? It can because all of those are emergent properties of the closing of a loop on itself. As far as we know, the Ouroboros originated in ancient Egypt and the idea it expresses is probably older than that.

It's both esoteric and simultaneously strangely obvious and commonplace, and it crops up elsewhere too. The Norse myth of Jormungandr or Midgard Serpent is exactly the same – a serpent that surrounds the world and eats its own tail. There's a lot of slightly technical systems theory on closure and boundaries, but the essential point is one that was very well understood thousands of years ago and was enshrined in several similar myths and legends lest we forget it.

The creation myth of Rome involved the twins Romulus & Remus who had a colourful upbringing being left out to die as babies and then suckled and brought up by a wolf. When the twins had survived childhood to become adults, Romulus started to build a wall to form the boundary of what was to become Rome. Remus refused to accept the validity of this boundary and jumped over the wall. So Romulus killed his twin. The significance of the boundary in the story is critical. It is not just a physical pile of masonry. It quite literally is the definition of Rome, marking the finite limits of Rome. Failure to respect the boundary was a

Boundaries

rejection of the identity of what was enclosed by it. For Remus this was a fatal decision. We still mostly construct our world in this way. In many countries, it is still a capital offence to refuse to recognise and work within the commonly accepted boundary, it's called treason.

That's three mythical references and it would be easy to list a lot more, but some aspects of the importance of boundary are banal everyday experience. You can see it in a group of kids picking sides for a game of football and the effect of being picked and included, or not and being excluded. You can see it in tribalism in all sorts of contexts, in the visceral drive to be included on the one hand and the need to defend the boundaries of our identity on the other.

From the myth to the science, the two laws in the Grammar that are most relevant here are the **Law of Calling** – the act of making a distinction, carving out a boundary and defining that which is within the boundary, and the **Law of Crossing** – the act of moving across the boundary from one state to a different state. This moving from one state to another has two meanings, that the observer has gone from being in state A on one side of a boundary to state B on the other side, and also that the state of the observer has changed by the process of crossing over. You are no longer the same observer once you cross the Rubicon (to slip in another Roman boundary reference). As Spencer-Brown put it: *"...the first distinction, the Mark and the observer are not only interchangeable, but, in the form, identical"*.

And the end of all our exploring
Will be to arrive where we started
And know the place for the first time.
                                    Eliot

⌐ Spencer-Brown's 'Mark' or 'Cross', the minimalist boundary symbol used in the algebra of 'Laws of Form'

Wholeness & Identity

Whenever we put a boundary around something, and in our case around a system or part of an organisation, we are defining something. We are deliberately separating what is inside from what is outside the boundary. We are saying that inside the boundary is different in some way from everything else outside. This creates an identity for what is inside. This

Boundaries

happens whether we like it or not, every time we build a boundary. Every time we set up a new team or department, we create a new identity. So, identity is an aspect of structure and of the boundaries we create or the ones that we or other people recognise.

Where you are positioned, or position yourself relative to the system boundary, has a profound effect on your degree of individuation, what you are able to see and how you see what you can see. I find the easiest way to describe this is how we do it in Patterns of Strategy – by reference to herds.

If you are in the middle of a herd – whether that's a herd of wildebeest, or a company in a mainstream business sector – mostly what you see is your peers. You're surrounded by them and remote from the edge of the herd. Your world is mostly your peers, the other herd members and whatever is immediately in front of you. They limit your long-term view and you tend to take your direction from what everyone else is doing. For the wildebeest if the herd runs in a particular direction, then you do, and for the mainstream business, if all your peers jump on the latest management fad, so do you. There's safety in numbers.

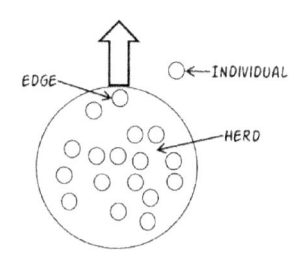

At the edge of the herd, there's more of the world to see and possibly some interesting opportunities, or worrying threats from outside. Your perspective is still that of a member of the herd, but you can see more and act on what you see, provided you don't get too far from where everyone else is, or charge off in the wrong direction. And it's to make sure that doesn't happen that you continue to see as a member of the herd – precisely so you can see things as the rest do and respond the way they will, so you don't get disconnected.

For those outside the boundary of the herd, the world looks and is very different. They can see a much broader range of possibilities and have much more freedom since they don't have to fit in with the rest of the herd. They also see the herd from the outside, not the inside. Their view of the herd is objective – seeing it as an object 'out there' rather than subjective – where their view is subject to and conditioned by the view of the system. The outsider is individuated in a way that that the insider cannot be and with that come advantages and disadvantages. The price of freedom is exposure, or to quote Richard Thompson: *"maybe that's just the price you pay for the chains you refuse."*

This goes back to emergence and the aspect of emergence which is changing the nature of a system's element to fit in with the rest of the system. Inside the boundary we are constrained by it, we are bounded or bound by the boundary. Not just our perspective (literally what we can see from inside) but also how we are able to think and how we feel is bound up by the boundary. Outside we are not bound and that changes what we can see and how we can think. Many of the seminal thinkers in systems were professional boundary hoppers – John von Neumann from working on the Manhattan project developing the atom bomb, to developing Game Theory, cellular automata and the architecture of computers that we still use to this day; Gregory Bateson from anthropology to sociology, psychology, ecology, learning theory, cybernetics, the double bind, schizmogenesis, military intelligence in WWII in the OSS and then proposing the U.S. resurrect that and set up the CIA and then playing a pivotal role initiating the hippie counter-culture; Warren McCulloch from marlinspike seamanship to blacksmithing to neural networks and several points in between.

Boundaries differ massively in terms of their hardness and porosity. Generally, the harder the boundary the greater the internal cohesion that can be and needs to be maintained. Hard boundaries are harder to cross in both directions, so they hold members better than porous ones, and you can see that with religious sects and management gurus where conformance can involve burning at the stake (sometimes literally for religious types, metaphorically for those seen as enemies of management gurus). In many social systems, rituals of conformance serve to harden the boundary and to reinforce the identity of members as parts of the system, and shibboleths or key phrases are used by system members to identify non-members so they can be castigated or expelled. In seeing boundaries, the fact that they tend to be well signposted and passionately defended makes them much easier to spot.

Boundaries

One of the things that the Ouroboros symbol makes clear is that the boundary is a loop, so naturally, any discussion of boundaries is also about loops and the properties of loops. Loops are covered in the chapter on dynamics, so I don't want to repeat all that here, but some of the ideas mentioned here are directly to do with properties of loops. The hardness or porosity of a system boundary is partly a function of how frequently the boundary is maintained – of the dynamics of the boundary loop and of the cohesion and coherence within the boundary relative to the outside – i.e. how different it is either side of the boundary. The more cohesive the system, the easier it is to differentiate from outside, the easier it is to identify differences entering the system and to force conformance – the 'difference that makes a difference' is clearer. Hard boundaries tend to become harder through time because they are reinforced repeatedly. In social or organisational systems, boundaries are frequently marked and defended with shibboleths – key terms or watchwords that have particular meaning for insider and that are used to identify outsiders. Porous boundaries tend to become more porous as the degree of difference between inside and outside gradually dissolves the boundary. Where you stand on porosity/openness vs conformance often depends on where you happen to stand relative to any particular boundary and whether you are habituated with being inside, outside or on the edge.

Boundary setting in systems practice

A vast amount of ink, sweat and tears has gone into debate within the systems community over boundaries. Most of that ink has been spilled over how to go about boundary setting. Where there has been almost no disagreement is that boundary setting is an important aspect of systems modelling. As an aside, much of the debate has been based around an assumption that doing boundary setting in a different way to the protagonist is somehow 'wrong', yet those tribal assumptions are a function of being within that tribe's boundary.

Putting factionalism aside, the necessity of taking boundary setting seriously when modelling should be fairly obvious. Models are abstractions and what you choose to include or exclude in your model is a matter of choice and one of the biggest and most important modelling decisions you will take. Unlike many other disciplines, where the

Boundaries

boundary of what you choose to look at may be obvious or simply one of scale, for systems thinkers the choice is rather more open. If, for example, the system in question is a school, where to draw the boundary may be obvious to an accountant, but it's far from obvious to a systems thinker and is largely dependent on perspective and your rationale for doing the modelling. For other disciplines, the nature of the boundary is largely defined by the discipline. For an accountant looking at a school, the boundary includes everything pertinent to the school's finances, whereas for the systems thinker, it is likely to be not just broader, but a decision that has to be thought seriously about.

There are various approaches to setting the boundary of any system to be studied and I'm not going to fall into the trap of advocating one over another, not least because I use several – and choose the most appropriate depending on the rationale for doing the modelling. Rather than conducting internecine warfare over preferred approaches to boundary definition, a smart way to take advantage of them is to use more than one and compare the results. Apart from this being basic good practice, it can also be a sobering reminder of how different the results can be that you get from using different boundary setting approaches. The real Systems Thinking skill here is both sensitivity to boundaries where you come across these, and also to consciously manage your boundary setting. Familiarity and use of more than one approach helps you to develop the ability to define boundaries in a formal sense, but sensitising yourself to recognise them at work in the real world is much more subtle.

Although the formal, methodological approaches to boundary definition in modelling are essential, they are about how we choose to model the world. The reality of boundaries as they are lived and maintained in the real world is a different beast to grapple with and is both rather better armed and a lot slipperier. If you try to rely on the formal approaches to tell you how to behave in the real world, they are likely to be both too crude and too slow. Dealing with the reality requires a more felt sensitivity to conditions, mood and subtle signals on the ground.

Sensitising

Every boundary encapsulates a more or less coherent domain, and because it is more or less coherent, it has a consistent and recognisable logic to it. The logic of a finance department is not the same as that of a marketing team. The logic prevailing in a gang of kids is not the same as that which operates in a community choir. Each boundaried logic is a stable way of seeing the world, it helps us filter and make sense of what we see and it's reasonably consistent and makes sense to us. Whenever we cross a boundary, we are moving away from a logically coherent position and inevitably and always there is an emotional charge. Emotion carries us from one stable, logically coherent, bounded state to another, but the transition across the boundary *always* involves emotion. Emotional charge is one of the surest signs of intangible boundaries. If you learn to spot it happening in yourself, that helps you sensitise yourself to be able to spot it more easily in others. Conversely, a failure to cross a boundary is often characterised by distancing – the moment in a conversation when someone stops talking about 'we' and switches unconsciously to talking about 'you' – indicating that whilst they think you may have crossed a boundary, they haven't, they are no longer seeing themselves as being in the same system as you.

The system + boundary + coherent logic + accompanying emotion complex is behind the phenomenon of 'undiscussables' and 'undiscussable undiscussables' as described by Argyris and Schon. The point they were making with the discussion of undiscussable undiscussables was that these exist in all organisations and you raise them at your peril. They are usually those topics that challenge the existing boundary of the system and the logic and stability of the system within the boundary. Sadly for the systems thinker and practitioner, it's often the case that you are working across boundaries – if you're not, it almost always means you're not in the right place. That in turn means that you're frequently walking a tightrope between what is and what is not discussable, so becoming acutely sensitive to where that boundary lies, to what is undiscussable, is both a matter of survival and also key to doing good work.

As a practitioner, the degree to which you can 'see' the system depends on being outside it, ability to communicate depends on being 'in' it. Boundary hopping is key. If you can't consciously shift your perspective at will, you are lost. And shifting perspective – à la **Law of Crossing** – means having the ability to change yourself at will from an outsider to an insider with the emotions and logic of an insider and back again.

One useful heuristic for practitioners trying to manage perspectives is what I call the 'Cracket model'. A cracket is a three-legged milking stool – three legged, because three lags can stabilise no matter how uneven the surface, whilst four legs are unstable on anything less than perfectly flat. In this case, in the context of an intervention in an organisation, the three legs are three critical perspectives: the managers / sponsors who have asked you in, those you're expected to intervene with – often staff, and your own. All three are legitimate, but different practitioners tend to have different biases between these three. Some assume that as experts, they are right. Some identify with staff and adopt the fairly widespread denigration of management as ignorant bullies. Some take the Machiavellian view that the 'Prince' is right and it's their job to do as asked. In reality, all of these perspectives can, and do, align with the long-term interests of the system as a whole, or can collapse into narrow self-interest. Learning to feel the pulls that each of these perspectives exerts, and to balance yourself between them, not only helps with managing your practice, but also helps sensitise you to perspective alignment in a wider range of contexts.

Boundaries, identity and communication

One of the effects that boundaries have is about communication and follows from the separation they impose. Communicating within a system is different to communicating across a boundary. And since I can't better the way that Spencer-Brown made the point, I'll hand over to him and his cat:

Amongst the other distinctions that are not commonly made, or, if they are made, are not made consistently, is the distinction between communication and communion. Communication happens according to physical existence, in some physically detachable sense, and the characteristic of communication is that what goes on goes on at the same

Boundaries

level. One can take at the level of physical existence, nervous events ordered by sound waves. For example, wireless waves, or what have you, all detectable in physical existence, followed by a perceptor of information, etc. etc. etc.

Now, it is my thesis that communication is superficial to communion, and without communion, there is no communication, really, at all. That is to say, if there were no communion, which I will now define as a fitting on another level between the communicants—if there is no communion as indeed there sometimes is not, then what is communicated, when it reaches the other end, it not understood.

The more perfect the fit on the communion level, the less needs to be communicated, the more that can be crossed from one being to another in fewer actual communicated acts. In Laws of Form, this is expressed in these two laws—or at least there are pictures of it in the two laws early on, in the canon of contraction of reference, whereby, as people get to know each other better—a gang of kids go about and one word or even half a word is used to express a whole community between them. Whereas when people do not know each other, this has to be expressed in a whole book. But between people who do know one another, however, there is no need for a book, it can all go in half a syllable.

Now when one is communicating, for example, with one's cat, that doesn't have the sort of language we have, or if it does, we don't know it, then it is done in this kind of way. It is done because you know each other. And when my cat says "Meouw," I sometimes say, "What do you mean, 'meouw'" But this is a game, because if I consider it, there is never a time when my cat says "Meouw" that I don't know exactly what he means. Why I sometimes say, "What do you mean, 'meouw'?" is because I can't be bothered to get up and give it the fish or open the door or pet it. If I am honest with myself, there is never any doubt whatever. Although it says "Meouw," it makes it quite plain to me, by the context in which it says it, exactly what it means. And if I pretend that I don't understand, it knows perfectly well that I am being awkward."

His point about communion is about boundary – within a boundary there is a shared identity, and the strength of that identity is a function of how closed the boundary is. Where there is a shared identity, that is communion, and communication is relatively easy. Across a boundary there is always a disconnect. We all recognize the degree to which we share identity with others by how easy it is to commune, whether the bond (boundary) is formal or intangible – we both belong to the set of people who have had 'this experience' or like 'this music'. Conversely, when communication becomes hard, we know there isn't communion – we're not part of the same shared identity, we are part of different systems and there are boundaries that separate us. The phenomenon of non-communication across boundaries is known in cybernetics as transduction, the degree to which messages are distorted as they go across the boundary.

In practical terms you can use this in two ways. First, where you observe communion, you know there is some sort of unity within a boundary. That unity, that system, may be transient and indeed may be just one of multiple system boundaries operating in the space, but it's there and you can identify that there is something there by virtue of the communion. Secondly, if you identify a system, the nature of the communion will tell you something about the meaning of the system. If *"one word or even half a word"* can communicate a world of understanding about topic A whereas for topic B we require *"a whole book",* you know full well that the system is about A and not B – even if this is a work team in an office that can actually only commune about football. The quality of the communication will tell you a lot. And that's true for us in our practice as well.

The ins and outs of it

As a Systems Thinker and especially as a practitioner, you can calibrate your position relative to the boundary by the ease of communication – 'contraction of reference' or communion – by sensitivity to emotional expressions and by the degree of alignment to a dominant logic. The dilemma is the need to be able to cross boundaries and the risks associated with that, because there are risks when you get it right and risks when you get it wrong.

The risk associated with successfully crossing a boundary is that you 'go native', you lose yourself within the identity of the system you've entered and become subject to it and can only see it subjectively. The risk of failing to cross is that you remain forever an outsider – blessed with a degree of objectivity but cursed with an inability to really understand the system and to change it. To cross from outside to inside is to intrude and because, by definition, an outsider does not fit the coherence of the whole, they challenge that when they come in, which is both good and bad. The value the outsider brings when they cross is to import new forms – new perspectives, new ideas, new values and emotions and that only really works when they manage to be simultaneously both a part and apart.

Changing Boundaries

At a practical level, changing boundaries is one of the most impactful interventions you can do. Designing systems involves deciding what to group together and what to separate – lumping and splitting. Most organisational restructures are about just this – reshaping the internal boundaries of the system to make it easier for some things to work together and contrariwise to make it harder for other things to work together. It's a choice of focus. And in the process of changing the boundaries, the identity, logics and languages of sub-systems are changed – for better and ill. At another level, many strategies involve shifting boundaries – IKEA's revolutionary business model involved shifting the boundary of the business, so that their customers assembled their products rather than IKEA having to do it.

Every boundary shift changes relationships making some easier and others harder and changes identity and purpose. Part of the problem, of course, is that we tend to design for what we want and ignore the negative impacts that may also be entailed – the relationship that now becomes much harder, and similarly we tend to see what is, not what is not there but could have been had different boundaries been built, different choices made.

The Difference that makes a Difference

Difference and systems

One of the most oft quoted phrases from Gregory Bateson is *"the difference that makes a difference."* It's also typically both blindingly obvious and at the same time opaque and its deeper meaning is hidden in plain sight beneath the obviousness. In any comparison, there may be many differences between what's being compared, but only some of them are significant, only some of the differences make a difference.

Let's start with the obvious end of this. Any system is differentiated from its environment externally by the difference between the two. All systems have an internal structure that separates parts of the system into different sub-systems. And the different sub-systems are different from one another, and different from the system they are part of because …. they are different. Differences that make a difference form (literally form) the structure of the system and the differences are marked as boundaries. What is one side of the boundary is different to what is the other side of the boundary. Inside you as a biological system, your liver is different to your heart. It has a different structure, its cells are different (they have a different structure and have a different pattern of relationships to one another) and each organ has different emergent properties – they do different things. Each has a boundary, they are distinct physical systems with their own physical boundary that separates them as a coherent whole from different systems that are structured differently and do different things.

Without difference, there is no boundary and without boundaries there is no structure – there is no system, just randomness. The two concepts of the difference that makes a difference and boundary cannot be understood separately and they are fundamental to systems and to Systems Thinking.

The differences that make a difference mark the boundaries of systems and hence the system structure but also the system's emergent properties. An emergent property is a property of the system that is not a property of the parts of the system. Emergence is that which is different about the

Difference

system. Emergence is one of the ways we distinguish a system, and it is done on the basis of difference – what is the difference that makes a difference about *this*? Generally, the system's emergent properties are the most important aspect of the system to us. It's what our liver does which is different to what the heart is able to do that we actually care most about and which is most important systemically – if it doesn't work, it's not just the liver that is affected, the whole system is.

That was the obvious part. The slightly less obvious part is neatly summed up by Francisco Varela: *"…what is the meaning of 'wholeness'? This relates to two key processes. One is the process of recognizing the stable properties of wholes, by interacting with them. The other is the recognition that the stability we see arises from the self-referential, mutual, reciprocal interactions that constitute the system. Thus, the three notions I mentioned are* **distinction**, *stability and closure, and are really one and the same."* The **emphasis** there is mine.

Difference and complexity
The difference that makes the difference is at the heart of understanding complexity. If complexity is measured as 'the number of possible states of the system' then theoretically the complexity of any system is infinite – ultimately at the quantum level, but in most cases long before that. From a practical perspective though, it's a very different picture. In practice, the number of possible states depends on the number we can usefully distinguish and this is straightforwardly a 'difference that makes a difference' question. If the difference between two states is insignificant, if it isn't one that makes a difference, then we can ignore it. In getting a handle on the relative complexity within systems, we only need to take into account the number of states that are distinguished by actually making a difference. As Ashby said: *"a system's complexity is purely relative to a given observer; I reject the attempt to measure an absolute, or intrinsic, complexity; but this acceptance of complexity as something in the eye of the beholder is, in my opinion, the only workable way of measuring complexity"* and it's *"purely relative to a given observer"* because it's the given observer who decides what differences make a difference and therefore how many states we need to distinguish and therefore what the complexity is. And the value set that the observer uses – what basis they have for deciding which differences make a

Difference

difference – will depend on where within or outwith the system they stand, specifically where relative to system boundaries they stand.

You can think about complexity – the number of states of the system – as a function of structure, or dynamics, or perception, or all three. Structural boundaries mean separating things that are different. Differentials in dynamics create difference – if we move at different rates or in different directions, then staying the same as one another isn't going to happen. Perception can follow or initiate either the structural driver or the dynamic driver of difference. These three are distinguishable, but inseparable. If dynamics drive apart, then a structural boundary emerges and is perceived and to some extent, the order in which these three are operating often doesn't matter and usually isn't discernible.

As well as dynamics driving difference, difference drives dynamics. When you have two systems with high differentials across the boundary, those differences, that lack of fit, creates points of relative instability. The less system A fits system B, the more unstable and therefore the more dynamic, the relationship between them is. Differences exacerbate difference across the boundary and that can create escalating (positive) feedback loops in the relationship that amplify the differentials. Conversely, where the level of difference is low, the level of fit is greater, the stability is greater and that injects less energy into the dynamics. Accommodating low levels of difference is easier and homeostatic loops can form that stabilise the relationship.

Difference and exchange

Because differences create and mark system and sub-system boundaries (and then the boundaries mark the difference) you can think of the structure of a system as a mosaic of differences. As discussed in the chapter on boundaries, boundaries are barriers to relating. Because the world is different either side of the boundary, connecting is harder and signals are distorted as they pass across the boundary and it's the level of difference that causes that distortion.

But it's precisely those differences that make exchanges possible and worthwhile. We take in from outside the system that which the system

Difference

lacks and the exchange of value across a boundary depends on difference. If I go to the pub and order a pint of beer, I give Anne the landlady money and in return she gives me the beer. The exchange relies on her valuing the money more than the beer and on me valuing the beer more than the money. Same beer, same money, but the exchange can only happen if there is a difference either side of the boundary in how we value these. All commerce, from local markets to globalised trade is built on this. Differences separate systems and simultaneously create the conditions for relating and exchange. The benefit of connection depends on difference and the ease of connection depends on sameness which means that pragmatically, there is a sweet spot – different enough to make connecting worthwhile but similar enough to make connecting possible.

Whilst on difference, wholeness, boundaries and exchange across the boundary, it's worth going back to Varela again: *"Now, a word of caution here. We are not: saying that such systems are closed for interactions. This is a point where there is much semantic confusion; when you say that a natural system has organizational closure, people think that you mean closed for interactions. Nothing of the sort, though this is the common meaning…. no system is closed for interactions, that is, it is not closed for matter and energy. But it can be organizationally closed, as was said by Ashby many years ago."* In other words, its boundary encloses the structure that embodies its difference from outside, but allows in elements from outside to maintain but also change that structure. Difference maintains stability by separation into stable wholes, but also drives change as difference is exchanged.

Difference and modelling

The modelling skill in making distinctions is really about recognising those differences that make a difference so you can build those into your model and forget the rest. This is one of the thinking traps discussed in the chapter on modelling: how do you select the relevant elements, relationships and variables to include in your model? To which the answer is that you select those that make the difference that makes the difference.

Difference

Making distinctions is so important that it forms the core tenet of Spencer-Brown's **Laws of Form** in his **Law of Calling**. Given how important this is as a skill, it may seem odd that there is relatively little guidance or technique on how to do it in systems methodologies. The impact of these distinction choices affects not just what aspects and elements of a system get picked up and which downplayed or ignored, it also forms the structuration of many systems models.

> *"a universe comes into being when a space is severed or taken apart… By tracing the way we represent such a severance, we can begin to reconstruct … the basic forms underlying linguistic, mathematical, physical, and biological science, and can begin to see how the familiar laws of our own experience follow inexorably from the original act of severance."*
>
> Spencer-Brown

The thinking skill of making distinctions and identifying which really matter is partly about recognising those differences that make a difference so you can build those into your model and forget the rest. Making distinctions is one of the most fundamental activities in modelling and the skill with which this is done is one of the biggest factors determining whether any model captures the essential and dispenses with the superficial or loses some vital factor or relationship – which in turn largely determines whether it is useful or misleading. It works at multiple levels: the level of deciding what this system is about, then where we should draw the boundary, then what are the critical elements, relationships and variables that we need to model, then how much detail do we need to go into in each of those. To some extent, the first of those is discussed in the chapter on emergence, the second in the chapter on boundaries and some of the third in the chapter on modelling.

> *"We select, from an infinite number of relations between things, a set which, because of coherence and pattern and purpose, permits an interpretation of what otherwise might be a meaningless cavalcade of arbitrary events. It follows that the detection of system in the world outside ourselves is a subjective matter. Two people will not necessarily agree on the existence, or nature, or boundaries of any systems so detected."*
>
> Stafford Beer

Many or most systems approaches involve grouping system elements into coherent sub-systems and how you choose to do this is a problem of

65

Difference

making distinctions: why practitioner A will group according to one set of criteria and practitioner B will do it in a different way is about how we make distinctions. If you change this basic structuring, then essentially you have built a different model and you will draw different conclusions. The natural way to do the grouping is by level of difference, so the system structure (the boundary) is set by the degree of difference within and outwith the boundary and if the level of difference within a model boundary is greater than the level of difference across the boundary then you've probably got the boundary wrong. And those 'bogus' boundary identifications are all around us: racism depends on believing that differences between groups are greater than differences between individuals within each group and that is clearly not the case, although that was probably less obvious 200 years ago when cultural, racial, religious and technological boundaries were often contiguous, so the inter-group differences were much stronger.

In terms of process, because identifying differences works at multiple levels of a model and in all areas of a model, this pretty much has to be an iterative rather than a linear process. The identification of the relevant system elements depends on the identification of the relevant whole and the identification of the whole depends on the boundary, as Varela helpfully points out, but then the identification of a boundary can depend on the sameness or difference of sets of elements. Sometimes you can work back in a relatively linear way from an emergent property that you want to explain, identify the difference which characterises that property and then work from that to identify the identity, the boundary and the elements of the system. Sometimes.

Methodologically, one of the principal ways in which seeing difference is brought into systems practice is by stakeholder modelling and multiple perspectives. Technically what we're doing there is to pick representatives from across that mosaic of differences within and outwith the system and get a fix on the range of difference at work.

Seeing Difference

We tend to think of seeing differences as an act of cognition, as a thinking process, and it can be, but unless you are explicit with yourself

Difference

about the basis on which you are making distinctions, the reality is that what drives your choices isn't cognitive, it's driven by much deeper, subconscious value judgements. It's very easy to assume that these implicit judgements are 'true' or are based on some validity simply because they seem obvious – to us, but instead they are based on personal values. Here as elsewhere, the foundation of this skill is in being conscious of the distinctions you make and more importantly being conscious of the basis of your distinction making.

One of the best techniques I've seen for getting at the values that lie under the skin is from George Kelly. Kelly's grid takes a set of cognitive elements at play in a situation, shuffles those randomly into sets of three and then asks: of these three, which two are similar and which is different and why? The 'why A & B are similar and C is different' is the difference that makes a difference to that stakeholder and exposes their values in respect of this situation. This shuffled triples exercise is done repeatedly and the value set emerges. The differences that we are able to see are much deeper than merely cognitive, they are built into our system structures.

In thinking about how to see difference I find it useful to look at four different theories of perceiving, and recognise that how people *think* they perceive varies a lot and has an effect on what we perceive.
1. Reality is out there, we sense what is there
2. Reality is out there, we sense some of what is there
3. Reality is out there, we sense some of what is there and what we are able to sense is limited by what we are able to make sense of and that depends on the mental models we use and the mental models we use depend on what we sense
4. Reality is out there, but instead of sensing it directly, what we do is find a model that could fit the reality and use that to prejudge the situation and that is what we perceive.

3 and 4 can sound very similar, but the sequencing is different, because the way the actions relate to one another is different, so the emergent property is different. In 3, our models are filtering our perceptions of reality, whereas in 4, our models and past experiences are actually constructing our perception of reality. We build a prediction of what we see based on past experience and that prediction is confirmed or denied

Difference

by how much the world is similar or different to it. As Harnden put it: *"From Pask and Maturana (and Bateson and von Foerster) we have it that mind does not work as a mirror of nature, and indeed, is not a representative function (representative of what is 'outside it'), but instead forms (in Maturana's language) a 'languaging' function. By this he means that mind is something that works for humans NOT by capturing or picturing or representing what is outside it, but, instead, by enabling recurrent human interactions with all that is 'outside'. It is not so much how mind 'represents' reflects, but how mind enables the in every sense isomorphism (one-to-one correspondence) of what is within and what is not. So the systemic nature of things is not something constructed or imagined or willed (by human beings), but is the experience of being fitted to what is anyway going on."*

In that process of construction, the drive is for similarity, what we perceive is what we know, we structure our perception as a kind of collage of things we already know and for that to work the reality has to be similar enough to our past experiences for our perception to work in the world.

At the same time, as the most basic cognitive act is to see difference, most of our cognition is based on seeing sameness. Sameness and difference are just two sides of the same coin and in fact they are just the two sides of the boundary that is created by the act of distinguishing. As Spencer-Brown pointed out, every distinction creates a boundary – on one side 'this' and on the other 'not this' and everything that is on the 'this' side of the boundary is there by virtue of sameness and everything on the other side is there because of its difference or not-sameness. Sameness and difference may be two sides of the same coin, but they are not equivalently easy.

It is much easier to see sameness after having seen difference than it is the other way around. Seeing sameness first captures and anchors our thinking in a way that makes it harder to see differences until they are so overwhelming they make themselves obvious. Sameness and difference is a lobster trap, the entrance to sameness is wide and the access easy, but it is much harder to get out of. Going from difference to sameness is less trapping.

Difference

There is a whole field of psychology – Perceptual Control Theory (PCT), which Powers developed from the work of Weiner and Ashby, and the findings of PCT are that we act in the world so as to not overstretch the tolerance limits of our perceptions. If the cognitive load of perceiving using past experience becomes too hard, then we move to reduce it – we move into safer territory. The more commonly known behavioural theories in psychology argue that our behaviour in the world is driven

> "…the organism's stability produces certain levels to be maintained, and all the nervous system does is to maintain those internally generated levels in the face of perturbations. So behavior becomes the compensation for those perturbations. This was first proposed by H. Maturana, and followed by W. Powers in his book Behavior: The Control of Perception. "Perception" in this context means the organism's view of whatever impinges on it. And his view is precisely dependent upon the reference levels he is set up to maintain, rather than on an externally defined "stimulus" that is to be "processed," as defined by an external agent."
>
> Varela

by our perceptions, whereas PCT reverses that logic and argues that our behaviour drives (controls) our perception. In behavioural psychology the thesis is that stimulus outside in the world affects perception which affects behaviour which affects the world. The PCT thesis is that external stimulus or not, we behave in the world so as to keep our perceptions within homeostatic limits – we behave to reduce the need to perceive difference. Now both of these are loops, so you could take the view that it doesn't matter where you start, but the loops run in different directions, so it does matter. One way in which it matters is the understanding of purpose, so in PCT, purpose is intrinsic to the system; it is to move to reduce the perceptual load, the load of maintaining perceptions when the reality doesn't fit them, whereas in a behavioural model, purpose is extrinsic. Practically, for the subject of this section of the book, this means that we constantly drive towards being able to perceive more easily, and that means being able to get away with perceiving sameness rather than difference. We are naturally difference avoiders.

This means that seeing difference is a skill that has to be developed and extended. This is naturally and inevitably uncomfortable. If our natural behaviour is to reduce perceptual load and to move to be able to perceive sameness, then going the other way is hard and if you can't feel the discomfort of the stretching, then you're probably not stretching. It's the mental equivalent of 'feeling the burn', the burn that is muscle fibres tearing and healing stronger. One of the emotional and mental traps here is what I call the externalising trap. There are some people who have developed the habit of pointing out difference to others whilst staying firmly within their own comfort zone and it's often possible to detect a whiff of smugness about them as they cause discomfort for everyone else whose mental equilibrium they've just destabilised. If you learn to spot this trait in others, you can learn to spot it in yourself. The critical issue is not so much that doing it is bad for others, because usually the effect on them will be temporary; the critical issue is that it's bad for the person who does it because it is self-limiting and the emotional reward for doing it can become addictive.

All this has massive implications for the systems practitioner. Our job often involves seeing disparities between our perception of the world and that of others which we think have implications either good or bad for them, then destabilising their perceptions so that they can move in a direction that will restore equilibrium. One of the risks is that the client retreats and uses cognitive dissonance to ignore the source of discomfort – at which point you have failed as a practitioner, and as the bringer of discomfort you get booted out. Doing the job well is walking a tightrope – overstretch their perceptions and they reject the message, under-stretch them and they may keep you forever, but you have become part of the problem and are contributing to a possibly fatal delusion about the reality of the world they are in. The nature of discomfort is a difference in the world that is being ignored, i.e. a difference that makes a difference that is not being recognised and is being perceived and treated as a sameness. To walk the tightrope, to do the job well, then, requires understanding what the differences are that you are seeing that they are not, what those differences mean in terms of consequences for them – 'if we continue to ignore this then x will / might happen' and also what they mean perceptually and emotionally. Why have they not recognised this new difference before? What will it cost them to have to recognise it now? What will it cost them to deal with it?

Get to notice the cosy feeling you get when you can identify something unfamiliar as being like something familiar, that moment when you can

Difference

offload the discomfort and restore equanimity. Then compare that with the feeling of unease you get when you look for the mis-fitting of the new to the familiar. The spikiness of the misfitting, the particular emotions it triggers in you, and in a PCT way, the characteristic behaviours you use to dismiss or ignore difference. Get to feel the degree to which seeing misfitting makes you a misfit. Seeing difference puts you on the other side of the boundary of the known system, both in terms of perceiving and emotionally. It's the disparity between the comfort of familiarity versus the discomfort of unfamiliarity. We talk about this more in the chapter on uncertainty: in terms of McGilchrist, this is a switch of hemisphere, in terms of Boyd, it's the rigorous mental discipline of making yourself actively look for differences between your model of the world and the reality of the world and in terms of Korzybski, it's consciously flipping from map to territory.

Sameness, difference and learning

A common learning fault is to compare something new to what you already know. The most consistently extreme example of this I've seen was a professional group who followed the teachings of a management guru. If you presented an idea or model with which they weren't familiar, then the invariant response was to compare it to the teachings of the great man – if they could find a way to say it was the same as what he had said then they accepted the idea – but of course they had learned nothing, merely confirmed what they already knew (and that there was nothing new to learn). If they couldn't reconcile it with what the great man had said, then they rejected the idea. Either way, they'd learned nothing new. My experience is that this particular anti-learning trait is endemic in some groups and is maintained by strong negative feedback loops, often encoded in ritualised repetition of existing patterns of thought – it's really no different to the chanting of mantras.

"...Information consists of differences that make a difference..."
Bateson

'Single loop learning' – a negative feedback loop that either confirms or doesn't that you got what you expected, is essentially re-learning what you already knew. 'Double loop learning' – where there is a further loop

Difference

questioning the parameters of your expectation, takes you into some new territory. It's about learning anew.

If you want to learn new things, then handling difference is critically important and is a skill that can be learned. Most people presented with something new will compare it to something they already know and look for similarities.

> "What passes for planning is frequently the projection of the familiar into the future."
> Kissinger

This is a way to fit it into our world, to literally assimilate it. The alternative is to look for difference, for the way this new thing is different to what we already know. Most people can do both, but around 95% of people look for similarity first and only consider difference as an afterthought or not at all. Naturally, once you have located the new things and identified it with something known, then you minimise the need to spot differences. Both cognitively and emotionally, it's easy to gloss over difference – sameness creates harmony, difference creates discord. In the chapter on uncertainty, I mention McGilchrist's theory about the two hemispheres of the brain – his Master and Emissary model, in which one hemisphere deals with the known, the familiar and the other with the novel and unfamiliar. From that perspective, anchoring something new into the realm of the known means that we consign it to the hemisphere that deals with routine and consequently we are less likely to be able to spot differences.

Relating

"Because you understand one, you think you understand two because one and one is two, but first you must understand and."

Of all the Systems Thinking skills in this book, this one is, in my view, the hardest both to get your head around and also the hardest to hang on to in practice. Superficially it's easy, but for most people the reality is something else entirely and one that can be deeply disorientating.

The thinking skill is to focus ***primarily*** on relationships rather than on the things the relationship is between, and to focus on how the relationships define the things rather than the other way around. Obviously, both thing and relationship can be important, but in terms of where we choose to focus, we study the nature of the connection more than what it is that is being connected.

Understand 'and'

If we start with a simple example, a connection or relationship between two people, the natural tendency is to think about the people themselves rather than the nature of the relationship that is between them. We naturally fall into seeing the world in terms of the 'things' in it, in this case, the two people. In some ways, we don't even have a vocabulary in the English language to discuss this easily or sensibly, so even in terms of the language we use If we want to talk about how people relate to one another, we use a noun 'relationship' to speak of it as if it was itself a thing, because the alternative to it being a thing is that it is 'no-thing', it is nothing – non-existent.

And of course, this isn't simply linguistic. Things are material – our two people have physical bodies, we can see, touch, smell them, whereas their relating is partly intangible and even when it is sensed – for example when we can hear them talking – it is ephemeral, impermanent, so our natural bias towards concentrating on things is understandable.

Relating

And yet the impermanence of our perception, the intangibility of relating, has nothing to do with the importance or indeed the longevity of the relationship. The most important thing for me about anyone else is my relationship to them – even when that is distant in time or locality. Time is no barrier – many people are affected by their relationship to their parents long after their parents are dead. The relationship can be real even though the 'thing' the relationship was with may have long since gone. As for the past, so for the future, some of our most powerful emotions are about relationships that are not but which might be or which might become. Some people live their entire emotional lives based on hope. Nor does our thing-centric bias have anything to do with importance, from the dog I meet walking down the street, to my closest friends. The nature of how we relate is what is most important: will the dog bite or wag its tail, are friends 'there for one another' irrespective of gaps in time, fortune and circumstance? Even with something more banal, the way I relate to a car or computer can be as important as the thing itself.

The 'things' world view dominates whole sectors. Just as one example, the linked fields of organisational development and occupational or business psychology are heavily dependent on psychometric testing. Psychometrics seeks to type people and to provide a way to understand them, their strengths and weaknesses and to predict how they will behave. It is in essence a pigeonholing exercise. One of the most popular approaches is Myers Briggs and this has 16 types, and everyone fits into one of these. This is a things view of people, it sees people as inherently and inalienably 'being like X', as having fixed characteristics which in turn, define what they are like. In this view, individuals have fixed qualities that can be used to define them 'Fred is an ESTJ' and also predict and drive behaviour – 'Fred will do x / think y because he's an ESTJ'.

This is despite the fact that one of the giants who founded the field of OD, Kurt Lewin, saw things very differently. Lewin's formula $B = f(P, E)$ states that an individual's behaviour (B) is a function (f) of the person (P), including their characteristics, and their environment E. For Lewin, both an individual's internal state and their external context were important, but behaviour is driven by how individual and external environment relate to one another. It's how P and E relate to one another that drives the behaviour, not either P or E, or even P and E as entities. And here I think you can see how easy it is to slip from a relating world view to a things-based one – the field is based on a negation of the basic tenet of one of its founding fathers and yet pays lip service to it.

From a systems perspective this looks very different, as Roger Harnden commented: *"one of the intrinsic conditions for systemic thinking is that it refuses labels as fixed attributes and also refuses linear causality. It doesn't say 'they are wrong', but (merely and crucially) they are nothing to do with systemic thinking. So if I read something that (say) Nick, or Maurice or Russell or Luc has written, and I respond by a conclusion that Nick is W, Maurice is X, Russell is Y and Luc is Z, then that is NOT systemic thinking (whether or not it reflects my deep-seated prejudices is a completely different matter). Systemic thinking does not resort to such labels and such a demand for a never shifting identity."*

A relational view is totally different to the things view. From a systems perspective, we'd look at people's behaviour and traits as being a product *"how can we know the dancer from the dance?"* Yeats of their interaction with other people in their environment and the focus of attention shifts from the individual and their characteristics to the pattern and nature of relationships and its characteristics. If the world of occupational psychology is built around a things view, what's the evidence for the relational view? Does this have any validity in psychology, or is it simply a nice idea from systems thinkers who don't really understand people? Well, there are several very substantial sets of evidence and practice to support the relational view.

Most dramatic are the famous Stanford experiments. A group of students was divided into two groups, prisoners and guards. Each group then started to behave in stereotypical ways associated with structure of the relationship they were in. The guards became increasingly controlling and the prisoners became increasingly rebellious. The story goes that before long, the prisoners had gone feral and were out of control and the guards had turned sadistic (and were equally out of control) and the experiment had to be stopped before someone got hurt. The behaviour of the individuals in the two groups was conditioned far more by the situation

Relating

they'd been put in than any sort of inherent internal characteristics. The structure of relationships was stronger than personality.

Lest you think that is a one off, anyone who has worked with management teams using simulations will be aware just how fast and powerfully an individual's situation in the simulation will determine their behaviour. In the MIT Beer Game, even when players understand the dynamics of the game, they feel powerless to not respond to the messages they are getting. The structure of relationships in the game is stronger than their own knowledge and common sense. Barry Oshry's Power lab is similar in some ways to the Stanford experiment (but less dangerous). In it, people are split into three groups, tops middles and bottoms and behave in stereotypical ways that are consistent within those roles across thousands of participants. The relationships we are in drive how we think, how we feel and, going back to Lewin' formula, how we behave.

The differences are profound, not just conceptually, but practically. If we assume that it's an individual's inherent characteristics that are dominant, then we tend to see individuals as fixed entities and our focus is on square pegs and round holes. If on the other hand we see individuals' behaviours as being shaped by the relationships they are in, then our priority is on understanding those relationships and changing them where appropriate. That opens up a completely different set of options for us.

"We live in a world which is only made of relationships. And when you think you can talk about the table, you say it's hard, all you are saying is that in conflict, in confrontation between the table and your hand, your hand had to stop moving at a certain point, the table won. If the table was soft, your hand would have won. But you are talking about something between the two of them."

Nora Bateson

The traditional and non-systemic view of a customer-supplier relationship was crudely 'we make stuff, we push it towards the market and the people who buy it are customers, and the nature of the relationship is that we give them goods, they give us money'. Structurally, the value is generated in the two entities (goods or services are generated in the provider and money is separately generated by the customer). The relationship is a simple act of exchange of the value each has generated independently (the act of exchanging may be repeated, but each is a singular event) and the nature of the relationship is essentially linear and is seen in contractual terms.

If you look at it systemically, then you focus on the relationship and the value inherent in that and you view the relationship as a dynamic rather than a single contractual act or series of single acts. You look at how each party affects the other, you focus on how to enrich the nature of the exchange, exploring and bringing in different types of value that can be generated, you look at the potential of the relationship to generate value rather than just the two entities at either end of the relationship and you see the relationship as a continuing loop rather than a linear exchange.

And when you look for that pattern, you can see it everywhere now. Customers paying Apple to contribute to Apple's market research makes no sense from a traditional view of the nature and role of 'customer', but it makes perfect sense if we view the relationship systemically, as one where together they are co-developing something of mutual value and the customer is enriched by the act of relating closely with Apple. When you take the relational view, you multiply the options for change.

A pattern of relating

More broadly within Systems Thinking, a system is a structure of connections, a pattern of relations. This is so within the system boundary, between the levels of a system and across the system's boundary between the system and its environment. It's the pattern of those relations that drives emergent properties. The internal relations determine how the system is able to act in relation to its environment and the relationship with the environment affects the behaviour of both the system and the environment. This is not merely a philosophical issue. Within Systems Thinking, what a system *is* depends on its connections – both internal and external – but as importantly, what it *does* depends entirely on those connections and so does what it becomes. There is no such thing as a system that can be seen distinct from its environment. There is no 'system within a boundary' without there being an environment outwith the boundary. The relationship across the boundary stimulates change in the system and the nature of that change is a function of the relationship between its internal configuration of connections and the nature of the connection across the boundary. Which is very close to the Lewin model of behaviour. Systems are structurally coupled to their environments and this coupling is a type of connection that drives structural changes in both the system and its environment, and the trajectory of change is determined by the pattern of connections.

The system's identity, behaviour, and direction of change are all functions of the pattern of connections. As Gregory Bateson said: *"The horse didn't evolve, the field grass didn't evolve. It is the relationship that evolved. The horse and the tundra with grassy plains are interlocked. It's an evolution in which the grass needs the horse as much as the horse needs the grass. And you want grass, you want what's called a lawn, in the suburbs, so you will first of all go and buy a mower which will be the teeth of the horse, cut that grass. You will then go and you'll buy a roller, and the roller crushes the grass down and makes it make turf. Then finally you end up going and buying a sack of manure because you have to be at least the other half of the horse too."*

How it's hard….

Given that this is the thought pattern needed for Systems Thinking that is arguably the hardest to hold onto, the question of how to not just develop this as a skill, but also how to check you're using it is fairly important. If you're using many of the classic systems methodologies, then these support this type of thinking but it's easy to follow the methodology whilst thinking things rather than relating. In a System Dynamics 'stocks and flows' model, the essence of the model and the modelling is the flows, not the stocks, but it's easy to reverse your focus. In Soft Systems, stakeholders are classified by how they relate to the system, but it's common for people doing stakeholder models to drop the connectivity and simply list stakeholders. The props to thinking are there, but easily bypassed. In Viable Systems, it's easy to focus on the content of the boxes and circles in the model, and fill these with the names of 'things' such as agencies, departments, and teams rather than sets of activities and it's easy to skate over the nature of the connections between them. The essence of the Viable System Model is that it's a set of complexity balances along those connections within the system and between the system and its environment, and the boxes are really just anchor points for the connections describing the activities engendered by connecting. In that case there's commonly a three-level debasement or downgrading of the model from its systemic nature: from focus on the complexity balance of a relationship, to the activity at each end, and from that to ignoring the activity and the connection to the tangible resources – the things – that carry out the activities. And you can easily do this and still kid yourself that, because you're using a bona fide systems approach, you really are doing Systems Thinking. The obvious answer is simply to check your thinking periodically: am I thinking about this as a set of entities or as a set of relationships?

There's an interesting parallel here with the problems that holistic thinking poses for reductionists and it's a common complaint that you can't think about a relationship without first thinking about the things the relationship is between. Of course, that isn't true, most of us go through life seeking out things: people / causes which we can affix to a type of relating that we need to maintain. Lose a boyfriend / girlfriend / partner and acquire another on the bounce, often with similar characteristics (for better or worse); lose a job and if you can't find another, fill the space with a hobby or charity work, anything to maintain the relating because it is the relating that matters above all else. The relating is primary, the object of the relating is often secondary, both in importance and in time sequence. Learning how to see the nature and pattern of relating isn't easy or natural for everyone, however.

Although several of the commonly used systems methodologies act as a crutch to thinking about connections, there are other ways to develop the skill. I find Gregory Bateson's writing particularly effective for insinuating this type of thinking into your deep thought patterns. Many of the arts help. Music, painting and poetry– all rely on relationships for their effect. It's not the notes in a piece of music, it's the relationship between them that engenders an emotional reaction. It's not just a block of colour in a painting that creates tension, movement and mood, it's the juxtaposition or distance from other elements of the painting. I was introduced to a discipline as a teenager part of which involved visualising spaces between things and forcing yourself to focus on the space whilst holding the things in the 'peripheral vision' of your imagination. The tendency is to slide attention onto one or other of the things rather than keeping it on

Relating

the space they share. It was a hard and surprisingly disturbing exercise but did help with the control of focus. There's a bit of a parallel with the 'gyre problem' I mention in the chapter on holism. There it's about seeing enough of the wider context without losing sight of your reference centre and here, it's about focusing in on the relationship without losing sight of the entities at either end of the relationship.

But more prosaically than art or mental gymnastics, then as a quick mental checklist, are you looking at flows, balances, reciprocities, exchanges and changes within and outwith the system? If you are not, then go back and try again. Are you thinking solid entities or static characteristics, or are you categorising by type, are you using one of those 2x2 taxonomic frameworks beloved by consultants the world over? If you are then, go back and think again.

... and how it's easy

Having ramped up the 'this is really hard' I thought it worth spending a bit of time on how it's also easy. To qualify the 'it's hard' bit, what's actually hard is doing it consistently and bringing it into consciousness.

The 'it's also easy' part is because we do do this naturally, but not always consciously. Our personal lives are bound by the connections we live within: relating is our everyday life. At the level of organisations, our experience of using a systemic approach to strategy based on modelling relationships has shown that the vast majority of people find this approach easy to grasp, intuitive to use and disarmingly obvious once it's available. For us as practitioners this was a totally unexpected finding, we'd assumed the structural coupling paradigm – so different to a conventional strategy perspective – would prove too alien, but the reverse was the case.

Many issues are actually much simpler once you take the view that it's the connections that are of primary importance. Ackoff's DIKW pyramid is pretty esoteric if you think about Data, Information, Knowledge and Wisdom as things. It's also painful to watch people trying to wrangle this as a taxonomic structure into which they plug types of assets, and you get all sorts of weird inversions as people swap data and information (it tends to be data and information because the people who look at this in a things way tend to skip past knowledge and wisdom).

Looked at from a connections point of view it's much simpler, and a lot more useful. The Ackoff progression is both one of ascending levels of abstraction, in a holistic up and down way, and the different levels of the pyramid are different because they have different connections. So 'data' is only data if it is connected to something specific and real – the measurement of a concrete pipe, for example. The word data means reference points and a datum line is still used to mean that fixed reference in some contexts. If you don't know what the number in a database refers to, then it isn't data, it's just a number. Information is abstracted from that to (literally) form a pattern of understanding about those things, and it qualifies as information if and only if it 'in-forms' thinking. Whereas data's defining connection is to some actual thing in the world, the defining connection that makes 'information' information is to a person, typically a decision maker, and it qualifies as information by (in)forming their thinking. Knowledge is understanding that is portable from situation A to situation B and context X to context Y, so the defining connection that makes 'knowledge' knowledge is similarities between situations and contexts. And wisdom is the understanding of when you can and can no longer apply knowledge across totally different domains or situations (e.g. knowing when we have to think of a political movement like a wave and when we can think of it like a machine, say a gearbox) so the defining connection here is differences between contexts.

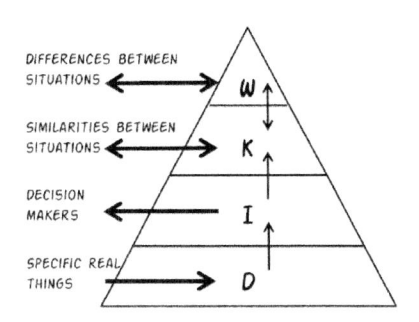

"Knowledge comes from but one perspective. Wisdom comes from multiple perspectives".
Bateson

As well as the relationship being the defining characteristic, this helps us manage more holistically and to deal with complexity. As we go up from information to knowledge to wisdom, so the range of applications increases.

Relating

Conversely, as we go down to data, the sheer volume and variety goes up dramatically and so does the load of handling this – hence the current fixation on the new IT holy trinity of 'big data', AI and Cloud. Big data because if you think in terms of things, then data is the raw material (and never mind that most of it is corrupted to some degree so it doesn't actually represent what you think it does), AI to try to make sense of that data and hope to turn it into information that someone could actually use, and cloud to store the big data on. Which is why all those AI algorithms built on the work of von Neumann and the neural network pioneers have suddenly been pulled from dusty filing cabinets where they had languished decades.

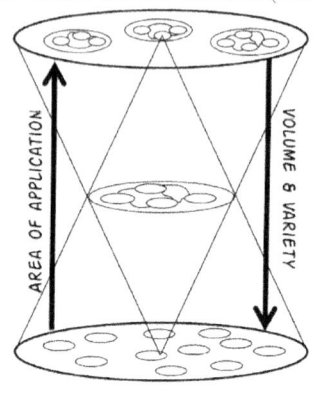

As with the comments earlier about the fixation of OD on seeing people as things or, let's be generous, as types, rather than seeing our behaviour as context dependent, so there is a similar issue within the IT industry and it is the objectification of information. This has had massive consequences, just one of which is that much of what passes for 'data' in knowledge industries is corrupted to some degree. It's very difficult to solve this sort of problem if you imagine that data and information are things rather than defined by their connections.

A few years back I was chatting with a colleague who asked me about a recent sailing trip I'd done. It was a long trip, across one ocean and passing through two others. He asked me about the ends – the port of embarkation and the destination and then he talked about those. The journey itself was totally ignored. Only the fixed things registered with him and the whole meaning of the trip, pretty much everything that mattered, was ignored. All the meaning was in the connection between start and finish.

Dynamics and loops

One of the breakthroughs that Systems Thinking made was to move from looking at the world in terms of linear cause and effect relationships to looking at it as sets of loops or circular relationships. In terms of philosophy or indeed religion or mysticism, the idea wasn't remotely new; in the 5th century BC, three contemporaries in different parts of the world, Confucius, Buddha and Heraclitus, all developed systems of thought around this. But Systems brought a different rigour and precision to the study of circular relationships as being essential.

It was tempting to pull apart this section and treat dynamics and loops separately. It was also tempting to bundle the loops element of this chapter into the chapter on relating, since part of the point is that the nature of the relating we're talking about there is that is about loops. So it may seem perverse to deal with loops alongside dynamics rather than with relating. To some extent, the awkwardness of the separation is the reason for doing it here. It would be really easy to dismiss the loop element of relating as nothing more than an 'and also...' And it's not that at all.

If thinking holistically requires precision to navigate levels well and if thinking about relating before the things they relate to is the slipperiest mental skill, then thinking about dynamic loops is probably the most complex. And that is because it involves taking into account multiple effects, and sometimes you have to do that simultaneously. There's the reciprocal nature of a loop: thinking about how X affects Y at the same time as you think about how Y affects X. There's the consequences and implications of what gets created when a loop closes. There is the effect that the dynamic of a loop has in perpetuating that loop and what that means for persistence through time and stability. And there's the effect that the dynamic of a loop has in propelling the system along a trajectory and changing it through time. And all of these are happening at the same time and as a consequence of the same pattern. In terms of the demand this puts on thinking, splicing together those different aspects or implications of dynamic loops demands a flexibility and suppleness that is as intertwined as the aspects themselves. Ideally you think about these

Dynamics & Loops

strands at the same time as a sort of gestalt, but thinking about them sequentially and iteratively is a good preparation, and usually good enough; so as you deal with one strand, say closure, then think about the next strand it's spliced with, maybe persistence, and then the next, trajectory, then….

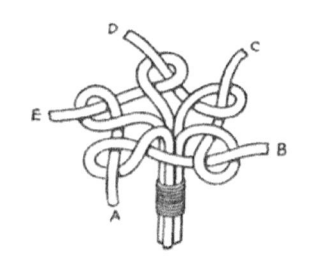

So, let's look at those five strands in turn.

A   Reciprocal effects

As we've said above, the shift from seeing the world in terms of linear causation to seeing it in terms of circular causality was one of the biggest differences systems brought. In practical terms, there are well established methodologies for understanding this, notably Jay Forrester's System Dynamics, and much of the cybernetic tradition focused on the understanding of feedback in systems. Those two cross over, so System Dynamics is primarily the study of the effect of positive and negative feedback loops, positive feedback driving divergence from a stable or normative state and negative feedback driving the dynamics towards stability and self-regulating return to a normal or normed state. These two effects are captured in the two **Circular Causality Principles** in the Grammar. For a lot of people, causal loops and causal loop diagrams will have been their first introduction to systems, possibly via Peter Senge's popular book 'Fifth Discipline'. I first stumbled across systems in the form of System Dynamics when I was at school in the form of the book 'Limits to Growth'.

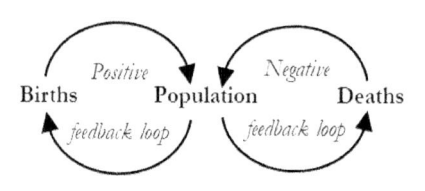

Senge's book does a good job of explaining what both positive and negative feedback loops are, and how they work, using two metaphors – a snowball for positive feedback and a seesaw for negative. The snowball rolling downhill gets bigger as it picks up more snow and the bigger it gets the faster it rolls and the faster it picks up snow. With the seesaw, as

Dynamics & Loops

one side goes down, the potential energy of the other side increases until it pushes down and returns the seesaw to level.

Although understanding both positive and negative feedback effects is relatively simple it is often ignored. Exponential growth in an economy is driven by positive feedback, as is the exponential reduction in productivity in the pharmaceutical industry (productivity halves roughly every 9 years, so it's now around 1% as efficient as it was in the 1950s), but in both cases, the nature of the feedback loop and how it could be altered is rarely discussed. Similarly, negative feedback driving boom-bust cycles in the economy is seen as a disaster rather than as a natural corrective process.

Whilst understanding the effect of either a single positive or negative feedback loop is relatively simple, understanding what is likely to happen in a system where you have both is not. And having both is typical. Where you have a positive feedback loop driving economic booms, and negative feedback that corrects that growth via a bust, these two dynamics, these two forces are in conflict and it's not simple to understand which will prevail at any point in time. Nor is it enough to simply tackle this in an arm-waving way by talking generalities about 'at some point, the negative feedback will dampen the effect of the positive feedback'. Does the negative feedback loop actually have the power to dampen the positive? And if so, roughly when and how might that happen and how will that change the dynamics of the positive feedback loop? The problem is that once you get past a simple single positive or negative loop and into a combination, our brains are simply not up to dealing with how loop A affects loop B and vice versa and you have to build a proper model to work this out.

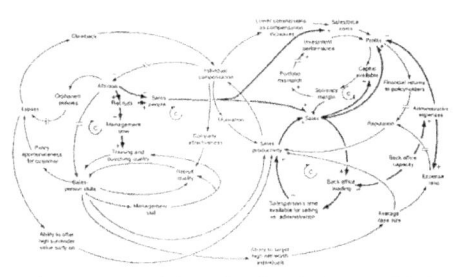

A brief comment here on this and emergence; because we talk about feedback loops as causal, some people assume that this means they are deterministic. They are not, the properties of loop structures are

Dynamics & Loops

emergent and part of the learning of System Dynamics is precisely that beyond a single simple loop, we cannot intuit the properties of the system because it isn't linear and deterministic.

If systems introduced the idea of circular causality as a scientific approach – obviously it's been around forever in art, mysticism and philosophy – then what of the more traditional approaches based on linear causality that have driven technological and social change for generations? Viewed through the lens of circular causality, looking at linear causality is simply to focus on one 'side' of a loop. To look at how X affects Y, but to ignore how Y affects X and indeed how the effect Y has on X will in turn change how X affects Y. The obvious consequences of that ignoring are unintended consequences. The 'serious' news bulletins (as opposed to 'cat rescued from tree' stories) are largely composed of these unintended consequences coming back to us. Sometimes they come back immediately, sometimes years, decades or even centuries later. Some loops are asymmetrical, so the power of X to Y may be far more than the power of Y to X. Or the Y to X effects may have a delay and in those cases it's easy to persuade yourself that you can afford to look at the relationship as linear. But if the feedback has a delay, then you may appear to get away with treating something non-linear as if it was linear, but only for a time.

B Closure

We discuss this in the section on boundaries, so I'm not going to dwell on it here, except to say that the formation of a boundary *is* the closure of a loop. Ouroboros, the serpent feeding on itself (or for those of a Viking disposition, the Midgard Serpent), is a feedback loop.

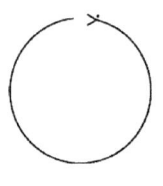

The point here is not so much to think about boundaries in terms of loops, but the reverse – to remember that every closed loop forms a boundary, it creates a dynamic system and that has its own properties. This means that when we look at a dynamic loop, or especially if we construct one, the questions that must be asked are 'what closure does this make?' and 'what is the system that has been called into being by this

Dynamics & Loops

closure?' The closure, the formation of a system through the closure, creates an identity and part of that identity is the emergent properties driven by the dynamics of the loops, and you can't really understand any of those fully without considering the others – hence the need to think of these together.

C   The arc of being

The phrase 'close the loop' implies that it's finished or 'case closed', but the opposite is true, the closing of the loop provides the impetus for driving the cycle again… and again. Loops have longevity precisely because they keep themselves going. Therefore, counterintuitively, the dynamic of a loop is the stability of the system. Systems are by their nature dynamic and instinctively that takes us towards thinking about change and how the dynamics create change – which they do.

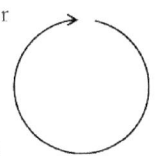

But they also do the exact opposite, and it's not always obvious to look for and understand stability in terms of dynamics and loops. Which is odd, because perhaps the most obvious thing about a loop is that it goes round. It repeats itself. It comes back to where it started and then it does it again, and again and again, round and round. Dynamic loops are the engine of persistence in systems, they are what contains (through the boundary loop) and maintains (through repetition) the identity of the system. It's the dynamics that drives stability and identity – as Aristotle put it: *"We are what we repeatedly do"*.

Loops repeat by their nature, and in doing that, they entrain energy into persisting structures of relationship and they create, recreate and maintain themselves – they drive autopoiesis, the property of living systems to create and recreate themselves.

As well as a way to understand the dynamics of systems, feedback loops have some critically important and often not well understood properties. Memory is comprised of feedback loops. We tend to think about how we think in terms of the technology of the day, so back in the 19th Century, people thought about our minds as machines and memory as a library, in the electronic and then computer age, people talk about 'hard wired'

Dynamics & Loops

thinking, short term memory as if it's RAM (invented incidentally by Jay Forrester of System Dynamics fame) and long-term memory like a file storage system. Actual memory isn't like that, it's not a thing that is fixed and lodged somewhere in your skull. Memory is the running of a loop – we recreate our memories every time we run that loop, it's plastic (which is why witnesses to accidents or crimes can be so unreliable); and it's dynamic.

The memory effect of loops operates at multiple levels. In fact, it works at every level where there are loops, which is all levels everywhere, whether that is in a biological system, from a cell to an ecosystem or in organisations. At a cellular level, organisms' immune systems depend on having a model of the system and this is maintained by feedback loops. Population migrations in ecosystems run on memory at the species or ecosystemic level: in the US, the monarch butterfly's migration requires several generations to complete a cycle; individuals don't make a full migration, but the population remembers how to do it.

In organisation and social systems, from habits, though operational processes (repetition of activities) to repeating patterns of strategies, organisations constantly construct, reinforce and renew their memory through repeatedly running loops of behaviours, actions and relationships. One organisation we looked at had run two strategies for 200 years of its history, oscillating between the two in a cycle that the trained eye immediately spots as a feedback loop. A colleague working in a big international development agency spotted a seven-year recurring pattern of centralisation and decentralisation. Doing the sums, he realised that they were due another swing to decentralisation and talked to the other group directors about this, but they dismissed the idea – there had been no hint of change in the air. Two weeks later the announcement came down from head office – a radical restructuring to a decentralised organisational model. Like the Monarch butterfly, the recurring pattern isn't held in the minds of individuals, rather it is the minds of the individuals that are held within the recurring pattern of the system.

A huge amount of energy and ink is expended by people complaining about how hard it is to change organisations and societies and the reason is simple: organisations and societies are made up of self-perpetuating, self-reinforcing dynamic loops that provide them with their stability, and the stability provides them with their identity. None of that goes away on its own. The identity, initiated by the closure of a loop on itself, creates memory through the repetition of running the loop and the memory recreates the identity.

There is nothing inherently good or bad about this, it just is. 'Bad' systems self-stabilise just as 'good' ones do. Alcoholics get trapped in cycles of alcohol abuse, same for drug users, same for domestic abuse victims, same for child abuse, same for gang violence. If you want to change it, you have to look at 'decommissioning' the stability loops, understanding and then unpicking them.

In terms of thinking about dynamic loops, there's reciprocity: when you're dealing with a relationship where you can see that X has an effect on Y then as a system thinker you have to always ask yourself 'what's going the other way and how does it do that?', there's closure: 'what system is created here?' and there's stability: 'how is that identity built and maintained?'. But there's another aspect to the whole cycle or arc of being which is to think about time in a different way.

We're accustomed in the west to think of time as essentially linear, as 'Time's arrow' moves inexorably forward. But the whole point about the repetition created by circular causality is that the past repeats. Activities repeat. Events repeat. History repeats. When I carry out the same operational process that is locked into my personal and the organisation's memory, I am repeating history. When the business does the same flip from employing one of the two strategies it's been using for 200 years, to the other one, it's repeating history. After the 2008 financial crash, I was doing a talk on systems to some MEPs and financiers and they insisted, and presumably believed, that the crisis had been unprecedented, unforeseen and unforeseeable. One of my co-presenters, a founder of the Institute for Fiscal Studies, pointed out that 2008 was just the latest in a recurring pattern of hundreds of bank collapses. Bank crises are a recurrent behaviour because the structure of feedback loops drives them in a fairly reliable way, the pattern of banking crises is itself stable. Once you start to look for the recurring pattern, they are often not that hard to

Dynamics & Loops

spot, but they may require you to stand further back to see them. Some cycles can be very long.

This non-linear view of time and history is perhaps easier in some eastern traditions of thought.

D   The arc of becoming

Loops are also the engine of self-organisation. When two or more free elements connect, if they don't just bounce off one another, and if there is a strong enough resonance, then that forms a loop and that becomes a recurring pattern, a self-organised system.

Elements find themselves in relationships and the loop of that relationship is formed and once it goes around again, each element is changed by the relationship and becomes different, both less and more. Less because each is now to some degree constrained by being in the relationship and more because it also takes on the emergent properties of the system that has just been created. This happens for better or worse, and intentionally or not and both the better / worse and intentional / accidental become near impossible to separate out since what we see as better or worse is changed by being in the system and our intent is also changed as our identity is changed by being part of the system. The 'thinking like a systems thinker' part of this involves spotting the dynamics of becoming, of spotting what is coming into being, and also, how the elements are changed in the process of becoming, a property of emergence. Specifically when we're considering human systems, it's about understanding how the thoughts, feelings and values of individuals are changed by the process of being bound up in a bigger system.

E   Trajectory of change

Where you have a system coupled to its environment – and by definition, all systems are coupled to their environment – then the relationship will drive change in both. For Maturana in biological systems, this is 'structural coupling', and as Bateson described it: *"The horse didn't evolve; the field grass didn't evolve. It is the relationship that evolved"*. There is a natural

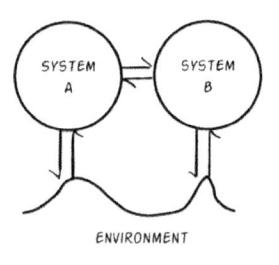

Dynamics & Loops

trajectory to both system ↔ system and system ↔ environment relationships, they evolve as an emergent property of the dynamics of their interaction. We tend to assume that this is inherently unpredictable and ultimately it is, but in very many cases, the natural trajectory can be deduced. The identity that is created by the closure of the interaction loop tends to be reinforced the longer the loop runs – the longer an alcoholic's relationship with alcohol continues, the more of an alcoholic they become. There is a sort of creeping change that is going on all the time.

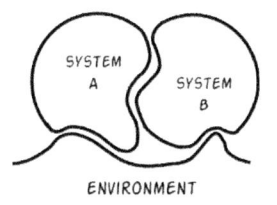

But then there's also the flip from stable evolution to more dramatic transformation. And you can think of this as a bit like the slow pressure of tectonic plates apparently suddenly turning into an earthquake as the build-up of pressure overtops the capacity of the forces restraining it. In exactly the same way, in a system where there are both positive and negative feedback loops, unless these are perfectly calibrated – and in a natural system, why would they be? – then flips in state can happen.

When does a stabilising dynamic flip into a transformational dynamic? Like the earthquake, that is really hard to predict. Marxism was predicated on Marx & Engels experience of the awful living and working conditions in the hyper-growth of 19th century Manchester – the world's first industrial city. Manchester was growing so fast that the exchange building, Manchester's trading floor, had to be rebuilt three times in around 70 years because the numbers of traders outgrew the premises even before work on each version was finished. The speed of growth of the city resulted in squalid conditions and deplorable health and little safety. Marx concluded that conditions were so bad and the capitalists so oppressive that the workers would revolt. He was right about the oppressive conditions and completely wrong about the predicted transformation. Mancunians maintained and were maintained by the dynamic that powered the astonishing rate of growth.

Dynamics & Loops

On August 19th 1989, there was a picnic at the border between Austria and Hungary. The border was part of the iron curtain that had split Europe in two. Two ideologically split armed camps faced off across the border with conventional and nuclear weapons primed and ready to use. To the west were the capitalist and largely NATO countries and to the east the communist countries of the Warsaw Pact and between them a 7,000-kilometre-long physical boundary with fences, walls and minefields built by the Warsaw Pact less for defence than to keep their citizens from escaping to the more prosperous west. The picnic had been advertised amongst East Germans holidaying in Hungary as well as to Hungarians and with the tacit agreement of the Hungarian and Austrian authorities as well as the East German Military, the wire was cut and people started to cross the border to the west. With the border open in Hungary, East Germans and Czechs crossed into Hungary and then to the west. Czechoslovakia was next to relax border controls, and after protests at the border, East Germany gave way in November 1989 and the Berlin wall was broken down by protestors from both sides. Political transformations followed as communist governments from the Baltic to the Black Sea were replaced. A tightly integrated political, economic, military and social system that had been rigorously controlled and defended for decades, unravelled within a few months. The pressure for change had been there from the beginning, so there was nothing new about that. The speed of the unravelling was because the system was maintained by an interlocking and tightly coupled set of control loops and once one was loosened, it caused a chain reaction across the lot.

The last aspect of transformative dynamics to keep in mind is the Triggering of network effects. The sorts of seismic changes that ripple through systems – including social systems – tend to happen when there is a chain reaction between and across interlocking loops, when the destabilisation of one system triggers the destabilisation of others.

Complexity

'Systems' is the study of systems that sit between inert and chaotic, those which are, to use Weinberg's phrase, 'medium sized', and is a discipline that looks below surface effects to see the underlying system that generates those effects. At first glance, these can seem quite different parameters, but they are all really to do with complexity.

First, Weinberg's size dimension. His law of medium numbers applies to systems too large to study exactly and too small to study statistically. If you are trying to understand the behaviour of a nation you can use statistics, and if you are trying to understand the behaviour of an individual or a small social group you can use ethnography. But if you are trying to understand the dynamics of a shoal of fish, an organisation, or a market, then statistics tends to be too blunt an instrument and specific observation doesn't give you the overall picture, and systems give you a better way to understand what's going on. Obviously, there are overlaps – sizes of system where you can usefully use statistics together with systems approaches, or systems approaches together with individual analysis – but generally Weinberg's dictum is intended as a heuristic for the practitioner and the reason it works is because it uses size as a crude proxy measure for relative complexity.

Weinberg's observation is that physics is the study of things that are susceptible to the techniques of physics, just as mechanics is a practice applied to things that are susceptible to the techniques of mechanics. In the same way, systems is the study of things that are susceptible to the techniques of systems and it's where there is complexity and the generation of emergent properties that makes systems applicable to the sorts of issues it's helpful with. No discipline is universal and its limitations are an aspect of itself.

Second, the 'between inert or static and chaotic' dimension. Many of the systems laws described in the Grammar part are concerned with how, when and why systems are stable, or unstable or fall into chaos. The **System Stability Principle** is critical here and states that '*for any system to be recognisable as a system it must remain stable for long enough to be recognisable as a*

Complexity

system'. Whilst systems is *really* interested in how and when systems fall into chaos, or conversely, how systems can self-organise out of chaos, the actual state of chaos is generally outside of the brief.

Systems (and complexity theory) are interested in, and in a Weinberg way, have approaches designed to work for, the continuum between static and chaotic. They really don't have a lot to say about totally static systems where there may be structure, but no dynamics, or chaos where there's lots of dynamic, but no discernible structure, but if you have anything that has discernible structure and is dynamic, then that is a legitimate target to use systems with.

And the third element is that we are looking at the underlying systemic drivers rather than at surface effects. We're interested not just in observing that a system creates an emergent property, but in how, in a system, the structure and dynamics do that. Whilst a (brilliant) economist like Pareto points out the '80/20 rule', a system thinker would look beyond the phenomenon of uneven distribution to the dynamics and relationships that drive that inequality – the 'winner's loops' and 'loser's loops', for example.

'Medium sized numbers' is helpful because it's an easy proxy for the probable level of complexity, and underlying drivers are helpful because they take us to how complexity is generated. Both are about the third – complexity itself, and complexity is central to any systems approach since it underpins emergence.

Given the medium sized numbers heuristic, which uses size as an approximation for complexity, why not just use size? Why trouble to understand complexity any further? Well, partly because size doesn't get under the skin to the systemic drivers – size is itself an emergent property – and partly because size is a really crude proxy. Elephants are significantly bigger than mice, but not proportionately more complex. Lots of large organisations massively reduce their complexity by fractalising themselves – a big bank has lots of branches which are essentially the same as one another so the complexities driven by difference are reduced. Doubling the number of branches doesn't double the complexity of operations. To understand complexity, you have to go deeper.

Why it matters

Ross Ashby used 'variety' as the measure of complexity and his eponymous **Law of Requisite Variety** follows from that, and for those suffering from physics envy, there is a mathematical proof. Ashby defined variety and therefore measured complexity as *"the number of possible states of the system"*, which rather begs the questions – what are 'states of the system'? what causes them to increase or decrease? How would we spot a state of the system or fail to spot it? And why does it matter? There are three main factors that drive the number of states of the system. One is its structure, another is its dynamics (and of course those two are related) and the third is perspective. But we'll start with the last question first – why does it matter?

The point, or the boundary of Requisite Variety, marks what complexity theorists call, or used to call, 'the edge of chaos' because once you step beyond it, that's what you get. So, since two of the main things that we're interested in in systems are emergent properties (and chaos or the transition to or from chaos would be a significant emergent property) and whether a system is stable, unstable or chaotic, then understanding where it is relative to the edge is critically important. Once you have a model of your system and have identified some areas where there isn't requisite variety, you can follow that chaos through the system to see where it flows and what it does on the way. Mythologically, dragons symbolised chaos and it's no accident that in many cultures they were depicted as convoluted intertwining forms. Following the chaos through the system – 'chasing the dragon' – is a critical part of some areas of systems practice.

The relationship between emergence and complexity flows both ways, you can start with complexity and work to emergence or start with emergence and work through to complexity. It's this level of complexity in a system that creates this emergent property, so we're interested in complexity because it drives emergence and you can study the complexity to find out what is likely to emerge from that. Working the other way, the question is: given this perceived emergent property, what is the complexity that creates that? Or you can tackle it from both ends at once. Whichever, complexity and emergence are tightly related.

If we want to change a system, and a lot of systems practice is concerned with that, then understanding the complexity of why the system is as it is and how that would have to change for it to be different is key. If complexity is the number of possible states of the system, but at any point in time the system is in one of those states, it follows that the number of ways the system could have been, but wasn't, is much greater than the number of ways that it actually is. Understanding how and why the system is as it is rather than as it might have been is a critical part of understanding. As Gordon Pask said, the systems practitioner should "*approach their work like Sherlock Holmes*".

Structural Complexity

There's a pseudo-systems adage that 'everything is connected to everything' which at one level is true, but isn't literally true. Every thing isn't actually connected to every other thing, or at least not directly. Separating things and breaking connections is a structure of boundaries. Structure – whether of a natural system or one designed – is about complexity and specifically about how to reduce complexity so the system doesn't become chaotic. Structural boundaries make some connections easier and others harder and in the process they reduce the number of connections that are possible both within and outwith the system. Different structures – putting the boundaries to divide the whole up in a different place – has a huge impact on the number of connections that are possible within the system and therefore on the system's complexity. Because in looking at structural complexity, what we're interested in is the number of possible permutations of connections, or how many parts of the system can connect to other parts, and the basic formula for calculating structural complexity is $2^n - (n+1)$ where n is the number of elements in the system. Because it's a factorial, the number of possible connections goes up dramatically with the number of elements. Structure, the system's pattern of boundaries, reduces the number of elements that can connect and so constrains the overall complexity.

Complexity

You can do 'static', point-in-time calculations of structural complexity and in many systems, the numbers ramp up and down dramatically. To take a real life case, running a set of typical products through a manufacturing plant structured in one way had a variety of 27.5 x 10^9 and structuring it a different way you could bring the variety – the total number of ways those products could flow through that factory – down to 70, and that is a big difference, and a big difference not just numerically, but also in terms of whether the structure and the people in it are overwhelmed by the complexity of operations. Thinking about boundaries and connections is also thinking about complexity, since where the boundaries are determines the number of possible connections which affects the systems complexity. For better or worse. In software, the biggest determinant of buggy software is the complexity of the organisational structure the code was written in. Where work has to cross multiple boundaries, it's harder to have the communications to enable that to happen well and the result is inevitably miscommunication and poor work. Fractured structures produce fractured products – as McCulloch's **Law of Sufficient Complexity** has it: '*A complex system constitutes its own simplest behavioural description*' or more prosaically, a system does what it does because it's structured like it is.

"Your organisation is perfectly designed for the results, outcomes and performance you are getting from it."
Galbraith

Ultimately, the complexity of any system is well beyond the level at which we can reckon it – it just depends on how deeply you choose to look into it. Even the most 'simple' and inert system is almost infinitely complex at the molecular and sub-atomic level and most are incalculable long before that. Getting a handle on the complexity starts to look like an impossible task. But then in comes Ashby's Law which sets down the critical importance of Requisite Variety or in other words: have you got enough responses to deal with the number of states the system can have? To which the answer is either yes or no. So, in many practical situations, the complexity calculation boils down to an 'are we're OK or not OK?' binary question. And once you get your eye in, in a lot of cases, you can go a long way towards knowing pretty quickly whether a system or a relationship does or doesn't have requisite variety without having to do difficult complexity calculations and partly this is because the numbers ramp up and down really fast. This is one of those places in systems where it's really helpful to focus on the relationship rather than on the things the relationship is between. Requisite variety is about the balance of complexity across a relationship: is A significantly more or less complex than B? and that comparison is usually much easier to make than having to be precise about the level of complexity of either A or B.

There is no shrink-wrapped approach to measuring structural complexity and it's essentially an exercise in working out the number of possible states of the system. The formula mentioned above is useful as a way to get a handle on the number of possible permutations, but the choice of what it's useful to count is a judgement based on understanding the difference that makes a difference. In theory, structural complexity is always infinite, but practically it isn't, it's a measure of the complexity that matters *here*. The number of possible states is about the number of different states that we need to distinguish and so this is about which differences in state make a difference.

The thinking skill around structural complexity is really about: having a basic understanding of how to assess the number of states, being aware of the choices you are making about what differences in state you think matter and understanding the interplay between complexity and structure.

Different structural options result in massively different levels of structural complexity as the number and pattern of possible connections are increased or reduced by the pattern of boundaries. Too much structure restricts connectivity and reduces the dynamism and options available to the system and ultimately drives towards stasis. Too little structure increases the level of connectivity which in turn increases the number of options, the dynamism, and ultimately leads to chaos. Structure serves the purpose of absorbing complexity and complexity mirrors the structure of boundaries. You cannot understand the one without simultaneously understanding the other. The **Root Structuration Theorem** gives an 'ideal' ratio of structural boundaries to reduce complexity and you can use that as a benchmark against which to assesses any pattern you are presented with – bearing in mind that there are almost always really good reasons why the ideal in theory isn't ideal in practice in most actual situations. At the other extreme, the **Complexity**

Instability Principle is about how structural complexity can drive a system up to and beyond the edge of chaos.

Dynamic Complexity

So that's structural complexity and if the world stood still, that would be all we needed to get a grip on complexity. But it's almost never a static game and the relative dynamics of different parts of the system and its environment will increase or decrease the variety of the system for any given period of time. Every change to the system means the system is now in a different state, so the link between dynamics and complexity in an Ashby 'number of possible states of the system' way is obvious. In terms of grasping this intuitively, I think this is easier than structural complexity and there are a number of standard systems approaches – most notably system dynamics – that help with understanding this with more rigour for any particular situation.

Outside of applying the standard approaches and just in terms of thinking systemically, this is largely about relative rates and rates of rates. How fast is this system spinning relative to the rest of the system it's a part of? How fast is it changing relative to its environment? What do those differentials mean, what are the consequences of them? In many cases there are at least two aspects to this which I'll call cadence and change rate. Since dynamic complexity relates closely to the chapter on dynamic loops, I'll talk about the issue of cadence in relation to that. If you have a dynamic loop it has a cadence, it 'spins' at a particular rate, the time it takes for it to complete a revolution. Your heart has a natural rhythm, its cadence, as does a business process or a societal or an economic system. Where two systems with different cadences are coupled, the differential affects both. The faster may experience the slower as a brake or as a source of stability, and the difference between those is a perception about the value or not of the difference, but the effect is the same irrespective of perception. The slower exerts a drag on the faster. Conversely the faster may be perceived by the slower as an irritant or as a welcome stimulus, but irrespective of value judgements the actual effect is the same. The faster exerts an impetus on the slower.

Complexity

You can think of this in terms of value, or almost in terms of mechanics, like gears locked together and spinning at different rates. Except that most system couplings are not actually as tight as gears and the values are not actually independent of the cadence itself. Why would the slower see the faster as an irritant or a helpful stimulus? It could be a helpful stimulus if the slower system was also coupled to other systems where it was too slow and needed to speed itself up or lose its fit.

Values are not systemically independent, they are systemically dependent and they are particularly dependent on perceived differentials in speed and change. In many systems, synchronisation is common. It's common in ecosystems where one species times its reproductive cycle to coincide with the activity of other species. It's common in socioeconomic systems where organisations across whole sectors synchronise their change rates to ensure the cohesion of the sector. They may shout 'competition' but collaborate in synchronising. The effect of differentials in cadence can be to drive towards synchronisation, or where this doesn't happen, can be a sort of dislocation or decoupling as the fast and the slow part ways.

The importance of differentials in change is fairly intuitive; systems which change slower than their environment lose their fit and then at some point it's usually game over. The actual end may be dramatically fast or a long time coming, but unless there is enough of the environment to which the system can maintain a fit such that it can be sustained, the end will come as the system dies. Differentials in change rates are a matter of life and death as the **Viability Principle, Conservation of Adaptation Principle, System Survival Theorem and Structural Viability Theorem** all discuss.

You can think of cadence and change rate as separate elements of dynamics, but they are closely linked. Evolutionary biologists traditionally used fruit flies to study evolution – why? Because their reproductive cycle is astonishingly quick, from eggs being laid to those eggs turning into larvae then pupae then into adult flies laying their own eggs is around three weeks. Which is several hundreds of times faster than the reproductive cycle of the biologists studying them, where from birth to being able to reproduce takes tens of years. Because the reproductive

Complexity

cadence of the fruit flies is fast, their rate of change is also fast – they evolve faster, hence why they are beloved of evolutionary biologists.

In terms of thinking about dynamic complexity, change rates mean change, which means more 'possible states of the system' and differentials in cadence between coupled systems are themselves a different 'state of the system' and also cause change, triggering more 'possible states'. And it's not just cadence and change rates, but also changes in the rate of both of those that need to be kept in mind: is the rate of change speeding up or slowing down, is the cadence increasing or decreasing?

In structural complexity we have **Root structuration theorem** that describes an ideal ratio for a system structure to absorb complexity. The equivalents in dynamic complexity are the **Viability Principle, Conservation of Adaptation Principle, System Survival Theorem** and **Structural Viability Theorem,** all of which are about the balance of dynamics within systems and between systems and their environments.

Dynamics within dynamics
The natural harmonics of complex dynamic systems

As with **Root** these all act as useful hooks on which to hang your thinking, but the basic issue in all of these is asking what happens to A if it's moving at one speed and is coupled to B which is moving at a different rate. And also asking what happens to B. Since synchronisation in systems is common, but rarely perfect, the 'what happens?' questions are often around whether the drive to synchronize is likely to be strong enough or work fast enough for the system to hold together. Which

Complexity

means it's about rates of rates – the rate at which the faster decelerates to stay coupled to the slower, or the slower accelerates to stay coupled to the faster. Where this doesn't happen, something generally has to give and just as in structural complexity we have the **Complexity Instability Principle**, in dynamics, the equivalent is **Self-organised Criticality** which describes how dynamics drive systems to the edge of chaos.

Perception ...

Depending on how you choose to look at any system, the level of complexity will vary dramatically. Similarly, if you look in the other direction and ask about the emergent properties of any system, then which emergent property you pick to study will alter the complexity within the system that is relevant to driving that emergence. Complexity for the practitioner is a real facet of real systems, but the study of it is subjective. As Ashby said: *"a system's complexity is purely relative to a given observer; I reject the attempt to measure an absolute, or intrinsic, complexity; but this acceptance of complexity as something in the eye of the beholder is, in my opinion, the only workable way of measuring complexity"*. I'd caveat that by saying that a system's complexity isn't actually purely relative to a given observer, but for all practical purposes it is, and if you think you've actually measured it, or captured it, you're wrong.

In terms of getting a grip on your own perceiving and how this affects the apparent level of complexity, this comes back to being aware of two things. The first is the emergent properties you're interested in and therefore the system generating those emergent properties and values. The other is the basis on which you make distinctions or, to put it another way, what differences you think make a difference here. In most cases, neither of those two is independent of the other and neither is independent of the system being observed. Both are conditioned by the structural and dynamic complexity experienced. You can't really understand structural or dynamic complexity without understanding how you perceive those, and how you perceive them depends on both types of complexity. Where you stand relative to the structure (i.e. which side of a boundary), will affect your perception, and the dynamics of the system relative to your own dynamics as an observer will affect how you perceive

Complexity

the dynamics. Observers are not independent of what they observe, and the observed is not independent of the observer.

The question of whether complexity is real or perceived and whether reality or perception matters all goes back to the Korzybski 'map-territory' issue. System complexity *is* real, but what we are able to perceive of it is what we are able to perceive. Where the difference matters depends on what we're trying to do. The reality of complexity matters when you try to change something. The perception matters when you try to understand. As ever, distinguishing when you are dealing with the map from when you are dealing with the territory is critical and people very often get this wrong.

If we take a car as an example, then do I want to understand how to design a car to go faster on a racetrack, or do I just want to understand how to drive to the shops? Both involve the same car with the same inherent structural complexity, the same parts in the same relationships to one another. They may involve different dynamics, so racing will put the parts of the car into different dynamic relationships and you're likely to run the engine at higher revs. But perceptually, the complexity is totally different in each case and how much of the complexity of the car I need to perceive is massively different. Similarly, if we take the weather as an example, technically weather is a chaotic system, but effectively it's complex, it is more or less predictable because the prediction period of the weather's dynamics matches my 'action period', i.e. it's stable enough for long enough for the time I need as an observer, à la **System Stability Principle**.

... and misperception...

There are a couple of approaches that have come out of complexity theory that argue that this domain can be neatly subdivided into categories: simple, complicated, complex, chaotic.

Would that it were that simple. This is a thinking trap since pretty much nothing in the domain we're interested in (i.e. between static and chaotic) fits into any of those categories, everything is more or less complex. The

Complexity

sorts of systems to which you can apply systems or complexity theory are simple, complicated and complex all at the same time.

If we take a factory producing widgets as an example (a real one, not a made up one), then for the managing director, the factory was simple, it was a money pump. He put money in at one end to buy time and skills and materials, and widgets came out the other end that customers paid for and the difference between what went in and what came out was profit. For the machine operators, it was complicated – a set of interlocking procedures, standards and schedules. For the operations director it was complex, a set of interdependent dynamic flows of orders, materials, jobs, products that had to be juggled and coaxed through a set of constraints. For the production planners the factory was a complex monster that regularly collapsed into chaos as their production schedules were continually overtaken by urgent customer demands, unstable production volumes and variable quality. All of those were legitimate views of exactly the same system. All described where the factory sat for them on the continuum of complexity and how it behaved. All were simultaneously true – the factory did behave as a simple system and a chaotic one and everything in between and it did that most of the time. If you think it's any one, then you've missed the point.

The weather is the archetypal chaotic system – it's the system that gave rise to chaos theory in the first place when Lorenz realised that even tiny differences in starting conditions could lead to dramatic differences in actual weather – hence *"Does the flap of a butterfly's wings in Brazil set off a tornado in Texas?"*.

Weather is definitively chaotic, but it's also 'just' complex, forecasters model weather systems as complex dynamic systems, mostly successfully.

Weather is also simultaneously complicated and stable, as sailors have operated for centuries using maps of weather sub-systems – the trade winds – which were mostly reliable but were not deterministic or predictable in detail. And weather is also simple – 'is it raining or not?' and 'how hard is the wind blowing?' are questions that have definitive answers and are about as complex as the weather system is for most of us most of the time.

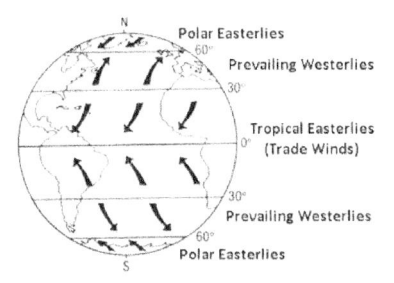

All systems that we're interested in studying using systems or complexity theory are somewhere on the continuum of complexity and are by definition dynamic, so they will be moving up and down that continuum and as per the **System Stability Principle** will be stable enough for long enough for us to be able to recognise some sort of pattern. All of them are simultaneously simple through to the border of chaotic. When you categorise any system as 'simple', 'complicated', 'complex' or 'chaotic', that isn't actually a statement about the reality of the system itself, because it's all of those. Instead, it's a statement about you as an observer. The complexity classification approaches are not a telescope that you use to see the world better, they are a mirror that tells you how you are choosing to view the world. Now there is nothing wrong with having a mirror as long as you realise that what it's showing you is a picture of you, not the reality out there.

Leaving aside categorisation approaches, the thinking problem of wrestling with complexity remains and it can be hard to not fall into the mental and emotional trap of defaulting to certainty which is, after all, the attraction of categories. If you take a system where you're trying to understand why it behaves the way it does, where its complexity is and what it's doing, and you sit down and do some Ashby type variety calculations and come up with some really clear conclusions, it's very tempting to believe that you've nailed it. You haven't, it's like putting a marker post in a stream running through shifting sandbanks. It's valid up to a point and for a period, but the picture will change. In terms of how

Complexity

you know you're thinking about complexity well, in systems thinking and practice you need to think about complexity as being in constant flux. If you've slipped into the certainty of categorising the complexity, then you've lost your grip on it. If you are totally bewildered, and it feels totally chaotic then either it actually is chaotic, or much more likely you just haven't got to grips with it. If it feels a bit like wrestling a snake in mud, but your head is above water and you can keep your hands around something slippery but solid, then you might be doing OK.

That makes it sound a lot harder than it really is. The good thing about it is that thinking about variety – the number of possible states of the system and specifically about requisite variety across a relationship – makes things much easier. With practice it's often possible to look at a system or a relationship in a system and be reasonably sure that it either does or does not have requisite variety and from there go on to work out what the consequences will be for the system in terms of its trajectory towards stability or chaos.

Last word on this I think goes to Oliver Wendell Holmes, a US Supreme Court justice who said: *"For the simplicity that lies this side of complexity, I would not give a fig, but for the simplicity that lies on the other side of complexity, I would give my life."* There is often a moment in wrestling with the complexity of a situation or system when suddenly it resolves itself, when the essence of it becomes clear, when everything falls into place and all the confusion evaporates. Then, there is a sense of completion rather like the experience when the build-up of tension in a piece of music is resolved. And at that point, it's hard not to feel that you've done it, you've understood the complexity, you've untied the knot, solved the riddle. And you may well have done, such feelings are important in the work, because when you do resolve the complexity, that *is* how it feels. But this is an aesthetic reaction and as Churchman pointed out, aesthetics is one of the enemies of systems thinking. And it's an enemy because that feeling of 'simplicity the other side of complexity' can be genuine or can be a mirage – or in the case of the categorisation approaches, a reflection of you rather than anything meaningful about the world. Don't be too quick to shout 'Eureka'.

Uncertainty

As Voltaire said: *"Uncertainty is an uncomfortable position, but certainty is an absurd one"* and this is particularly true for systems thinking and practice. In fact, it's doubly true, so having ways to deal with uncertainty is vital.

The reason it's doubly true is that we're forced to consciously deal with two sources of uncertainty. The first is the uncertainty of the real world and of the systems in it. The second source is the uncertainty of the modelling process that we use to make sense of systems in the world, and the uncertainty of the first can compound the uncertainty of the second. These two are not the same thing and both need to be actively managed.

For the first, the uncertainty of systems in the real world, pretty much everything we're interested in about systems has uncertainty around it. We study systems to understand emergence and systems' emergent properties. Given that these, by definition, are not properties of any of the parts of the system, emergent properties often have an elusive quality to them. If you take a living system, its most 'obvious' emergent property is life itself. But there is nothing obvious about the nature of life; what actually constitutes 'life', and how you recognise it, are both debatable and hotly debated. Even when an emergent property is itself unambiguously an emergent property, its inherent nature often isn't. And many emergent properties are more elusive than that. What is the system which has war as an emergent property? It's not at all clear what the boundaries, or the components, or the relationships or the dynamics are.

Emergence, a major concern for systems practice, is often shrouded in uncertainty and so is the very nature of systems, balanced as these are in a dynamic stability between stasis and chaos. Not just the sources of their stability can be uncertain, but critically the sources of their collapse are often highly uncertain. We can often work out how, why and under what conditions systems will fail, but knowing when is a whole different matter. Since, following the **System Stability Principle**, a system is something that is stable enough for long enough for a pattern to be recognisable, and one of our prime concerns in systems practice is how systems are stable when they are and how they flip into instability when

Uncertainty

they do, this basic uncertainty about their continuity of stability and even existence is fundamental. The drivers of instability that are built into some systems – their structural complexity and dynamics – can sit there like time bombs. Both are inherently uncertain, we can model them and calculate variables and rates, but ultimately both are unknowable in an absolute sense (**Darkness Principle**) and just how close to the edge these take the system is always uncertain.

And the mention of modelling takes us to the other source of uncertainty we have to wrestle with – how good are our models?

As described in the modelling chapter, we understand systems using models, and models are always simplifications of reality. As George Box observed, *"all models are wrong, but some are useful"*. All models are necessarily wrong precisely because they are simplifications. It's the simplifying that makes models usable and useful because when you get it right, essential aspects of the world are retained and noise is dispensed with. So if, in model building, we're in the game of simplifying, then the critical question becomes: what do we choose to include and what do we choose to leave out? What do we class as essential and what do we class as irrelevant? And it's this that determines whether a simplification is an over-simplification or not. Picking the right elements, relationships, dynamics and variables to include in your model is one of the key skills in modelling. You can think of the modelling process as an economy of what to know and what not to know.

We all have biases in how we see the world and that means those biases are tacit models – which means that we tend to see what we expect to see and then confirm our own biases. And because this is us, our thought processes, our own emotions, it's difficult to see beyond them, to see them as biases. It's really easy to build a model – whether tacit or formal – and see the world using that and assume that what's in it are the essential elements, relationships and variables and therefore that it's a good model. But it may miss out something really key, or indeed point you in totally the wrong direction. This is a self-referencing system of thought and the trick of dealing with the slipperiness of this is to constantly check the validity of the models you are using. This is 'second order cybernetics,' the cybernetics of the observer, the modelling of your

Uncertainty

own modelling, the art of becoming self-aware of what you actually think and why you think what you do.

In modelling, there is always uncertainty about whether or not you've got it right – whether you've included an element that misleads or missed out a relationship that is critically important. Uncertainty comes with the territory and their uncertainty is something that systems thinkers have to learn to feel the edges of – it's the warning that you may have got it wrong. As per the Voltaire comment, most people find *"Uncertainty is an uncomfortable position"* but for the systems thinker, working as we do with inherently uncertain models about inherently uncertain systems, for us, uncertainty is our friend and companion and should be carefully cultivated. Ultimately uncertainty is the only thing that allows us to maintain a sense of perspective.

There's a symptom that crops up in several categories of mental illness which is a separation from reality and a reliance on the internalised picture of reality rather than relying on directly experiencing the external world. Whether full blown psychosis, delusion, dissociation or common cognitive dissonance, all feature a preference for the 'controllable' internal landscape rather than the external. For quite different reasons, there is a similar syndrome that can afflict systems thinkers when they become too attached to their own models. When that happens, they tend to stop questioning their assumptions, and most critically when information appears that contradicts or invalidates their model, they discount it or fail to even spot it: *"Whether you can observe a thing or not depends on the theory which you use. It is the theory which decides what can be observed,"* to revisit Einstein, and at that point, as a systems thinker, you have quite literally lost the plot.

Just as too little uncertainty can lead the systems thinker down a false trail, so too much can be crippling. Systems thinkers can suffer the equivalent of 'paralysis by analysis'. In analysis, each new level of detail opens up still more questions and drives the analyst to seek out more and more detail. Hopefully the systems thinker – using holistic thinking – isn't going to fall into quite the same trap, but the equivalent is to strive to extend the scope and depth of the model, to include more variables, more

Uncertainty

stakeholders, more factors, more....in the hope that this will bring the uncertainty down and back to comfortable levels.

There's an adage from Korzybski that is much used and misused in systems that *"the map is not the territory"*. What Korzybski was talking about is the healthy level of scepticism we should have about all our maps or models because our processes of observing and knowing are based not on directly observing reality, but observation filtered through our pre-existing understanding – we project our models and then see the world through them. Unfortunately, this phrase gets twisted in two ways. It's used as a shibboleth to identify and denounce people suspected of assuming that we do see objective and unfiltered reality – for some in the systems movement, this is considered a thought crime. Secondly, it's used by some to dismiss the idea of reality altogether. In an Alice in Wonderland sort of way, they'll argue that since the map is not the territory (true), and we cannot ultimately know all the reality of the territory (also true), therefore there is no territory, there is only the map. Both these positions are traps for the unwary. Many of the people who profess these arguments don't actually practice as if they are true, but they are still pitfalls.

Helpful, I think, to go back to what Korzybski actually said and meant: *"A map is not the territory it represents, but, if correct, it has a similar structure to the territory, which accounts for its usefulness."* The only reason for using systems approaches to better understand the world is if the world is at least partly systemic in its nature. The validity of systems as an approach and our individual practice depends on the models having *"a similar structure to the territory"*.

There are nine mental techniques and an emotional one that help to maintain a balance and that help the systems thinker to use their uncertainty to their advantage.

1. The balance of probability: Bayes & Boyd

Thomas Bayes was an 18th Century clergyman and John Boyd was a 20th Century fighter pilot, so not obvious stablemates. The reverend Bayes laid down some of the basic tenets of probability theory and usefully, how to

Uncertainty

deal with it. As a clergyman, he was interested in how we can have faith – other than blind faith – in the absence of proof. So how is it that a thinking chap – like himself – can believe in God when there is no proof that God exists and when according to the religious doctrine of the day, there couldn't be any proof, because that would remove the need for faith? Bayes' answer to this conundrum about uncertainty was a theorem that takes his name. Essentially, Bayes' theorem takes an uncertain proposition and requires you to look for evidence that the proposition is true and also evidence that it is not true and to progressively compare the two sets of evidence through time to continuously recalibrate your strength of belief.

Bayes' theorem forms the basis of drugs testing, where evidence of efficacy is counterbalanced by evidence of ineffectiveness: positives are balanced against negative results, false positives, false negatives and placebo effects are all factored in. In the world of systems practice, in some cases, it helps to actually do the maths – to work out the indicators confirming and denying the validity of your model and feed them into the structure of Bayes' formula, but often it's enough to merely work out the indicators, watch for them and keep a running count. As Korzybski said: "*There are two ways to slide easily through life; to believe everything or to doubt everything. Both ways save us from thinking.*" The Bayes recipe is to decide to not "*slide easily through life*".

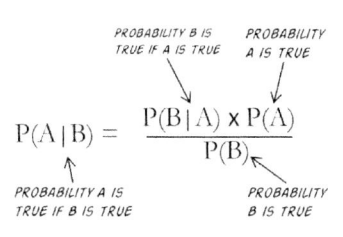

$$P(A\mid B) = \frac{P(B\mid A) \times P(A)}{P(B)}$$

(PROBABILITY B IS TRUE IF A IS TRUE) (PROBABILITY A IS TRUE)
(PROBABILITY A IS TRUE IF B IS TRUE) (PROBABILITY B IS TRUE)

For the mental discipline for actually thinking in a Bayesian way, we turn to Boyd, an individual just about as far removed from the reverend Bayes as it's possible to imagine, but who was also interested in grappling with uncertainty. Boyd was a fighter pilot and wrote the manual for fighter combat manoeuvres used by NATO and went on to become one of the most influential theorists on military strategy of the post WWII era. Boyd taught dogfighting in the US Air Force and had a standing bet that he could beat anyone in a dogfight within 40 seconds – hence one of his nicknames of '40 second Boyd'. Allegedly, he never lost his bet. In the split-second world of fighter dogfights, being able to handle uncertainty was a matter of life or death – quite literally. Boyd's OODA loop

Uncertainty

(Observe, Orientate, Decide, Act) is immediately recognisable to any systems practitioner as a cybernetic learning loop and Boyd referenced Ashby. At the core of the model is the second O, Orientate, by which Boyd meant 'have and use a model of the situation' and naturally, the validity of the model in a situation that was unfolding at supersonic speeds was critically important.

Boyd's answer to this was to do two things – split your thinking processes and actively look for evidence the model is wrong. The thinking split was because for observations that fitted your model you already knew what to do, so the decision and action should be reflexive, instantaneous. For

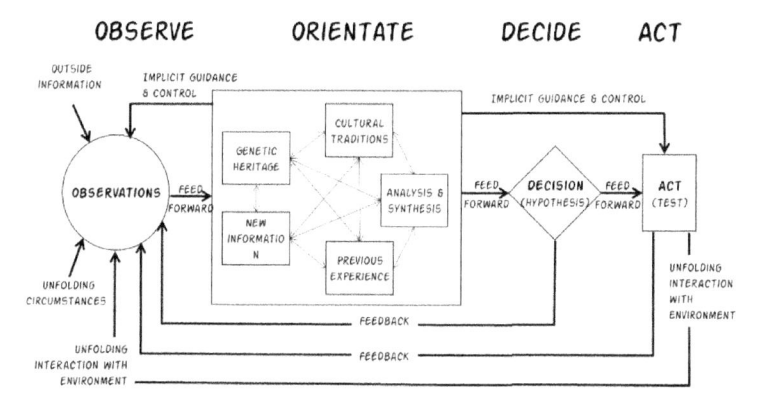

OBSERVE   **ORIENTATE**   **DECIDE**   **ACT**

anything that doesn't fit the model, you actually have to rethink, and this takes longer. The 'doesn't fit the model' requires that you look for evidence that contradicts the model. And here is the Bayesian approach instilled into a mental practice carried out in fractions of a second. The technique is quite simple to describe, but rather harder to practise. First, be conscious of the model you are using, next work out what you would expect to see if it's true, then what you would expect not to see, then actively look for evidence that your model is wrong, next assess whether that is significant or a random occurrence, decide what to do about the new evidence and adjust your model to accommodate any significant discordant observations. The adjustment can involve recalibrating our model – 'oh it can change *that* fast!' or restructuring 'didn't realise it included that!' or altering the indicators to look for. This is a subtle and can be quite a difficult mental discipline, but remember we usually have

Uncertainty

the luxury of being able to do this at a snail's pace compared with the speed Boyd was doing it. So our task is relatively easy. As a basic rule of thumb though, the higher the level of uncertainty, the faster you need to run the feedback loop to check your models are good enough.

As an aside, Boyd's splitting thinking into reflexive, model driven and longer, re-orientating, is consistent with McGilchrist's explanation of the hemispherical split of our brains in 'The Master and his Emissary', where one hemisphere (the Emissary) deals with routinized decisions and tasks and the other (the Master) deals with the unexpected. As you might imagine, since lots of people are uncomfortable with uncertainty, there are two consequences. One is that many seek out situations where they live in routine so the capacity to deal with the unexpected atrophies. The second is that when the unexpected does occur, many people struggle to switch hemispheres and try to deal with the unexpected using routinized solutions. The feeling of using the Emissary is totally different to using the Master, so given that as systems practitioners, we are deliberately walking into a world of uncertainty, getting the feel of which you are using when, and why, is quite important.

2. Feedforward

The science of cybernetics that gave us feedback was born from work on trying to catch flying objects. The flying objects in question were enemy aircraft. But when it comes to catching things on the wing, the past masters are dragonflies. Dragonflies are the hunting animals with the highest success rate at around 95%. This compares to less than 20% for a lion, approximately 25% for greyhounds – the fastest dogs, 30% for cheetahs – the fastest land animals, and the fastest animal on earth which is the peregrine falcon has a measly success rate of less than 10%. So why are dragonflies so much better? Their success rate is partly because of their speed and agility – they can accelerate to 50kph in three wingbeats, fly forwards, backwards, upside down and hover, but mostly it is because they use a completely different technique to most hunters: feedforward. Most hunting animals use feedback to get to their prey, they follow the prey and sense its changes in direction and use that information to adjust their path in response to what the prey has done. Using feedforward on the other hand, dragonflies fly to where the prey is going to be in the

Uncertainty

future. As the ice-hockey player Wayne Gretzky put it: *"A good hockey player plays where the puck is. A great hockey player plays where the puck is going to be."*

What does this mean for our handling of uncertainty? In most cases, systems models can be used to make predictions. Typically, these won't be, and won't pretend to be, precision forecasts, and in many cases they'll be qualitative rather than quantitative, but predictions nevertheless. Building predictions sensitises you to signals that can confirm or deny your model which, without the prediction, would just appear as noise and be ignored.

3. Close the Loop

As Reg Revans the father of Action Leaning said: *"there is no action without learning and there is no learning without action"*.

The process of modelling is one that is separated from the real world, and for good reasons – so that we can experiment with the models before risking experimenting with the world, since experimenting on the world can go horribly wrong. And some systems thinkers find it much easier to live in their own modelling bubble than to engage with harsh reality. It's an environment where you can be in control, largely devoid of inconvenient truths or people. It's the same reason as people get immersed in computer games. The allure is seductive for those who enjoy the activity of modelling, and the risk is obvious – that the models and the modeller slip away from reality.

So, the Close the Loop dictum is about grounding the model into reality. It's actually about two loops and the connection between them: there's a modelling loop which is about whether our model appears to correspond to reality (which is where Bayes came in), and then there's an action loop which is about whether that apparent correspondence stands up to actual contact with reality. When we interact with the system using the model, does it actually work? Does the system behave the way we'd expect given what the model tells us, or does it do something completely different? Up to that point everything is just hypothesis – well, hypothesis if you've done it right and fantasy if you lost the plot.

Uncertainty

Failure to close the loop is a problem that is not confined to systems thinkers. Change management professionals have been using the same set of models and assumptions for decades and accompany this with the observation that it's really hard to do, and that around 70% of their change projects fail. If a model fails more than 50% of the time, the model is wrong. I don't mean it's wrong in a Box *"all models are wrong, but some are useful"* way, I mean that in a Bayesian way, it's wrong more than it's right. It means it doesn't actually reflect reality, it's a fantasy. In Korzybski terms it doesn't have *"a similar structure to the territory, which accounts for its usefulness."* It's incredibly easy to dissociate the model from the reality and in that dissociated state to be sure that the model is coherent and therefore must be true. It is only contact with reality that tells you whether it is or it isn't. Same thing happens in business strategy – around 90% of strategic plans don't work. The model is wrong. The assumptions on which the discipline of strategy has been built are totally plausible, internally consistent and coherent, but that consistency and coherence count for nothing – the model is wrong. If it wasn't wrong it would work and it just doesn't.

Conversely, checking against reality can resolve uncertainty in favour of the model. When Jay Forrester built a System Dynamics model of the economy, he found – as expected – a fairly regular roughly seven-year pattern we know as the business cycle, so far so expected. What he hadn't expected was a longer cyclical pattern of deeper growth and recession roughly every fifty years (or for beachcombers the seventh wave of a seven-year cycle). Forrester assumed the model was wrong and tried to alter it to get rid of this phenomenon but failed. Eventually he realised that the model was right and his assumptions about reality were wrong when he discovered that the historical evidence backs it up and that the same behaviour had been noticed independently by both Kondratieff and Schumpeter. Both of those ascribed it to other behavioural phenomena that are correlated, but Forrester's model shows the deep driving structure. But from an uncertainty point of view, closing the loop can either confirm or deny the validity of a suspect model and you need to be prepared for either outcome impartially. As Churchill put it: *"However beautiful the strategy, you should occasionally look at the results."*

Uncertainty

4. Experiment

Experimenting is a particular way to 'close the loop'. As we said with Bayes & Boyd, all other things being equal, the greater the level of uncertainty, the faster you should run feedback loops to speed up learning. Experimenting helps in speeding this up and it also helps to de-risk uncertainty through closing the loop at a level of risk that is manageable or acceptable. It speeds up the feedback loop because doing a relatively small experiment or pilot is likely to be very much faster to design, organise and get results from than doing a fully-fledged industrial strength implementation. It reduces risk because you can select the size of the experiment to match your risk appetite.

To some extent, experimenting is built into systems practice since the basic pattern is to build a model of the situation, experiment in the 'model space' before deciding what to actually do in the real world and that division is explicitly built into Soft Systems Methodology and implicitly built into all systems approaches. What we're talking about here is following the model-based experiments with experiments in the real world. There is some particular technique around this. Good experimentation has clarity on exactly what is being evaluated / what is being learned about. Less 'I wonder what would happen if…,' more 'do we get this anticipated result if we change x y z? and what else do we get that we didn't expect or possibly didn't want?'

5. Watching the Dark

"Is there any point to which you would wish to draw my attention?
To the curious incident of the dog in the night-time.
The dog did nothing in the night-time.
That was the curious incident."

Lots of disciplines rely as much on what is not there as what is. If you think of Michelangelo's Creation of Adam in the Sistine Chapel, the focal point of the painting is the gap between God's and Adam's outstretched fingers – the focus is on what isn't there. Artists learn to

Uncertainty

always consider the 'negative space', the shapes, tensions and emphasis created by what is not there.

Martial arts vary, but in most of them, it's not just about hitting your opponent; part of the art is in not being where your opponent is trying to hit you. Absence is as important as presence. Garden design usually involves working out which plants to put where, and architecture involves where to put walls, doors and windows but great garden design and architecture is about creating spaces – it's about where the plants and walls are not.

Most of us are trained to look for and think about 'things', about objects, about what actually is there, not about what isn't.

What isn't there is as much a part of the picture, or the model or the system as what is. We once did a project around binge drinking in a town in the UK and the authorities were concerned about several aspects of this – particularly the disorder. We built some models of what we thought was going on, and then we went to watch as thousands of party goers disgorge at 2 am from a string of nightclubs and bars lining the street of a once sleepy market town. And there were thousands of obviously quite drunken people, which is what we expected to see. But there was no disorder.

You can think about this in a Bayesian way as an absence of evidence of the emergent property of disorder, but it's not just that. The lack of disorder is an emergent property in its own right. This is very orderly mass party-going. It's not the system we thought it was, with the emergent property that we thought it had, it's something completely different. And you ask different questions as a result. A senior policeman had an 'aha' moment when he realised that the presence of the police was enabling the binge drinking. As he put it *"We're causing the problem – the fact that we're there to stop them getting hurt means that they can get s***faced safely and not worry. If they thought they might get mugged, raped or knifed, they wouldn't be*

Uncertainty

there." The 'problem' wasn't about disorder, it was about the absence of disorder – *'the curious incident of the riot in the night-time, there was no riot…'*.

Ashby said: *"A Cyberneticist observes what might have happened but did not"* and the point he was making was a slightly different one to the Sherlock Holmes' point about the dog in the night-time. Ashby was pointing to understanding the constraints the system was under.

It's easy to look at what is in systems: the boundaries, the relationships, the dynamics, the level of stability, the emergent properties, and to ignore the fact that whatever it is, it could have been totally different. More than that, there is only one way in which this system is as it is, but there is an infinite number of ways in which we could have been looking at something totally different and taking that for granted. Understanding *this* system depends on us understanding why not the others.

Ashby was interested in the set of constraints that led this system to have turned out as it currently is rather than as something else. That may sound both a bit esoteric and also fiendishly hard to do; after all, if there's a theoretically infinite number of 'could have been' systems, how do you understand the constraints that led to them not being? Luckily, that is itself a system question. What in the wider system(s) of which this system is a part, are the boundaries, structures, relationships and dynamics that a) keep this in being and b) prevent something different from being in its place? And that is a rather less daunting question.

6. The Law of Complementarity

Triangulation is a basic principle in navigation, where after all, you are wrestling with the uncertainty of where you are. If you take a single bearing on a landmark and plot that on a map or chart, all it tells you is that you are somewhere close to that line. Take two bearings on different points and where they cross *should* be your position. Except that taking bearings is a somewhat uncertain business where magnetic distortions, compass error, poor visibility, a pitching deck (if you're doing this at sea) and chart / map errors, can all affect the result.

You take three bearings, plot them on your chart and you should end up with a triangle or, as sailors call it a 'cocked hat' which dates the technique to the time when captains wore triangular hats. The truth of your actual position lies somewhere within that triangle and obviously the smaller the triangle, the more the bearings coincide, the more certain you can be.

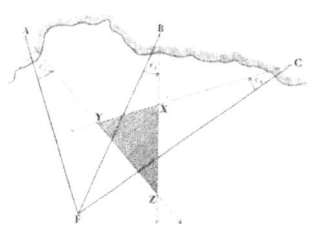

The same approach works in systems practice where it's known as Weinberg's **Law of Complementarity**: *"any two different perspectives (or models) about a system will reveal truths about that system that are neither entirely independent nor entirely compatible"*. Using one model or one modelling approach is inherently fallible. Cross-referencing two or three and looking for the degree of correspondence and contradiction between them will give you a much better sense of how much each can be trusted. On an organisational redesign project in a factory, doing a Viable Systems Model pointed towards one structural solution rather than another, but it was only once we'd also modelled the dynamics of the workflow through the alternative structures and cross- referenced the structures to HR's competency frameworks and checked that the models coincided, that we could be sure. And getting the design wrong isn't just an expensive mistake, experimenting with the real world could have killed the company.

7. The Rule of Three Levels
It's not a rule and it's not always three, but….

Because holistic thinking leads you into asking 'of what is this a part', the temptation is always to want to look at another level 'up' in the same way as analysts always want to look at another level 'down', at more detail. The rule of thumb here then is to look at three levels: the system we're interested in, the system of which it is part (the meta-system) and at the parts of the system (the sub-systems). Model just one level and you basically have something free-floating in a vacuum, model lots of levels and you've just magnified your task and lost your focus. The rule of three isn't hard and fast, but it's incorporated into several methodologies – it's built into the 'root definition' formulation in Soft Systems methodology, it's the normal approach in Viable Systems and it's described nicely by Ackoff as quoted in the chapter on Holistic thinking.

If you contrast systems approaches with many conventional management frameworks, two themes spring out. One is that traditional approaches are overwhelmingly linear (which systems and the world are not) and the other is that they are mostly flat, they treat the system as having only one level. EFQM, TOGAF MODAF, DODAF and all the other …AFs, ITIL, Agile, Balanced Scorecard, all struggle with being single-level models in a complex world and that creates distortions. There are complexities that they cannot handle. Doing a three, or thereabouts, level model will tell you a lot more.

8. Range not point

The next of the handful of ways to deal with uncertainty is to think about ranges of values, or outcomes, rather than points. There are two reasons for doing this. The first is technical, the second is emotional. Technically, in any uncertain situation, nailing anything precisely is orders of magnitude harder to get right than it is to arrive at a range with reasonable confidence. Think of a long car journey, the chances of getting the arrival time precisely right are negligible (unless you cheat by getting there early and waiting in a layby). The chances of getting your arrival time right to within, say, half an hour are very much higher. The siren call for precision is driven by the urge for certainty and it's a trap. Whether it's assumptions about input variables, or rates of change, or the Outcomes that might be achieved if we do X, unless you really can be sure, try to stick to a range. The second point is emotional – the urge for precision is the urge for certainty. Deliberately using ranges forces you to accept the uncertainty and work with it – feel out the edges of what the probable range could be.

9. Wisdom

Before we get too carried away with ourselves, this is wisdom in the technical sense described in the section on DIKW in the chapter on relating. Wisdom in this context is about understanding when a particular

Uncertainty

body of knowledge does or doesn't fit the situation and when you have to shift either technical discipline or perspective or paradigm. Commonly in systems work this shows up as a recognition that we need to apply the **Law of Complementarity** and use an additional or different approach and the tell-tale signs are your own sense of uncertainty at the point where what you are trying should be delivering some results you can trust. This can be really tricky because often it's critically important to trust your process and let it work the way it's supposed to, to take you through to 'simplicity the other side of complexity'. There is a risk of ditching an approach prematurely because it doesn't seem to be delivering and a risk of only switching approach when actually you need to switch paradigm altogether. Calibrating this is a matter of experience – I don't think there are any short cuts. There are however some sure-fire ways to prevent this working: being a one trick pony and not having alternative approaches to switch to means you are more likely to over-invest in the one approach you know, failing to use the other 8 approaches to managing uncertainty will also reduce your chances. But one of the biggest ways to deny yourself the benefit of this is by not familiarising yourself with how uncertainty feels.

10   Feel it

The other nine techniques are primarily cognitive, but none of them work, or work as well as they should, if you can't get emotionally attuned to uncertainty. Part of this is about just being more comfortable with it, more tolerant of your own uncertainty and this is because the more tolerant, the more you can challenge your certainties, the greater your chances of getting closer to the truth. Uncertainty is your friend. As Yeats put it: *"The best lack all conviction, while the worst are full of passionate intensity."*

But it's not just about upping your tolerance levels. Getting to know how you feel in conditions of relative certainty and uncertainty lets you use your emotions to help you navigate how much you should trust your own judgements. If you are *"full of passionate intensity"*, chances are you are too certain and in need of a dose of healthy scepticism or critical reflection. If you are dithering and unable to move beyond it, then you are no help to yourself or anyone else. Find ways to check your models, test their internal logic, cross reference, test them against reality, speed up your

Uncertainty

learning loop to reduce the uncertainty till it's within the workable range and you are sure enough to actually do something.

Your emotional state is one of the instruments for handling the uncertainty of knowing that can be the most highly tuned – if you learn how to use it and tune it.

As Francis Bacon (the politician and philosopher not the artist) said *"If a man will begin with certainties, he shall end in doubts; but if he will be content to begin with doubts, he shall end in certainties."*

He is quick, thinking in clear images;
I am slow, thinking in broken images.

He becomes dull, trusting to his clear images;
I becomes sharp, mistrusting my broken images.

Trusting his images, he assumes their relevance;
Mistrusting my images, I question their relevance.

Assuming their relevance, he assumes the fact;
Questioning their relevance, I question the fact.

When the fact fails him, he questions his senses;
When the fact fails me, I approve my senses.

He continues quick and dull in his clear images;
I continue slow and sharp in my broken images;

He in a new confusion of his understanding;
I in a new understanding of my confusion.
Robert Graves

Part 2

The Grammar of Systems

"The real world consists of a balanced adjustments of opposing tendencies. Behind the strife between opposites, there is a hidden harmony of attunement which is the world."

Heraclitus

The Laws as a Whole – Order to Chaos to Order

For me, this set of systems laws and principles is the bedrock, the foundation of systems thinking and practice. And yet it has lain mostly ignored and even disparaged for some time. Which begs a number of questions: why has it been neglected? why unearth it here? and, are the laws actually any use?

Part of the reason for that neglect is that they gave rise to a set of approaches and methodologies, each of which encapsulated a subset of the laws and principles, and these provided practitioners with a handy way to use the laws without ever having to deal with the laws in their raw state. To take a culinary metaphor, systems thinking and practice went from discovering new ingredients and coming up with recipes using those, to producing meals from a small set of favourite pre-set recipes and as with cooks everywhere, working from a pre-set recipe that is known to work makes life a lot easier. So people do System Dynamics, and in the process they incorporate the two circular causality principles and feedback dominance theorem, but they don't actually have to think about any of these as principles that govern the structure and behaviour of the system, all they have to do is follow the methodological approach. Methodologies do away with a lot of the conceptual thinking so you can concentrate on doing. They speed up and de-risk practice. They also de-skill it.

In the process, the scope narrowed so 'systems' became about the things the methodologies could do for you. In terms of practice, it became the use of those methodologies and in scope it became about the sorts of issues those methodologies could illuminate. It's a little bit like Abraham Kaplan's law of the instrument: *"Give a small boy a hammer, and he will find that everything he encounters needs pounding."* Would that this were only true of small boys. If you are lucky, a well-rounded systems practitioner might have both a hammer and a screwdriver. And here of course you start to hit the limitations of only using methodologies, of only following the recipes that are in the recipe book. Even if you have both a hammer and a screwdriver, that's not a whole lot of help when confronted for the first time with a nut and bolt. Your trusty book of meat & two vegetable recipes may not be much use if you suddenly have to cater for vegans. And for those tempted to wince at the mixed metaphors in this paragraph, sometimes a single metaphor isn't rich enough in the same way a single methodology isn't.

These laws and principles become particularly relevant whenever you hit a systemic problem for which there isn't already a suitable pre-prepared methodology. Say you wanted to develop a systemic approach to economics and used Viable System Modelling. That would lead you towards a focus on the organisation and regulation of socio-economic systems. If you took System Dynamics, that is relevant as a methodology, but it leads you to focus on the dynamics that drive the short business cycle and the much longer capital cycle. Soft Systems and Critical Systems Heuristics would lead you towards seeing it in terms of politics and power. Each is relevant, but all are partial and pull you away from taking a truly holistic view and towards a view based on the law of the instrument. If you really want to tackle an issue for which there isn't already a pre-set methodology that genuinely covers the ground, these laws are the place to start.

The next reason for knowing them and knowing how to use them is that they are immensely powerful and fast. In many cases, you can gain, in minutes, insights using these laws that you would struggle to achieve in ages any other way. As Buckminster Fuller said: *"Don't fight forces, use them"* and the laws describe systemic forces.

Most importantly I think, when you take them as a whole, this set of laws and principles tell their own story. I first came across them not as any sort of coherent set, which is what I'm trying to present them as here, but one by one. It's only when you put them together that the story they tell really emerges. And it's both a simple and an ancient one.

Despite their apparent diversity and despite having been developed by a wide range of people, they are remarkably coherent and fall into three main clusters and just two storylines. The clustering is perhaps not too surprising as some of them are really derivative – so for example there's a family of principles and theorems about structural complexity that derive

Grammar of Systems

from Ashby's law. And because of their familial connection, you'd expect those to hang together.

But taken as a whole the 33 laws, principles and theorems group into sets around structural complexity, dynamic complexity and understanding. The two dominant storylines are about the interplay between order and chaos – the subject of almost every epic and myth – and about the limits of knowing, the interplay between reality and our perception – the subject

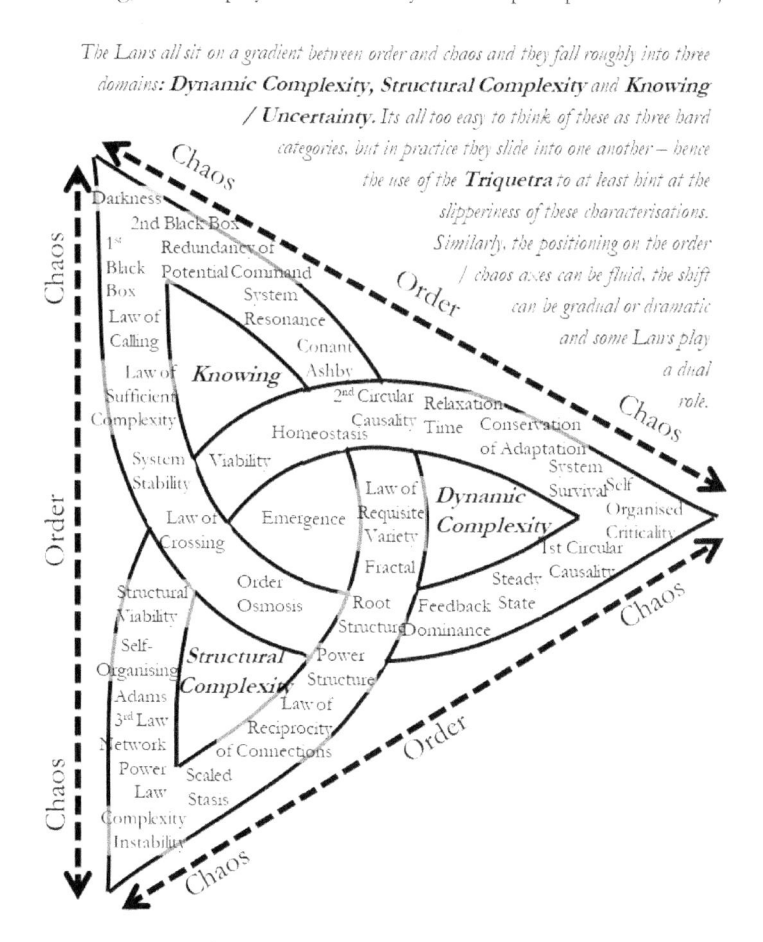

The Laws all sit on a gradient between order and chaos and they fall roughly into three domains: **Dynamic Complexity, Structural Complexity** *and* **Knowing / Uncertainty.** *Its all too easy to think of these as three hard categories, but in practice they slide into one another – hence the use of the* **Triquetra** *to at least hint at the slipperiness of these characterisations. Similarly, the positioning on the order / chaos axes can be fluid, the shift can be gradual or dramatic and some Laws play a dual role.*

of religious belief. Those are ancient themes and to some extent, you can

127

Grammar of Systems

see systems as a science that comes back to deal with some of the fundamental issues that people have always struggled with. You can legitimately argue that one of the big shifts systems made was to move science from a predominantly linear view of causation to a circular one.

But that linearity was a feature of post-enlightenment scientific thought; you only have to look at a Pictish or Viking rock carving to know they didn't see the world in straight lines. The artistic representation of thought from ancient cultures across the world shows the same themes – expressions of complexity, dynamics, stability, chaos and the labyrinthine nature of knowing.

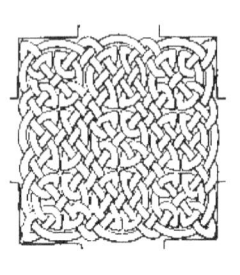

Taking these laws and principles as a whole, as a coherent body of thought, leads you to viewing the world as a dance of stability and instability, of structure, chaos and the re-forming into new structure.

Why this set? To some extent, this is a personal selection – it's those I use and have found useful. But I've also applied some selection rules. I've only included principles that have been developed within the systems community and which are used by the systems community – albeit almost exclusively once incorporated into methodologies. So there is a 'systems native' element to the selection and it doesn't include things that appear in other lists such as the Pareto principle (the 80/20 rule) because that didn't come from systems and it isn't systems based (i.e. it looks at surface phenomena not underlying structures). Fortunately, the 'systems native' criterion and my 'useful to me' criterion coincide, so there were very few boundary decisions. Most of the things that fell outside the boundary for inclusion here are in the 'miscellany' that follows, and they are there predominantly because they are ideas that are harder to express as a law or principle and

At the still point of the turning world.
Neither flesh nor fleshless;
Neither from nor towards;
At the still point, there the dance is,
But neither arrest nor movement.
And do not call it fixity,
Where past and future are gathered.
Neither movement from nor towards,
Neither ascent nor decline.
Except for the point, the still point,
There would be no dance,
And there is only the dance.

T.S. Eliot

tend to be ideas that make up some of the technical language of the systems thinker. A few of these laws and principles were fairly commonly used, but as far as I could see unnamed and for obvious reasons, I've named those in the way I thought most useful – conscious of Stigler's Law that no scientific discovery is named after its originator. Oh and Stigler's Law doesn't feature because he was a statistician rather than a systemist and his law isn't systemic any more than Pareto.

Grammar of Systems

The Law of Calling

"In the beginning was the logos". Logos in this phrase is usually translated as 'word', but it also means form – from which we get 'logic'. It's one of the simplest and yet most subtle and complex of ideas and it's fundamental in systems and gets expressed in several ways. I've chosen to express it as **The Law of Calling** which is how it gets named in Spencer-Brown's 'Laws of Form'. **The Law of Calling** is the making of distinction and Spencer-Brown makes the point that this is the most basic act of cognition. This is not an original idea – hence the biblical quotation, and it is a genuinely ancient concept.

DIFFERENCE CREATES BOUNDARIES AND BOUNDARIES CREATE DIFFERENCE

The Law of Calling says that *"when we make a distinction, we separate on the basis of perceived difference"* and the very act of doing this, of seeing something as distinct from everything else around it, is the act of drawing a boundary and of literally defining (setting down the finiteness) of the system. Despite its normality – a tadpole is able to distinguish food from not-food – this act of distinction is critically important in systems theory and practice precisely because the boundaries of most of the systems we're interested in cannot be taken for granted. The act of **Calling,** of distinguishing this as part of our system and that as not-part, as something outside in the environment of the system, is a matter of boundary judgement, it is as Gregory Bateson put it, about *"the difference that makes a difference"*. The first question then is 'on what basis do we draw a distinction?' – what is the logos, the logic of our **Calling** *this* distinction, of drawing a boundary *here* and defining a system in *this* way rather than any other? Since there are any number of distinctions we could make, which are the differences that we think make a difference here – and why do we think that?

The very ancient symbol of Ouroboros – the serpent eating its own tail – is an expression of this idea and is directly relevant to the issue in systems theory and practice. In the process of closing the loop with its body, the serpent forms a boundary that encloses a space and creates a distinction between that which is inside the boundary and the formless chaos outside. In systems we do the same thing and as in the **System Stability Principle**, our defined system is stable (non-chaotic) for long enough for us to recognise it as a system.

Implications
In systems practice, the definition of the system of interest, the setting of the boundary, is often a critical step. In many cases it is only too easy to accept the boundaries that are presented to us, whether that is the legal boundary of an organisation, or the membership boundary of a social group – all systems boundaries are debateable and the **Law of Calling** insists we choose with care. In addition, though, in many cases, **Calling** forth a different boundary can produce unexpected insights and opportunities and unlock problems held in place by outdated, or badly set boundaries.

Watch for
Where there are differences that make a difference.

Grammar of Systems

Viability Principle

Beer's **Viability Principle** states that *"the viability of a system is a function of the balance maintained along two dimensions: 1) the autonomy of sub-systems versus integration of the system as a whole and 2) stability versus adaptation"*. Each of these two dimensions represents a tension, neither of which is fixed through time and both of which are dynamically linked.

A SYSTEM'S VIABILITY DEPENDS ON HOW WELL IT CAN BALANCE AUTONOMY WITH COHESION AND STABILITY WITH CHANGE OVER TIME

The tension between the autonomy of the parts of the system and the cohesion of the whole shifts through time in response to shifts in the complexity of what the system is doing and the environment in which it is doing it. An increase in the complexity of the task tends to drive an increase in autonomy. However, if there is too much autonomy, the system can (literally) dis-integrate i.e. fall apart.

The tension between stability and change is also inherent in any complex system. As the environment changes, so the system needs to adapt, so there is pressure on the system to change. But change destabilises the system. Particularly in organisational systems, there is a pressure for efficiency, and since efficiency is defined as output divided by resource, highly efficient systems are ones that have very little spare resource. But the ability to change depends on having spare resource, so the more efficient the system, the less adaptable it is and the more adaptable, the less efficient.

The two dimensions are dynamically linked – as the environment changes so the system needs to adapt if it is to remain viable. Some adaptations require many localised changes – responses to local conditions and therefore more autonomy, but others require concentrated responses by the whole system working together – higher coherence and integration.

Grammar of Systems

Implications
These are the two most constant tensions in any organisations and they flex through time both in response to external changes and each in response to the other. What we often observe is that instead of active management of these critical tensions through adjustment, organisations will resist an increase in the tension until it is unavoidable and then swing wildly to an extreme position, and that extreme position is itself likely to contain the seeds of instability. You see organisations oscillating unstably between centralisation and decentralisation and between periods of stasis and change.

It's important to make the tensions overt, and to avoid polarisation: not everything needs to be centralised and equally not everything needs to be decentralised, for example. In most organisations, there will be some functions which have to be centralised for cohesion or compliance, and there will certainly be others where sub-system autonomy is important, so that a sub-system can maintain fit with its environment. What's appropriate in terms of amount of change or degree of autonomy may fluctuate through time. Debate those functions where the need for centralisation or autonomy is more finely balanced. Similarly for stasis and adaptation, it's helpful to be clear on which sub-systems are to change, and equally which are to remain stable to provide some much-needed organisational ballast.

Watch for
Relative autonomy between levels, what can each level decide over and act on AND the amount of change over what time frame.

Grammar of Systems

Homeostasis Principle

It's important to distinguish homeostasis from just stasis. And the difference is that homeostasis works dynamically. A brick doesn't fall over because of stasis, a cyclist doesn't fall over because of homeostasis.

A SYSTEM WILL BE STABLE IF ALL ITS KEY VARIABLES REMAIN WITHIN THEIR PHYSIOLOGICAL LIMITS

Homeostasis is a self-regulating dynamic equilibrium that systems run to keep themselves within the limits of viability. It's particularly relevant for biological systems, but also applies to social, organisational and even mechanistic systems. So, for example, human beings can only function or survive within a certain temperature range and our bodies have a set of responses that are deployed to keep our body temperature within that range despite the fact that the temperature of the environment fluctuates. When it's hot we sweat, when it's cold, we get goose pimples so our hair stands up to help insulate us, then we shiver to increase blood flow, eventually our bodies shut down the extremities to conserve the heat of our core where essential organs are. The **Homeostasis Principle** states *"that a system survives only so long as all essential variables are maintained within their physiological limits".*

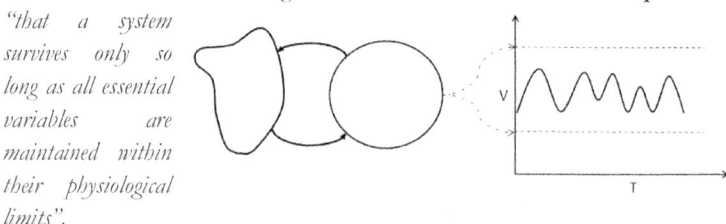

There is something both elusive and apparently magical about homeostasis – how does it come about? Do systems really self-adjust like that? But homeostasis is entirely natural and relates closely to the **System Stability Principle**, as systems which aren't homeostatic pretty quickly cease to be systems, or at least cease to be the same system, since they are incapable of maintaining stability for long enough to still be recognisable. The tendency towards stability and the tendency to change are fundamental to an understanding of how systems are systems, so understanding homeostasis is critical in that. Often people get the principle of homeostasis relatively easily – it is after all what keeps us alive, but being able to understand and map homeostatic mechanisms and processes is a different challenge. How do the homeostats that maintain gang violence or binge drinking actually work? If we want to change a stable but problematic pattern, it's essential to know how and why it's stable, otherwise any intervention is likely to be thwarted by the homeostat restoring the status quo and it is also important to know how strong the elastic is – what are the system's physiological limits, beyond which its nature will have changed or the homeostat will no longer function?

Implications
The implications of homeostasis – for better or worse – are all around us. Organisational change management theory and practice is dominated by concerns about 'resistance to change' – understandably it's frustrating if you want to change an organisation and it continually returns to its pre-intervention state, but that is just homeostasis doing its thing. And although it's irritating for change managers, it's also a good thing – if organisations responded to every stimulus for change that hit them, they'd simply disintegrate.

Practically then, if you want a system to survive, understanding how its homeostatic mechanisms work, or designing those in is critically important – the Viable system model provides a blueprint for that and the **2nd Circular Causality Principle** and the **Feedback Dominance Theorem** are useful. Contrariwise, if you want to change a system, then understanding how to neutralise or remove its homeostats may be all you need to do, and certainly is likely to be at least part of the answer.

Watch for
Which variables are key for the system' stability and what are their physiological limits and what are the measures on each of those.

System Stability Principle

Systems are sets of relationships within an environment that have emergent properties. There is always some dynamic resulting from both the system's internal relationships, and from change the environment causes in the system, and indeed

SYSTEMS ARE PATTERNS THAT ARE RECOGNISABLE OVER SEVERAL OBSERVATIONS

change the system causes in the environment (structural coupling) or any combination of those. So, systems are subject to change. Change, continuous, or cyclic, or sudden and discontinuous. It can be fast or glacially slow, but change there inevitably is. That rather begs the question of whether a system that has changed is still the same system.

The **System Stability Principle** states that *"for any system to be a system, rather than just a passing phenomenon, it must remain stable for long enough to be recognisable as a system"*. For a system to be recognised as a system it must also be dynamic. Systems inhabit the space between chaos where relationships are dynamic but unstable and stasis where relationships are stable but not dynamic. The **System Stability Principle** helps us to negotiate that dilemma – when we look at the system, is it recognisably the same and also recognisably different? This is of course something we do in normal life all the time, so when we meet an old friend, they will be different from the last time we saw them, but recognisably the same.

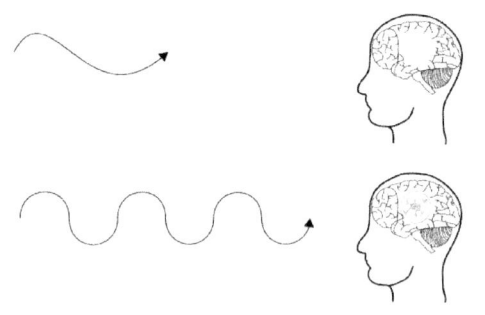

The question that the **System Stability Principle** begs is of course the existential one of: "so if it's different, how is it the same? What is its essential nature that makes this recognisably the same system?" When we do this everyday exercise with an old friend it's easier, they still have the same physical boundary, they inhabit the same skin – or at least they appear to. It's an illusion as many of the cells of their body will have been replaced if we haven't seen them for a while, so almost none of the 'same skin' will actually be the same skin cells, but they will inhabit the same boundary – they may have got fatter, but they are not likely to have suddenly grown six inches. When we do it with a system, it's harder, often the boundary may have changed, the constituent elements may have changed, the purpose may have changed, so what is it we recognise as the same? Often the **Emergence** and **Homeostasis Principles**, together with **Feedback Dominance Theorem** are useful – is the pattern of relationships and behaviours that drive emergent properties still basically the same? A behaviourist might talk about the value set of an organisation and of course values are the rules governing the action of feedback in a homeostat.

Implications
The first implication is a technical one for the systems practitioner – the need to periodically reassess whether the system you are working with is still the same system or has changed so much that it's no longer a case of updating your model, it's time to rip it up and start again. The second is less technical, but more existential - a system may have the same appearance, but have changed its essential identity, or keep its essential identity and completely changed not only its superficial appearance, but its structures, so it's important to understand its essential nature and there is no single touchstone for making that judgement. The third relates to 'Wicked Problems', one characteristic of which is that they morph whenever you intervene in them. Wicked Problems are a facet of a system that is on the borderline of being stable long enough to be recognisable.

Watch for
Consistency of the pattern of behaviour viewed from different levels of focus.

Law of Requisite Variety

Ashby's **Law of Requisite Variety** or **Ashby's law** as it is more commonly referred to, has been described as the management science equivalent of the second law of thermodynamics in physics. There is a mathematical proof of **Ashby's law**. The brief form of the law is that *"only variety can destroy variety"*.

HOW WELL ANY SYSTEM MANAGES DEPENDS ON HOW WELL IT MATCHES THE VARIETY IT FACES

The more extended form is: *"The control achievable by a given regulatory sub-system over a given system is limited by 1) the variety of the regulator and 2) the channel capacity between the regulator and the system. The upper limit on the amount of regulation achievable is given by the variety of the regulatory system divided by the variety of the regulated system".*

Essentially what the law states is that if a system has a number of possible states (variety) of 'n' then any attempt to regulate that system must be capable of matching that variety (so be able to respond to any state of the system) and therefore also has to have a variety of n.

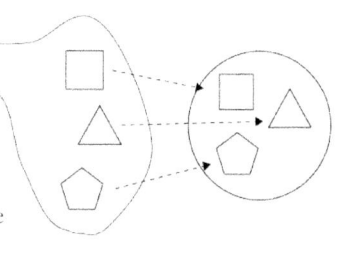

Ashby's Law has similarities to, but goes significantly beyond, Shannon's 10th theorem on which much modern telecommunications is based. In one sense it appears common sense and obvious, that in a managerial situation, if a system could do any one of 20 different things, then the manager needs to be able to respond to each of those eventualities to ensure that the system stays in control.

Implications

Although superficially obvious, **Ashby's law** is profound in its application and implications and is frequently not understood and ignored, the consequence of which is inevitably a failure to maintain the system in a state of control.

One of the implications is that there are inherent imbalances in variety between a system's environment, the organisational system itself and the

Grammar of Systems

management of that system, since the variety of the environment is theoretically infinite. Reconciling those imbalances requires the use of amplifiers to boost variety and attenuators to reduce it. Beer's Viable System Model is essentially a working out of **Ashby's law** and shows the mechanisms necessary to reconcile the inherent variety imbalances.

Another implication is that structure plays a very significant part in increasing or decreasing variety, since this can determine the number of system elements and their relationships to one another. The classic formula for calculating variety is $2^n - (n+1)$ where n is the number of interdependent elements. Because variety goes up by the square of the number of elements, variety can increase (or decrease) dramatically depending on the system's structure. Because of this, it's often not necessary to calculate the variety of a system precisely, in practice it's usually easy to spot where there is or is not requisite variety.

Watch for

Number of states of the system and percentage of those which can/can't be managed.

Grammar of Systems

1st Circular Causality Principle

Ashby's **1st Circular Causality Principle** is one of the two principles that really underpin System Dynamics and it deals with one of the two forms of feedback loop that make up a system dynamics model or indeed, most cybernetic feedback systems. This 1st Principle covers positive feedback loops which are feedback effects that tend to run out of control until stopped by external agency. The **1st Circular Causality Principle** states that *"Given positive feedback (i.e. a two part system in which each stimulates any initial change in the other), radically different end states are possible from the same initial conditions."*

POSITIVE FEEDBACK DRIVES STATE CHANGE.

In a positive feedback loop, an increase in A creates an increase in B which in turn increases A, driving a cycle of escalation. The term positive has no implication that the cycle is in any way good, it simply refers to the effect of the relationship in increasing a variable. As an example, a conflict spiral is a positive feedback loop even though the effect may be entirely harmful.

The principle was named by Ashby, but as with many principles in the Grammar, it permeated systems thinking before it was formally set down and you can trace it back to James Clerk Maxwell the father of modern physics and his work on governors in steam engines that then led through to the development of control theory. Clerk Maxwell put one of the consequences of positive feedback like this: *"when an infinitely small variation in the present state may bring about a finite difference in the state of the system in a finite time, the condition of the system is said to be unstable."* And this is the critical issue with positive feedback – it drives instability. That instability may be something we see as good or something we consider a disaster. Positive feedback and its instability is value free. Left to themselves, positive feedback loops produce exponential outcomes.

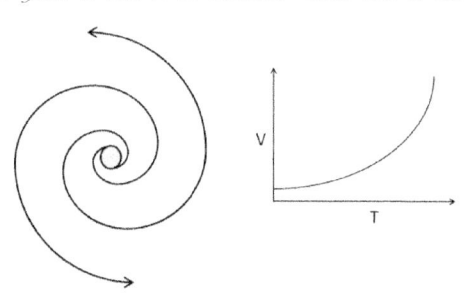

140

We're all familiar with positive feedback systems – compound interest works on positive feedback, the more capital you have the more interest you get, the more interest you get the more capital you have the more…. Fires work on positive feedback, the more of a building that is on fire, the faster the fire spreads, the more that catches fire…. Despite this, and despite how extremely common positive feedback is in all aspects of life, we are often slow to spot it, or to even consider where it might lead us.

Aside from the differences between the two types of feedback loop, modelling causality using loops rather than assuming that causality was linear in nature was itself a scientific breakthrough brought about by early systems practitioners. Whilst each side of a loop can be seen as causal in nature, the loop as a whole isn't deterministically causal. Its behaviour is emergent and, particularly for positive loops, the end state is explicitly unpredictable.

Implications
The whole of the climate change and global warming debate has been built on the back of positive and negative feedback loops, so demonstrably this has had a major impact on public policy internationally.

One of the implications of these two principles is that it's important to know whether you are dealing with positive or negative loops and if (as is normal) you are dealing with a combination, then understanding their relative power, rate and the gain on each loop is critical to understanding the probable behaviour of the system. To do this, you have to build a mathematical model, you can't just do it with causal loop diagrams. And then you're in a position to amplify or attenuate the loops as required, to get the effects that you want.

Watch for
A increases B increases A increases…
Any exponential outcomes.

2nd Circular Causality Principle

Ashby's **2nd Circular Causality Principle** is the counterpart and in some ways the opposite to the **1st Circular Causality Principle** at least in terms of its effect. Where the 1st describes the effect of positive feedback, the 2nd describes the effect of negative feedback loops, which is that they are self-correcting and drive towards stability. The **2nd Circular Causality Principle** states *"Given negative feedback (i.e. a two part system in which each part tends to offset any change in the other), the equilibrium state is invariant over a wide range of initial conditions."*

NEGATIVE FEEDBACK DRIVES STABILITY

In contrast to positive loops, negative loops self-correct to return to a stable state and again this is irrespective of whether we think that is a good thing or not. Bureaucracies tend to be built on negative loops that keep them in being, irrespective of whether what is being done is useful.

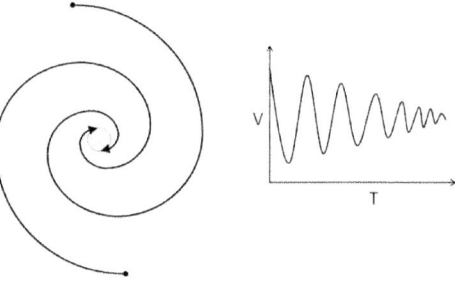

As with positive feedback, before system theory became established, James Clerk Maxwell grappled with the effect of feedback on stability: *"When the state of things is such that an infinitely small variation of the present state will alter only by an infinitely small quantity the state at some future time, the condition of the system, whether at rest or in motion, is said to be stable"*. Aside from the differences between the two types of feedback loop, modelling causality using loops rather than assuming that causality was linear in nature was itself a scientific breakthrough brought into the areas beyond the confines of mechanical control theory by the early systems practitioners. Whilst each side of a loop can be seen as causal in nature, the loop as a whole isn't deterministically causal, it's emergent.

Negative feedback underpins **Homeostasis** and is fundamental to understand the stability of any system. It is so ubiquitous we tend to not

Grammar of Systems

see it when it's there and take it for granted, so spotting negative feedback loops is harder than it really should be, not because they are actually difficult to discern, but just because we mostly don't even bother looking.

When working with these two principles it's important to know whether you are dealing with positive or negative loops and if (as is normal) you are dealing with a combination, then understanding their relative power, rate and the gain on each loop is critical to understanding the behaviour of the system. To do this, you have to build a mathematical model, you can't just do it with causal loop diagrams. And then you're in a position to amplify or attenuate the loops, to get the effects that you want.

Implications

The stability negative feedback loops create in a system conditions the value set of the system.

Most change approaches whether organisational or social change focus on moving a system towards a preferred alternative future state and fight against the negative feedback loops holding it where it is – and mostly they lose that fight. Which shouldn't be at all surprising, but apparently it is. The alternative approach is to de-commission or at least weaken the negative loops holding the present to unstick the situation before trying too hard to move it.

Conversely it is easy to destroy the source of stability that you rely on without realising it until too late. By actually looking for the negative feedback loops of stability, it is possible to safeguard those that are helpful. As Alfred North Whitehead put it: *"The art of progress is to preserve order amid change and to preserve change amid order."* So learning how to play both positive and negative feedback is a powerful combination.

Watch for
A increases B decreases A.
Any stable system.

The Law of Crossing

The Law of Crossing and **the Law of Calling** are expressions from Spencer-Brown's Laws of Form and share his dramatic, and whimsical language. But as with **Calling,** the idea in **Crossing** is much older and fundamental in systems. It is the partner law to **Calling**.

CROSSING A BOUNDARY IS A CHANGE OF STATE

The Law of Calling is about distinguishing a system and defining it and its boundary. **The Law of Crossing** is, as you might expect, about crossing that boundary, either from inside the system into its environment or from the environment into the system. In some ways this is mundane and obvious, but because of that we tend to take **Crossing** for granted and so ignore both its meaning and its implications. Being inside a system is fundamentally different to being outside, in terms of 'being' and also in observing and communicating.

Calling – distinguishing or defining a system – is different if it is done from within to if it is done from outside. A gang of kids define the boundaries of their gang system from within, and the process of doing that changes them as individuals and as a system. When a school defines a group of kids as a class, the effect is different because it's done from outside.

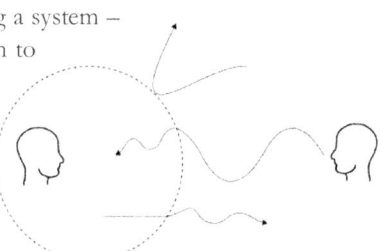

When Donne wrote: *"any man's death diminishes me, because I am involved in Mankinde; And therefore never send to know for whom the bell tolls; It tolls for thee",* that is a statement about the effect of where you stand relative to a boundary. **Crossing** the boundary changes the perspective and your identity from that of a participant to that of an observer of the system, or the other way round if you are moving into a system from outside it. Moving to an observer position brings distance, both perceptual and emotional and in terms of power. It's an easy trick to assume power, or at least authority, by **Crossing** to observe rather than participating; this is the stance of authority figures and of therapists. When defining, 'naming'

or describing a system from outside, there are choices on how we do that and there is a whole strand of systems theory and practice devoted to just that.

Similarly, when communications cross a system boundary they are changed and in systems this is transduction. Because inside and outside are not the same, the language is not the same, so signals mean something different. As Spencer-Brown says *"The more perfect the fit on the communion level, the less needs to be communicated, ….as people get to know each other better--a gang of kids go about and one word or even half a word is used to express a whole community between them. Whereas when people do not know each other, this has to be expressed in a whole book. But between people who do know one another, however, there is no need for a book, it can all go in half a syllable."*

Implications
Always know where you have chosen to stand relative to a system boundary and be conscious of the options that gives you and the choices it denies you – especially when defining the system. If you use the 'distancing trick' to gain power, be aware that is what you are doing and that others will also be aware of it – albeit often subconsciously. Being an effective agent of change requires you to see through the eyes of those on both sides of the boundary, understand the views and values of those and use that understanding to communicate in a way which will be heard.

More subtly, you need to manage transduction across boundaries. Communications are always distorted by boundaries, and, the more boundaries and the harder the boundary, the more distortion you can expect.

Watch for
Presence of a boundary and who is on which side of the boundary.
Signal / meaning distortions, inability / difficulty communicating.

Grammar of Systems

Network Power Law

This is often known as Metcalfe's law, but since Metcalfe's law as written didn't come out of systems theory and the basic proposition did come from systems and significantly earlier than Metcalfe named it, it's in here not under his name, but with a nod of acknowledgement for having popularised it. Metcalfe's law states that the utility of a network is equal to the square of the number of its users. More broadly in systems the **Network Power Law** it points to the exponential nature of much of complexity.

STRUCTURAL COMPLEXITY GOES UP EXPONENTIALLY WITH THE NUMBER OF ELEMENTS

The classic formula for this is $2^n - (n+1)$ where n is the number of elements or nodes in a system. So if you have two people in communication there is only one (bilateral) connection between them, with four people there are eleven: six bilateral, four triples and one involving all four. When you get to 16 nodes, there are 65,519 permutations of possible communications – so without some structure it's bedlam.

As a result, in many systems the complexity goes up exponentially and that can be good or bad depending on the context and what you are trying to do. Some of the most successful strategies for IT businesses harness the power of the **Network Power Law**.

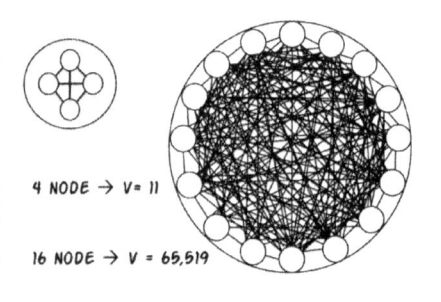

4 NODE → V = 11

16 NODE → V = 65,519

Which means that the first to build the network of users in a particular strategic arena has an advantage that is hard to beat. Having a network twice the size of a competitor doesn't give you twice the market power it gives you orders of magnitude more power – which is great if you are Facebook, but less good for a would-be competitor. Dealing with complexity is what organisation is about and understanding where complexity is generated in the business is critical to handling it well. Where it isn't handled well, you end up either with chaos where it unconstrained, or impoverished machine-like operations where it's over-constrained. On the negative side, failing to handle burgeoning complexity takes you into the **Complexity instability principle**.

Implications
Probably the biggest implication of this relates to the **Complexity Instability Principle** as mostly people don't understand how the complexity of networks goes up exponentially with their size and that over a certain level of complexity they become unstable.

As discussed above, it also has a huge impact on the effectiveness of organisations as their complexity (and its effects) are often not well understood.

Thirdly – again as discussed above, the hypergrowth of many internet based firms is largely dependent on the effect of The **Network Power Law**.

A critical implication is, though, that we can calculate complexity – it doesn't have to be just a rule of thumb or an accidental effect.

Watch for
The number of connected elements within a system boundary.

Grammar of Systems

System Survival Theorem

The **System Survival Theorem** follows from the **Conservation of Adaptation Principle** and sharpens up one of the implications of it – which is around how fast systems need to change if they need to maintain their fit with their environment through time.

SYSTEMS FAIL IF THEIR ENVIRONMENT CONSISTENTLY CHANGES MORE THAN THE SYSTEM

Both a system and its environment are changing and despite the fact that they co-evolve, it's unlikely they will change at the same constant rate. It's unlikely because their respective rates of change depend on their own internal state and, by definition, these are different, otherwise we wouldn't be able to distinguish the system from its environment. It follows then that we're usually dealing with two things, the system and the environment that are changing at different rates, but somehow need to fit together which means changing at the same rate through time. It is a tortoise and hare situation, where both run the same race, start and end up in the same places as one another but do it at different speeds.

The **System Survival Theorem** states that: *"to survive, the system must be capable of a rate of change that is greater than or equal to the rate of change in the environment on which it depends"*: $\Delta S \geq \Delta E$. If the environment *consistently* changes faster than the system, then the system will lose its fit with its environment and at some point will cease to be the same system – it will cease to exist other than as a thing. This is particularly critical in organisational systems, where of course once an organisation loses its fit with its environment, it tends to go out of business. The **System Survival Theorem** is closely related to the **Homeostasis principle** and follows logically from it once you take into account the fact that both systems and their environments are in a state of change.

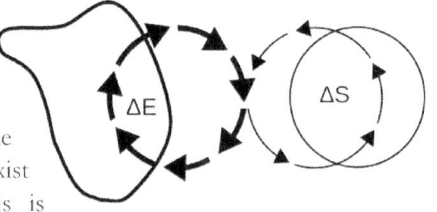

There's an odd bias in a lot of both systems practice and complexity theory towards adaptation and the phrase 'complex adaptive system' has been common currency for over 50 years, but there are three ways for systems to work the $\Delta S \geq \Delta E$ equation. The first is adaptation – change to match changes in the environment, the second is to retard changes in the environment – which works if the system has enough power relative to the environment and the third is pro-action – initiate changes which the environment will subsequently react to.

Implications
The rate at which the system, or particularly the organisation changes isn't something that people typically consider, except in a very loose way. In particular, the rate at which it needs to be able to change isn't thought of as a key metric. Often, the need for change, or the appreciation that the world is changing faster than we are, is something that is felt or intuited, but of course by the time it has been felt, it's often far too late. What we sense, what we intuit, is the existential shock of the essential bonds between the system and its environment ripping apart. But in almost all cases, it is possible to measure both sides of the $\Delta S \geq \Delta E$ equation and to know where you are on this survival critical metric. As Jack Welch said: *"When the rate of change inside an institution becomes slower than the rate of change outside, the end is in sight"*.

Whilst changing too slowly is fatal, so is changing too fast – there are two ways to lose fit and when the system loses its fit with its environment that is fatal. It isn't that both system and environment have to be perfectly synchronised, but the change rates must balance out over time.

$\Delta S \geq \Delta E$ is the basis for both measuring and understanding business agility. Using it you can dramatically increase the agility of organisations.

The **System Survival Theorem** together with the **Viability Principle** forms the basis of the **Structural Viability Theorem**.

Watch for
Rate of change of system relative to the rate of change of its environment.

System Resonance Principle

This is alluded to in the quotation in the section on the **Black Box Principles**: *"He knew that stimulus for a man or a machine must be shaped to match nearly some of his feature-filters"*. The degree to which two or more systems can communicate or relate to one another

`RESONANCE OCCURS BECAUSE OF SIMILARITIES IN SYSTEMS`

depends on them having similarities, either structural or in terms of their dynamics. Almost all of us know this at a personal level, we talk about 'having things in common' or 'being on the same wavelength' and you can think about this in quite superficial terms as having come into contact with similar things. But it isn't having seen or heard the same thing externally that counts, it's the commonality of patterns within each of us that has the effect. It's not that we heard the same concert, it's that we reacted in the same way and we cleave to that shared meaning because it implies that there is something essentially the same in each of us that causes us to make meaning in the same way. The effect that any stimulus has depends on the structure and dynamics of the receiving system – the filters that allow a signal to be recognised, the structure of feedback loops available to shape a meaning from it and the dynamics that govern that process. You can also think of the **System Resonance Principle** in terms of and as a consequence of the **Law of Sufficient Complexity**. The underlying structure and dynamics generates the behaviour and similarities of structure and dynamics between two systems generates resonance between them.

The **System Resonance Principle** relates to the **Law of Crossing** as it is about the degree to which any boundary can be crossed, or more accurately the degree to which any signal is distorted as it crosses. So it also lies behind the mystery of Spencer-Brown's cat mentioned in the chapter on Boundaries and perspective. What Spencer-Brown refers to as the quality of 'communion' is underpinned by the **Resonance Principle**.

"What an organism feeds upon is negative entropy."
Schrödinger

Grammar of Systems

Resonance is also behind the **Self-organising Principle**. And you can think of this as whether there is a fit as two systems come together. The co-respondence can be at the surface level or can be deeper and can be based on similarity or contrast / difference. Resonance can be by similarity – social groups that are formed and maintained by shared interest, taste for a particular music or style of clothes or value system or…. Contrariwise, it can result from useful difference - the fit between a nut and bolt is to do with how their surface structures fit one to another. Each is the reverse of the other, but the unity is their emergent property as 'a' fastener. For the bully or abuser who hunts out the weak, the fit between abuser and abused is also based on a matched pair of opposite characteristics. Once there is a resonance between two or more free-floating elements, then they are 'attracted' to one another which actually means that the fit increases the probability that they will stick together rather than simply glancing off and carrying on independently. Depending on the strength of that stickiness, that attraction, relative to momentum and other forces at work, the process of **Self-organisation** begins. Once it has begun, then the processes of structural coupling (underpinned by the **Conservation of Adaptation Principle**), where each part co-evolves to fit the other, progressively deepens the bond and strengthens and accelerates the process of self-organising.

Implications
The first implication is that the quality and effectiveness of communication depends on the **System Resonance Principle**. Where and to the degree there is resonance, communication is possible, and to the extent it is absent, communication will be lost in translation.

The second is that where resonance is strong, there is a greater propensity for **Self-organisation** to happen, whether that resonance is based on similarity or contrast.

Watch for
Ease of communicating, lack of distortion of meaning.

Grammar of Systems

Power Structuration Theorem

There are few issues in organisations and in theories about organising and managing that excite passion and anger quite as much as the issue of autonomy and particularly the tension between autonomy and centralisation. Some of
A SYSTEM HAS OPTIMAL AGENCY WHEN ITS NEEDS FOR AGENCY ARE BALANCED WITH THOSE OF ITS SUB-SYSTEMS
the debate is extremely partisan and quite a lot is self-contradicting. You hear people arguing for maximising autonomy for front line teams and at the same time arguing for more centralised leadership. The contradictions inherent in this have tied the whole field of leadership in knots. But arguments aside, the tension is real, ever present and a serious issue.

This tension is core to the **Viability Principle**, but that simply states it as one of two principal tensions that need to be reconciled in any organisational system and that leaves us with the problem of knowing how to resolve it any particular setting. There are two theorems that address knowing where to balance the tension: **Power Structuration Theorem** and **Structural Viability Theorem** so you can see this pair in part as derivatives of the **Viability Principle**. The first deals with differentials in power and autonomy between levels of a system and the second deals with differentials between levels in their rates of change.

The **Power Structuration Theorem** states that *"in a nested system, i.e. one with sub-systems, optimal agency is achieved when the need for agency by the system is in balance with the need for agency of the constituent sub-systems"*. Chris Alexander expressed it rather more elegantly as *"We define organic order as the kind of order that is achieved when there is a perfect balance between the needs of the parts, and the needs of the whole."*

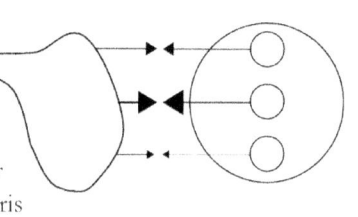

In the **Power Structuration Theorem** we're looking at this in terms of power, agency or autonomy – the capacity and freedom of action for different levels of the system to do what they need to do to address the demands on them. This is straightforwardly the application of **Ashby's Law** when this is applied to multiple levels of a system. The differentials in complexity and the respective need for agency between levels can be dramatic. It's not necessarily the case that higher levels of the system have more complexity to deal with than sub-systems or vice versa, each case can be different, although for organisations there are sectoral norms.

Implications
The first is that all dogmatic statements and theories about where the balance of power should be set should be taken lightly and that if you want to copy what works in a different situation, you should do your homework. Mostly the relative complexity of demands on different levels is unseen, but it's not that hard to get a grip of, as Beer put it: *"The cybernetic argument for autonomy is distinct from ethical, political, or psychological arguments. It has no emotive content. It is mathematical."*

The next implication is that you can increase the overall agency or power of your system if you get this right.

The third is that where there are strident calls that all organisations should recalibrate in a particular direction, that's often to redress a historic imbalance the other way, but the need shifts through time – hence the reason for the imbalance. It was there for a reason, it's not an accident.

Watch for
Relative need for agency between system levels and ability to redistribute agency between levels.

Grammar of Systems

Conservation of Adaptation Principle

At one level, this is an easy idea, but in two other ways it's quite hard. Superficially it's easy - not that much more than the truism that 'change is constant'. Hard because firstly change may be always going on but it's far from constant and secondly because you have to do a three-step shift from the normal perspective.

CHANGE IS THE ONLY CONSTANT IN THE RELATIONSHIP BETWEEN A SYSTEM AND ITS ENVIRONMENT

There's a things-based view of systems which holds that systems are like machines and that they are the same in any context. In that perspective, a car is a car and it doesn't matter if it's cruising down the road or at the bottom of a lake, it's still a car. And at a superficial level that's true. But from a systems thinking point of view, it's not true. Every system exists in relationship to an environment and the properties of the system depend on the environment as well as on the system itself; change the environment and you change the system. The car at the bottom of a lake doesn't have the same emergent properties or behave the same as the car on the road does, so it's not the same system. A tiger in a zoo and a tiger in the wild are not the same. The nature of the system – the nature of the system as we know it – depends on its relationship with its environment. If the relationship is broken, the nature of the system is inevitably changed, hence Donne's *"no man is an island, entire of itself"*. The second perspective shifts from thing to relationship and the focus shifts from the conservation of the system as an entity to the conservation of the relationships that keep the system in being.

Both systems and their environments change, some quickly, some slowly, some a lot, some a bit, some continuously, some abruptly and they tend to change at different rates. This in turn means that in the third perspective we're not just looking at the conservation of the relationships that keeps the system in being, we need to pay attention to whether and how change in those relationships is maintained. That takes us to the **Conservation of**

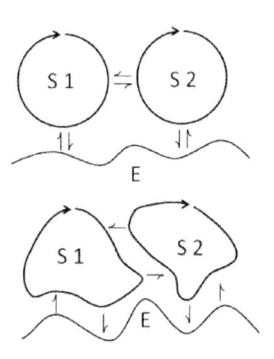

Adaptation Principle which says that *"to stay in being, any system needs to maintain change in its relationship with its environment."* The **Conservation of Adaptation Principle** lies behind Maturana's work on structural coupling and is nicely captured in Bateson's observation *"The horse didn't evolve; the field grass didn't evolve. It is the relationship that evolved"*. It links to the **System Survival Theorem**, and the **Viability principle**.

Implications
We tend to find it quite difficult to think about change and about rates of change. People are fond of saying that change today is faster than ever, and in some ways that's obviously true, the population is growing faster than ever, in other ways it's not obviously the case – I'd argue that the scale of innovation now is far lower than in WW2, for example. But opinions aside, we don't even have good language to describe change and are even less well equipped to talk – or think – about rates of change. So getting a good understanding of differential change rates in a relationship is hard and it's harder still with changes to the rate of change in relationships between entities that are changing at different rates. The **Conservation of Adaptation Principle** is both simple in concept and also hard to grapple with. Which is unfortunate given that it is the key to surviving.

For any system structurally coupled to its environment, changing too slowly can be fatal because the system loses its fit, conversely, so is changing too fast. These are the two ways to lose fit and once the system loses its fit with its environment, that is fatal. It isn't that both system and environment have to be perfectly synchronised, but the change rates must balance over time.

The **Conservation of Adaptation Principle** applies to any type of system – including people. The loss of the structurally coupled relationships on which we depend leads to an identity crisis or worse and that process of loss of fit starts with a failure to conserve adaptation.

Watch for
Frequency and rate of change of the relationship.

Darkness Principle

The **Darkness Principle** states that: *"No system can be known completely."* In some ways this may be obvious, as even 'simple' systems have multiple elements and interactions (by definition) and levels.

THERE IS ALWAYS SOMETHING ABOUT A SYSTEM YOU CAN'T KNOW

Even if you put aside the complexity generated by the dynamics of the system, just its material form is ultimately unknowable as you slip from the knowability of a Newtonian world view to the unknowability of a quantum one at lower levels. But that's at the level of theory, so what about practice?

In systems practice, systems are also ultimately unknowable for three reasons. Firstly because of their fractality – if you try to reduce them to parts, then as you go down levels from system to sub-system to sub-sub-system, the number and complexity of the parts increases and continues to do that indefinitely. Secondly in parallel, the number of interdependencies increase and, in many cases, exponentially. Thirdly and possibly most critically, systems are by their nature dynamic and change as you observe them – indeed the **System Stability Principle** defines a system as something that is dynamic yet stable enough for long enough for us to recognise its identifiable patterns and identity. Because of that dynamic nature, systems change and the longer you spend collecting information on the detail of the parts and their interdependencies, the more out of date that information becomes as the system changes underneath you.

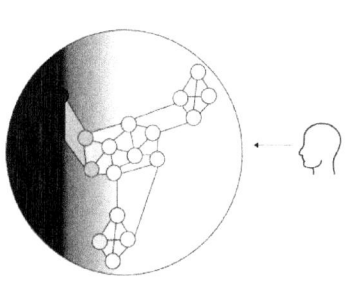

At this point some people throw up their hands with a 'so if it's unknowable, what's the point?' but of course it's true for every aspect of life and the fact that I don't understand everything about how I digest a cup of tea doesn't stop me wanting, drinking or indeed digesting tea. The **Darkness Principle** is no reason to not bother trying to understand systems. A word of caution here, there are a number of what you might call pop-scientists out there and particularly from some of the more arm-waving branches of complexity theory, who argue that since systems are ultimately unknowable, you should abandon all hope of trying to understand and simply rely on them to guide you through the mystery of complexity. Systems practice however takes a different view, and this leads us back to **Conant-Ashby Theorem** and the use of models and modelling to help us to understand systems' complexities.

Implications

The implication of the **Darkness Principle** is that since systems cannot be completely known, you have to:

a) abandon the belief that it is knowable if only we dig into a bit more detail.
b) stay aware that our knowledge is always bounded and never certain (so what's new?)
c) get comfortable with the uncertainty.
d) use a simplified representation of the system, AKA a model, to understand it.
e) choose carefully which aspects of the system to model and which to ignore.
f) work holistically – use the system's emergent properties to understand it.

Watch for

Percentage of observations of system which were surprising.

Grammar of Systems

Adams 3rd Law

Adams 3rd Law: states that *"a system composed of the lowest risk components available will be a high-risk system"*.

A SYSTEM'S OVERALL RISK DEPENDS ON BALANCING THE RISK ACROSS LEVELS OF THE SYSTEM

Adams 3rd Law is a thoroughly counter-intuitive, disruptive and insidious piece of thinking. Essentially it states that if you have a system that has been built from a set of components which have been selected on the basis that they are each the low-risk option, then the system overall will be subject to increased levels of overall risk. This seems so utterly contradictory that it takes a bit to get accustomed to it. Its relevance to the whole of the management of strategic risk is immense.

The logic is twofold. First is that the lowest risk components are low risk because they have been optimised for internal reliability. That means that they haven't been optimised for their systemic context. Building a component into a system inevitably involves some compromises being made in the design or in adaptation. The lowest risk components have the lowest risk because compromises have not been made, so when combined into a system, the system as a whole has to bear the risk of aggregated compromise that is the inevitable result of integration.

The second strand of the logic is related to that: if you have an organisation that relies on just pursuing low-risk options, then by definition, these have to be in long-term stable relationships. Such relationships are always vulnerable to being suddenly de-stabilised by changes outside the relationship. What these stable relationships generally don't offer is possibilities for adapting to new future opportunities. Without this, there can be a loss of confidence in the organisation by its various stakeholders. Developing and exploiting new opportunities is inevitably a risky business and by avoiding taking these risks, the risk-averse organisation effectively shuts itself out of new opportunities. It has unwittingly signed its own death warrant. To be sure, the death is sometimes a long one, but it is no less certain for that.

Implications
Many attempts to minimise risk carry with them the threat of higher levels of risk. The implication of this is that you need to choose – and are able to choose – the types of risk you want to engage with, but you can't eliminate risk. The focus needs to be on balancing the risk appetite for the overall system against the ability of each sub-system to compromise for the good of the whole.

Natural systems are often really good at managing **Adams 3rd Law**. Honey bees do a waggle dance to tell the other bees in the hive the precise directions to find a good source of pollen, so obviously the lowest risk option for each successive bee is to follow instructions, but despite this some bees ignore the flight instructions and go off in random directions. Each individual 'random' flight is higher risk, but of course if all the bees went to the same source, then once that was exhausted, the colony as a whole would be at major risk with no alternatives. Higher risk flights for the individual reduces the risk to the hive and conversely, minimising the risk for each individual flight increases the overall risk.

Watch for
Relative risk generated by and managed at different levels of the system.

Grammar of Systems

Self-organised Criticality

Self-organised Criticality is in some ways a counterpart to the **Complexity Instability Principle** but focusing on where the dynamics of a system are mainly responsible for driving instability rather than its structural complexity, although often it's difficult to separate these intertwined factors.

SYSTEMS WHOSE DYNAMICS DRIVE THE SYSTEM TO COLLAPSE

The term was first coined by three physicists: Bak, Tang and Wiesenfeld, but the idea was developed in systems theory somewhat earlier and the best description I know comes from Stafford Beer:

It is not difficult to recognize that the movement of water in this bay is the visible behaviour of a dynamic system: after all, the waves are steadily moving in and dissipating themselves along the shore. But please consider just one wave. ... the wave cannot be other than it is because a wave is a dynamic system. It consists of flows of water, which are its parts, and the relations between those flows, which are governed by the natural laws of systems of water that are investigated by the science of hydrodynamics. The appearances of the wave, its shape and the happy white crest, are actually outputs of this system. They are what they are because the system is organized in the way that it is, and this organization produces an inescapable kind of behaviour. The cross-section of the wave is parabolic, having two basic forms, the one dominating at the open-sea stage of the wave, and the other dominating later. As the second form is produced from the first, there is a moment when the wave holds the two forms: it has at this moment a wedge shape of 120°. And at this point, as the second form takes over, the wave begins to break—hence the happy white crest. Now in terms of the dynamic system that we call a wave, the happy white crest is not at all the pretty sign by which what we first called an entity signalizes its existence. For the wave, that crest is its personal catastrophe. What has happened is that the wave has a systemic conflict within it determined by its form of organization, and that this has produced a phase of instability. The happy white crest is the mark of doom upon the wave, because the instability feeds upon itself; and the catastrophic collapse of the wave is an inevitable output of the system.

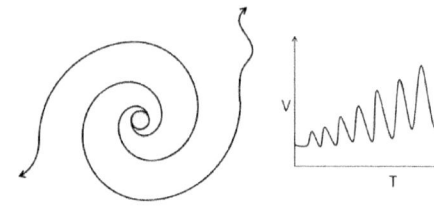

And that is the essence of **Self-organised Criticality** in systems – some systems are organised or self-organised with dynamics that ensure their own collapse. You can see this happening in natural systems, in social systems, in organisational systems, in financial and political systems. All systems are dynamic in their nature and those dynamics drive and are driven by tensions and pressures within and outwith the system and in the case of a **Self-organised Criticality,** those dynamics, tensions and pressures are organised in a way that destroys or changes the nature of the system.

Implications
The dynamics of systems can be modelled and understood, so typically it is possible to work out if a system is likely to go critical. Even without formal modelling, it is often possible to sensitise yourself to the tensions and pressures inherent in a system and to know when these are going critical. Criticality means a fundamental state change, that isn't necessarily a bad thing, it's just a different thing.

Watch for
Strong dynamic that will meet a limit to growth – unstoppable force meets immovable barrier.

Grammar of Systems

Complexity Instability Principle

This follows on from the calculation of system complexity embedded in the **Network Power Law**. The **Complexity Instability Principle** states that *"systems with too many active dependencies between their parts tend to become incipiently unstable"*, with each perturbation in one part of the system triggering a chain reaction of further perturbations in other parts, which in turn trigger more perturbations and so on, so the system may never stabilise.

SYSTEMS WITH TOO MANY CHANGING PARTS TEND TO BECOME UNSTABLE

As an issue it was understood fairly early on in network theory and Ross Ashby, Stafford Beer and Christopher Alexander all wrote about this as a problem, but despite this, it's not well understood in many fields. It's particularly problematic in organisation theory where there is a drive towards building flat networks as a 'solution' to organisational complexity. In this field there is often an assumption that because you don't always know who needs to connect to whom, everyone should be connected to everyone else and there should be no barriers to that. The **Complexity Instability Principle** shows that this is an inherently flawed proposition – building large flat networks may work, but it carries a very high risk. Critically, the variables that condition success or failure of a network that underpin the **Complexity Instability Principle** are not well understood. These are:

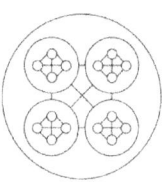

16 NODES
4X4 STRUCTURE
V= 55

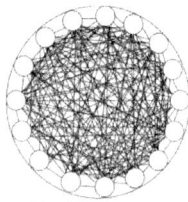

16 NODES
FLAT STRUCTURE
V= 65,519

1. the number of nodes in the network
2. the number of dependencies between those nodes – i.e. how many other nodes each is affected by
3. the frequency of signals / stimuli between those nodes
4. the **Relaxation Time** of the system

Because one of the most critical of these four variables is the number of dependencies and, as we've seen with the **Network Power Law,** this increases exponentially with the complexity of the system, flat networks are particularly unsuited to address high organisational complexity, as you tend to go over the instability threshold.

Implications
The solution to the **Complexity Instability Principle** is to organise or self-organise into sub-systems to reduce the number of interdependencies and therefore the complexity. You can do this by design, and Alexander made this the starting point for his treatise on systems design in 'Notes on the Synthesis of Form' or you can do it by **Self-organisation**. In both cases, the process is to work out the pattern of high dependencies, group together into sub-systems where the intensity of dependencies is higher within each sub-system than it is externally between the sub-systems and that dramatically reduces the overall complexity of a system. The difference between doing this by design or by **Self-organisation** is just who does it, on the basis of what information and how long it takes. Design is best if a design team can see the whole system and work to optimise the whole, **Self-organisation** is best if it isn't possible to get an overall view, or if the situation is (already) too unstable for an overview to be effective. As far as understanding how many sub-systems to divide a complex into to reduce the probability that it'll become unstable, **Root Structuration Theorem** acts as a guide.

Watch for
Systems with high numbers of interconnected elements within the same boundary. Systems with large imbalances in numbers of elements between levels.

Grammar of Systems

Order Osmosis Principle

Where a stable and organised system sits alongside a less stable and less organised system, elements from the less stable system will tend to move across the system boundary from the less ordered to become elements of the more organised one. It

SUB-SYSTEMS TEND TO MIGRATE FROM LESS ORDERED TO MORE ORDERED SYSTEMS

happens because elements in the less ordered system are less tightly bound into it and are therefore freer to move across the boundary. Firstly, the 'binding' is a function of the number and strength of the relationships with other system elements and by definition, a less ordered system has fewer and whilst naturally not all of these will be symmetrical, elements at the 'weak' end of the coupling are freer to move. Secondly the 'less stable' part of being a 'less stable and organised system' means that on average its dynamics are less bound into **Homeostatic** loops that maintain dynamic stability, and that in turn means that at least some elements will be driven by those dynamics out of the less stable system's structure. Conversely, in a more organised system, elements that enter in tend to be more tightly coupled into more relationships that are more homeostatically stable - because that's what makes more organised systems more organised.

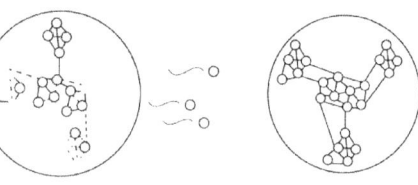

If the rate of osmosis is too high, this can destabilise the organised system so that the differential in structuration between the two balances out and osmosis stops. This relates to both the **Relaxation Time** of the system as well as its rate of change as described in the **System Survival Theorem** – in other words if the recipient system cannot adapt at a rate that at least matches the rate of perturbation, it will itself start to become disordered. Conversely, the more the less stable 'donor' system loses its looser element, it may become more organised and more stable – and again this can slow or stop the rate of osmosis.

It relates to the 2nd Law of Thermodynamics, but since that only applies to closed systems, and systems theory is concerned with open systems, this is as close as we get. So whereas the 2nd Law says heat cannot flow from a colder body to a hotter one, the **Order Osmosis Principle** is not that categorical. Generally, there is a flow both ways across the boundary, but it's not symmetrical. There's also a relation to Coase's law from economics: *"A firm tends to expand till the cost of organizing that extra transaction within the firm become equal to the cost of organizing the same transaction from the open market."*

Implications
One example of the **Order Osmosis Principle** is in population migration from failed or failing states. Less obvious is the migration from the countryside into cities that has been going on for centuries and then the migration from towns to cities and from cities to metropolises, where the power of structuration and dynamics follow the **Network Power Law**. Migration is a useful example of both the benefits and risks to the recipient system: positively, immigrants provide new resource to the recipient and stimulate change – historically this has been one of the richest sources of innovation, but too much too fast can create political, social and financial instability. Similarly, globalisation works because of the **Order Osmosis Principle** - not just work being exported to where labour or supply is cheapest, but it is also that low structure economies (where labour is cheapest) get sucked into more structured economic systems, and gradually become absorbed into that model. As they do, the differentials reduce, the advantage is lost and economic colonisation shifts somewhere else.

More broadly, the **Order Osmosis Principle** can be used and can be seen at work in many situations: destabilising previously stable systems, inflows from unstable systems moving stable ones in a particular direction, and conversely with stable systems being used to stabilise unstable ones. It is also critical to bear in mind in the design of system boundaries of all sorts and specifically how porous you want those to be.

Watch for
Net migration rates.

Grammar of Systems

The Two Black Box Principles

A 'black box' is a device where what it does is more or less understood, but how it does it is unknown. The 'black' signifies that the internal workings are invisible. **THE OUTPUTS OF A BLACK BOX ARE PREDICTABLE**
The two **Black Box Principles** follow on from the **Darkness Principle** and in one way provide a partial solution to the challenge that **Darkness** brings. The **1st Black Box Principle** states that: *"It is not necessary to enter the black box to understand the nature of the function it performs"* and the **2nd Black Box Principle** that**:** *"It is not necessary to enter the black box to calculate the variety that it may generate"* – obviously harking back to **Ashby's Law**.

The concept of the **Black Box** is superficially simple, but critically important in systems and in modelling complex systems. Essentially what it means is that if we know that given an input X and conditions Y a sub-system will generate output Z, we don't need to know how it does that. All we need to know is that it does - *Ye shall know them by their fruits.*

This is an absolutely normal state of affairs, I don't need to know why a piece of music has a particular emotional effect, just that it does, I don't need to understand the biochemistry of digestion to know to eat when I'm hungry. But in systems practice, the significance of the **Black Box** is more than just that. Because we understand the world through models and all models are simplifications, the key to good modelling is deciding what we can afford to leave out of the modelling and the **Black Box** is one of the keys to unpicking that. **Black Box** thinking means that we can ignore swathes of detail to focus on critical parameters and outputs.

I couldn't help including a quote from Warren McCulloch on a session at the Macy conferences on an actual physical black box.
"Lorente de Nó and I, as physiologists, were asked to consider the second of two black boxes that the allies had liberated from the Germans. No one knew what they were supposed to do or how they were to do it. The first box had been opened and exploded. Both had inputs and outputs, so labelled. The question was phrased unforgettably: "This is the enemy's machine. You have to find out what it does and how it does it. What shall we do?" By the time the question had become that well defined, Norbert (Wiener) was snoring at the top of his lungs and his cigar ashes were falling on his stomach. But when Lorente and I had tried to answer, Norbert rose abruptly and said:

Grammar of Systems

"You could of course give it all possible sinusoidal frequencies one after the other and record the output, but it would be better to feed it noise - say white noise......you might call this Rorschach." Before I could challenge his notion of a Rorschach, many engineer's voices broke in. Then, for the first time, I caught the sparkle in Johnny von Neumann's eye. I had never seen him before and I did not know who he was. He read my face like an open book. He knew that stimulus for a man or a machine must be shaped to match nearly some of his feature-filters, and that white noise would not do. There followed a wonderful duel: Norbert with an enormous club chasing Johnny, and Johnny with a rapier waltzing around Norbert.......at the end of which they went to lunch arm in arm."

Apart from being a fun story, it explains some theory behind the **Black Box.** It's not just about understanding a **Black Box's** outputs in a transactional sense – i.e. 'does it consistently deliver what the system needs?', it's also that the input-output characteristics are a reflection of its nature – the **Law of Sufficient Complexity.**

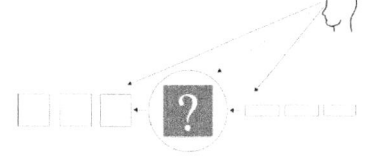

Implications
The implication for systems practice is that you can afford to not model in great detail IF you understand which parts of a system behave as a **Black Box.** So being able to work out which are **Black Boxes** is a critical skill.

For managers and regulators, the **Black Box** is also important. A system's effectiveness can be destroyed by prying too deeply into it – the box can explode. It's a key skill to distinguish those parts of the organisation where you really need to understand how they work from those where you simply need to know that they do work. Learn it and your staff will thank you for it.

Watch for
Consistency of outputs over time – in some contexts, this is what Statistical Process Control does for you.

Grammar of Systems

Self-organising Principle

This appears to be one of the hardest systems ideas for people to get their heads around, and I say that based on the fact that terms for this idea have been persistently downgraded to mean something else, something less threatening to conventional thinking. The original expression of this idea was from Jan Smuts and he coined the term holism to mean *"The tendency in nature to form wholes that are greater than the sum of its parts, through creative evolution"*. Because this idea of the self-creation of form is so difficult, the term holism got corrupted to mean something much less challenging – something more like 'looking at the whole thing". The term self-organising has suffered a similar fate, so it's widely been corrupted to mean self-managing, again a much less threatening idea. Language morphs through time, words change their meaning and that's fine, but in systems, the original concept is important and we a need a term for it, so by self-organising I mean what Smuts described.

PARTS GENERATE WHOLES

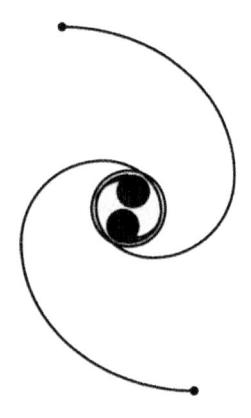

There are two critical aspects to this and they are actually the same thing, but appear as different depending on where you see them from. The first is the creation of a new higher-level structure of a system from previously disparate parts. To pick up on Smuts' political work, the creation of the League of Nations and then the United Nations as a meta-system made up from individual states coming together is an example of self-organisation. There was no higher authority to create this new system, the constituent states self-organised to create it. And evolutionary biology describes a similar process at work in the creation of life. The second aspect of this is the process of self-organisation within an existing system. This looks different, but is actually the same – sub-systems de-compose, dis-integrate (i.e. stop being part of an integral / composed whole) and their elements then recombine to form new sub-systems which may be similar or radically different to what went before. The actual mechanism of this is when 'free' elements engage with other elements to form relational loops and the closure of the loop is the formation of a new structure.

Philosophically, the biological self-organisation from single celled organisms to multi-celled, to next door's cat stands in contradiction to the creationist view. And similarly, self-organisation in organisational systems stands in contradiction to the leadership view. And that is one reason the idea is quite so threatening. Methodologically, socio-technical systems theory was largely based on studies showing self-organisation was common in work groups, but even here, the approach has largely walked away from focusing on understanding self-organisation.

What underpins the **Self-organising Principle** are the **Systems Resonance Principle** and what von Förster described as the 'order from noise' principle – it requires an environment in which there is a degree of randomness, or difference in a **Law of Calling** way.

Implications
The implications for organisational systems are profound. Once you realise that self-organising is going on in systems all the time, then it becomes something you have to take into account and it casts ideas about leadership in a totally different light. You start to see a lot of management effort as an attempt to fight the forces of self-organisation, rather than trying to harness them. Of course, to be able to harness them, you have to first recognise that they are there and secondly work out what sort of organisation is being created. But it's not just a question of the self-creation of structures, of organisational forms, because à la **Law of Sufficient Complexity**, those structures generate purpose(s) and follow them. Self-organisation is largely but indirectly responsible for direction setting in organisations, at all levels from micro-tactical to strategic.

Watch for
Systems becoming more tightly coupled to one another.
New structures and purposes emerging.

Grammar of Systems

Law of Reciprocity of Connections

There's a pop-systemist's saying that 'everything is connected to everything'. As written of course, that's simply not true, every thing isn't connected to every other thing, or at least it isn't directly connected. Indirectly though, it is and there are two aspects to this that are significant from a systems perspective.

IF 'A' CONNECTS TO 'B', THEN 'B' ALSO CONNECTS TO 'A'

The first is about reciprocity, as you'd expect given that it's the **Law of Reciprocity of Connections**. We tend naturally to think of relationships as one way, either as what someone else is doing to us, or what we are doing or would like to do to them. The **Law of Reciprocity of Connections** asks us to consider that instead of looking at any relationship as unilateral, to see it as bilateral, as reciprocal, as a loop. This is deceptively simple, but in reality, it's a fundamental shift. In every case you have to assume there is a reciprocal relationship and that for whatever goes out, you can expect something to come back. Which sounds very karmic, but of course, what comes back will – as per the **Law of Sufficient Complexity** – be a function of the system on the other end of the relationship. Just because you did something you thought was 'good' doesn't mean either that it will be received as good at the other end of the relational loop or indeed that what you get back will be 'good'.

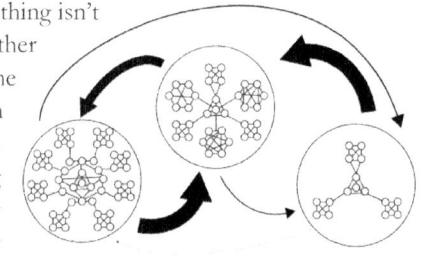

The shift from thinking of linear causality to affective loops is a profound one. Naturally, not all relational connections are equal, you can have a loop where one side of the relationship is dramatically more powerful than the other, but there's never nothing. And that brings us to the second significant aspect. Everything isn't directly connected to every other thing. In many cases the reciprocal loop passes through many other nodes before it is closed. The relative distancing this remote closure gives may appear reassuring – effects may be diluted and dissipate through the wider system. But conversely, what it means is that we're all part of the same system, we really are in the same boat. Up until fairly recently, we were able to run economies and foreign policies as if the effects wouldn't come back to us – despoiling a country either by war or exploitation of natural resources was fine, as long as it was someone else's country. Now that way of thinking is starting not to unravel, but actually to ravel up, as the connections close up and the world shrinks into a single economic, social and ecological system where nobody's actions have no consequences.

The **Law of Reciprocity of Connections** was developed by the neurologist Lorente de Nó and he was talking about neural connections in nervous systems: *"If a cell complex A sends fibres to cell or cell complex B, then B also sends fibres to A, either direct or by means of one internuncial neuron"*. The structure of systemic closure he was describing goes far beyond just our neural circuitry. Perhaps the most commonplace expression of it is in 'small world syndrome' or the six degrees of separation hypothesis – the idea that anyone on the planet is connected to anyone else by only six degrees of separation. Similarly in ecosystems, most trophic loops have relatively few nodes before the loop is closed and the eater at the apex of the food chain is eaten by the eaten at the bottom of the food chain.

Implications
The biggest implication is that we do not live in a world where our actions don't have consequences for us. The systemic closure of the **Law of Reciprocity of Connections** affects all systems. As systems thinkers, we need to think about the design of system communications and consider how communications might be received and interpreted. Equally, we need to be alert to responses, even when, especially when, they may be separated in time from the original system communication and may not initially appear to have any relation to the original system communication.

Watch for
Links that appear to be unilateral.

Grammar of Systems

Redundancy of Potential Command Principle

Warren McCulloch's **Redundancy of Potential Command Principle** states that *"in any complex decision network, the potential to act effectively is conferred by an adequate concatenation of information."* Put into plain English, our ability

YOUR ABILITY TO BE EFFECTIVE IN A COMPLEX SITUATION DEPENDS ON BRINGING TOGETHER THE RIGHT MIX OF INFORMATION

to act effectively depends on the decisions we make, and the quality of those decisions depends on bringing together the right set(s) of information. Which at one level is a statement of the obvious, but nevertheless is largely ignored. In Enterprise Architecture, for example, the discipline that claims to be able to design information systems, there is no real methodology for determining what information set(s) might be needed to take any decision and ensuring that this information is actually available.

The logic of this principle is that where there is an informational deficit, that will lead to significant factors being ignored in the decision and that in turn will lead to a decision that only partially fits the situation and *that* means the decision will not adequately address some aspects of the situation and is more likely to fail as a result.

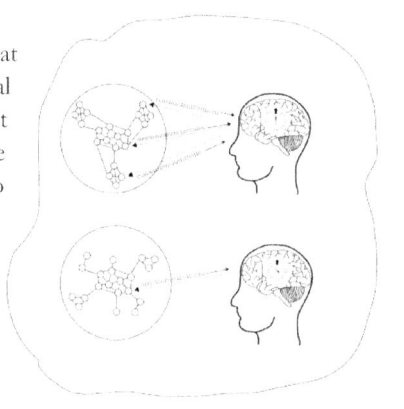

You can see the relationship to **Ashby's Law of Requisite Variety**. In terms of Ashby's Law, any decision that doesn't have 'an adequate concatenation' doesn't have requisite variety, pretty much by definition.

Implications
The most obvious implication is that understanding and providing for the information needs of any decision is critical for taking it well. Since it can be hard to pull together some information sets quickly, some information sets may need to be prepared in advance. To do that, you need to understand what decisions might be needed and therefore plan what

information might be needed. This is the reverse of normal IS / EA practice. Almost nobody plans information provision in this way.

The Hoverstadt corollary from the **Redundancy of Potential Command Principle** is: *"everything else being equal, organisations will take the decisions they have the information to take"* which in turn means that you can largely predict the decisions organisations will take if you know what information they are using to take them.

Watch for
Work from decision and the information needed back to supply. All decisions need a balance between information about the systems internal state and capabilities and also its present and future environment.

Grammar of Systems

Root Structuration Theorem

In one sense, **Root structuration theorem** is the obverse of the **Network Power Law** and an antidote to the **Complexity Instability Principle**. Where the **Network Power Law** (or at least the underlying formula) says that

STRUCTURING A SYSTEM TO HAVE THE SAME NUMBER OF SUB-SYSTEMS AT EACH LEVEL REDUCES ITS COMPLEXITY

complexity grows as the square of the number of system elements, **Root Structuration Theorem** says that *"complexity decreases as the number of sub-systems approaches the square root of the number of system elements."* And because the level of complexity is the driver of the **Complexity Instability Principle**, **Root Structuration Theorem** means that: all other factors being equal, the optimal level of structuration of a system to reduce the likelihood of becoming incipiently unstable will be when the number of sub-systems is the square root of the number of elements.

If we take a simple example of a system with 100 elements and each of those is able to interact directly with any of the others, then the complexity (the number of possible ways those elements can connect) is $2^{100} - 101$ or 1.2×10^{30}. If instead you group the 100 into 10 sub-systems, then each of those sub-systems has a complexity of 1.02×10^3 and the complexity of the system as a whole is just under 1.1×10^4 (because there is the complexity of each of the 10 sub-systems + the complexity of the interdependence between those 10). Compared to 1.2×10^{30}, 1.1×10^4 is a huge reduction in the complexity and therefore the incipient instability – the instability that can be generated from within the system itself.

Implications
From the point of view of system design and diagnosis, **Root Structuration Theorem** provides a guide to how structured systems need to be and roughly what that structuring should look like.

Obviously, whilst **Root Structuration Theorem** says that: all other factors being equal, the optimal level of structuration of a system will be when the number of sub-systems is the square root of the number of elements, in real life, the 'all other factors being equal' is almost never true. Whether you are talking about how many engineering sub-systems to divide a complex machine into, or how many software modules to divide a complex program into, or how many departments or teams to divide an organisation into, in almost all cases, there are other factors that need to be taken into account in deciding the structural split – complex systems are not homogeneous so you can't just make arbitrary mathematical divisions. Nevertheless, **Root Structuration Theorem** does help guide you to how many sub-systems we should be looking for in deciding the structure. That said, Genghis Khan did use a strict mathematical division system to organise his armies and empire and they seemed to do quite well. Oh and of course, following the **Law of Sufficient Complexity**, the structuring of the organisation and the software or engineered product it produces are likely to be the same.

Watch for

Balance in the number of sub-systems per level.

Grammar of Systems

Structural Viability Theorem

Power Structuration Theorem and the **Structural Viability Theorem** complement one another. The first deals with differentials in power and autonomy between levels of a system and the second deals with differentials in their rates of change.

A SYSTEM HAS OPTIMAL VIABILITY WHEN ITS CHANGE RATE / ENVIRONMENTAL CHANGE RATE IS SIMILAR TO THAT OF ITS SUB-SYSTEMS

The problem **Structural Viability Theorem** deals with is that, as the **System Survival Theorem** says, systems need to be able to change at a rate that matches the rate of change in their environment. But any complex system – i.e. one with sub-systems – is coupled to multiple parts of its environment and by definition, these are not the same (otherwise there'd be no need to structure the system) which means they are likely to have different change rates. That in turn means that different sub-systems of our system might need to be able to change at different rates. This is a problem for organisational systems as it is for biological systems and is the problem that led Cuvier to conclude that evolution was impossible (pre-Darwin, of course).

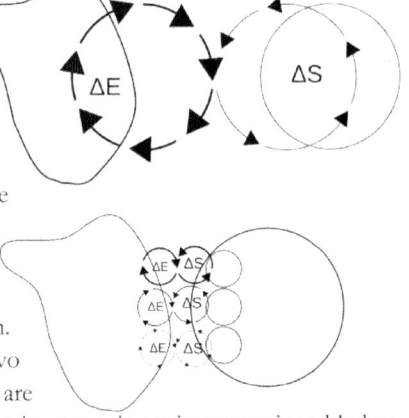

Sometimes in dealing with a changing environment, when the system faces lots of change at the sub-system level (e.g. changes and fluctuations in operational demands), and then there are times when it faces a seismic shift in the environment and the whole system needs to move together or face disintegration. And the balance between the two can flip unpredictably. There are times in an organisation's life when its strategic environment is stable but its operational environment is bubbling with small scale changes so maximising change capacity at the lower levels works well and then there are times when the strategic environment suddenly shifts and demands that the whole system changes.

Clearly, as with the **Power Structuration Theorem,** this is driven by **Ashby's Law** since the tension depends on differentials in the variety in the environment at operational and strategic levels, but it also relates to the **System Survival Theorem**. The **Structural Viability Theorem** takes the formula from the **System Survival Theorem** and articulates that across multiple levels of a system, so it states that optimal viability between structural levels is when $\Delta S/\Delta E$ for level 1 $\approx \Delta S/\Delta E$ for level 2. In other words, we have equalised the tension and are as viable as we can be, when our capacity to match the demand for change at one level is balanced with our capacity to match the demand for change at another level. Obviously, since different parts of the environment change at different rates, and they are connected, this balance will be in a state of flux and therefore the level of change capacity in an organisation also needs continuous adjustment.

Implications
As with the **Power Structuration Theorem,** all dogmatic statements and theories about where the balance should be set should be taken lightly. They are almost certainly true and valid in some circumstances but cannot possibly be universally true for all situations. We've seen organisations that were fantastic at responding to fast changing operational demands but caught flat-footed by strategic shifts that posed an existential threat and showed a $\Delta S/\Delta E$ for level 1 : $\Delta S/\Delta E$ for level 2 balance of 1 : 0.17. Asymmetries like this can be fatal, especially when they're biased against existential threats.

The second implication is the need to a) periodically review the relative demand for change pressing at different levels and the rate at which it is changing and b) adjust the system's change capacity at different levels to match.

Watch for
Balance in the relative rate of change facing system at multiple levels.

Grammar of Systems

Steady State Principle

There's a mental trap built into the **Steady State Principle**. It tends to lure you into thinking about systems as being static, but that's absolutely what it's not about. It's about how complex dynamic systems can remain as coherent systems when both the system as a whole and the sub-systems are changing and moreover likely to be changing at different rates. The **Steady State Principle** says that *"if a system is in a state of equilibrium (a steady state), then all sub-systems must be in equilibrium. If all sub-systems are in a state of equilibrium, then the system must be in equilibrium."* And the static vs dynamic mental trap is that we tend to think that equilibrium equals static, when actually it means a dynamic balance. Think less the equilibrium of bricks in a wall and more the equilibrium of a peleton of cyclists leaning to go round a corner.

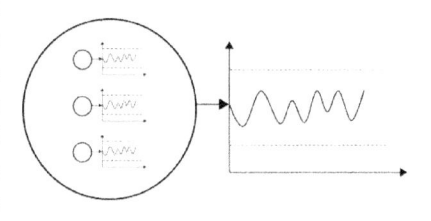

STABILITY OF THE SYSTEM DEPENDS ON THE LEVEL OF STABILITY OF ITS SUB-SYSTEMS AND VICE VERSA

I confess to having a bit of a problem with the way the **Steady State Principle** is phrased. Systems theory and Complexity theory largely cover the same ground, they are both interested in how systems are stable and dynamic, and change or collapse. But partly for historical reasons they have slightly different flavours. Systems tends to talk more about how systems are stable when they are, and Complexity tends to talk more about moments of transformation and the slide into chaos. Two sides of exactly the same coin. For me, the way the **Steady State Principle** is written sounds as though it's about the stability side of this – which of course it is, but its real message is about the chaos or not-chaos of a system.

The not chaos bit obviously relates directly to the **Homeostasis Principle** since it's the dynamic balance of **Homeostasis** maintaining equilibrium, and also because of that to the 2nd **Circular Causality Principle** since negative feedback drives **Homeostasis**. But overall, there's a relationship to the **System Stability Principle, Viability**

Principle, **Structural Viability Theorem** and the **Relaxation Time Principle**. The stability demanded by the **System Stability Principle** (stable enough for long enough to be recognizable) is conferred by the **Steady State**. This connects to the **Viability Principle**, and **Structural Viability Theorem**, because those, like the **Steady State Principle**, are about how dynamic change ripples through complex systems and what happens to the system as it does that. These two viability ones focus on balancing change through levels of a system, whereas **Steady State** focuses on the limits of those changes through time if the system is not to shake itself to pieces. It's related to the **Relaxation Time Principle** because when you have multiple changing elements in a system, the equilibrium, the overall stability & rate of change depend on how fast different sub-systems can relax post-change.

Implications

The basic problem which the **Steady State Principle** addresses is how the system continues to exist when its different interconnected sub-systems are all changing and at different rates. It requires that you can, in some way, assess the equilibrium of the system and its sub-systems.

It's relevant in all types of systems, mechanical, biological and socio/organisational. The French naturalist Cuvier dismissed the idea of evolution because he believed it was impossible for a system to change elements at different rates. In every field of engineering from problems of resonance in bridges to the synchromesh of a gearbox, overall integrity with differential change rates is a design issue. And in organisations and societies, the **Steady State Principle** asks you to think about organisational systems as sets of interdependent sub-systems all changing at different rates and the ripples of change that creates. As Whitehead said: *"The art of progress is to preserve order amid change and to preserve change amid order."*

Watch for
Relative stability of system at different levels.

Grammar of Systems

Law of Sufficient Complexity

There's a saying in systems that 'systems drive behaviour' and it speaks to that core systems idea that it's about looking at the underlying structure, not just surface behaviours. The **Law of Sufficient Complexity** is the formal expression of that idea.

THE SYSTEM DOES WHAT IT DOES BECAUSE IT IS WHAT IT IS

The **Law of Sufficient Complexity** comes out of Warren McCulloch's work on neurology and neural networks and says that *"A complex system constitutes its own simplest behavioural description"*. Which means that, if the system remains the same, with the same structure, and inputs, then it's likely to carry on doing the same thing. To adapt the popular phrase 'if you do what you always do you'll get what you always got', the **Law of Sufficient Complexity** argues that 'if you are what you've always been you'll do what you've always done'. Which perhaps isn't as neat in terms of phrasing, but is a slightly scarier message. The **Law of Sufficient Complexity** explains the **Black Box Principles**. It relates to **Homeostasis** and the **Feedback Dominance Theorem** and the propensity of systems to return to their previous stable state. The **Law of Sufficient Complexity** speaks to the need to change the systems structure if you want its behaviour to change.

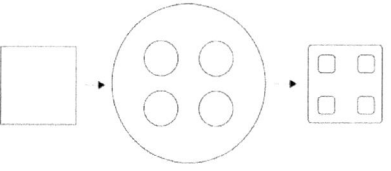

When we're talking about changing the system, that can take several forms: changing the actual structure – changing how the system is divided up, or changing the connections and relationships, or changing the dynamics – both volumes and flow rates, or changing the inputs, or the information flows or structure of decision making or…. But whatever the approach we take, if the system doesn't itself change, its behaviours aren't likely to.

Implications
One implication is that attempts to change the behaviour of a complex system without changing how it's constituted are likely to fail. The nature

of the system will reassert itself at some point. This has implications for a range of approaches in various fields that rely on surface effects.

Family therapy is based on the **Law of Sufficient Complexity** thesis that the behaviours and emotional states of members of a family are a function of the family system. If you remove one member of the family, typically someone else will step in and assume the relational roles the missing member was acting out. Management teams show the same characteristics, fire the troublemaker and someone else will often pick up that role.

In IT, Microsoft research has shown that the best predictor of the number of bugs in software is the complexity of the development organisation – the more fragmented the structure, the more fragmented the software. Also from IT, Conway's Law says that *"organizations which design systems ... are constrained to produce designs which are copies of the communication structures of these organizations."* When the behaviour of a system is to create another system, its structure will determine its behaviour and this will determine the design.

It contradicts the design rule that form follows function by pointing out that, function follows form. There's widespread belief that organisational structure should follow strategy, but strategy (a system output) is a mirror of the structure that formulates the strategy – and if you look at organisations developing strategies, you can see that at work very clearly.

Another implication is that if you just want the system to do what it reliably does, then you can operate in **Black Box** mode, you don't need to know how it does what it does. But if you want it to do something different, then you really do need to understand why it does what it does, which in turn, as the **Law of Sufficient Complexity** says, depends on how it's constituted. If you want to effect change, you'd better understand how it actually is constituted and how that relates to its behaviours – specifically the ones you want to change.

Watch for
Ability to account for system behaviour from system structure.

Grammar of Systems

Fractal Principle

Fractals are one of nature's ways of dealing with complexity. Fractals have the same basic structure at different levels, so the whole, the sub-systems and the sub-systems of the sub-systems are structurally self-similar. A twig has the same structural features as the branch it is on which has the same structural features as the bough which has…

SYSTEMS REPLICATE THEIR OWN FORM

The **Fractal Principle** relates to the **Law of Sufficient Complexity** and to the **Self-organising Principle**. Where a system creates new sub-systems, those tend to be a reflection of its own systemic structure and hence fractals. Where system elements self-organise to form a new system, a higher level of structure, that also follows the **Law of Sufficient Complexity** and the structure of the new higher-level system will also be a reflection of the systemic structure of combined elements. Since system elements that form a new higher structural level are different (by definition), what gets propagated through levels isn't likely to be a fractal of any one of the elements, but a bit like 'system sex', will be taken from key systemic features from across the set. What gets propagated will be a reflection of what binds them together and that of course depends on the **Resonance Principle**. In the context of the **Fractal Principle**, you can think of the resonance as part of the DNA of the system.

The self-similarity of fractals is not just a mechanism for creating complex systems, it's also a source of system stability. The self-similarity forms a basis for systemic coherence, as there is enough in common between system levels to mitigate the effects of the **Law of Crossing** – there is difference but enough similarity for resonance. Conversely, although there is self-similarity between levels, there is enough difference to allow for multiple levels of adaptation in accordance with the **Conservation of Adaptation Principle**. And that takes you to the **System Survival Theorem** and the

Structural Viability Theorem so the **Fractal Principle** provides a structural basis for adaptation at multiple levels. At the same time as that adaptation creates or enables system change, counterintuitively it also creates the basis for greater stability since, in a changing environment, as the **Conservation of Adaptation Principle** says, system viability depends on the system also changing.

Implications
There are two main practical implications. The first is that fractals are important in scaling systems

The second is in a sense the 'DNA' point. If you understand what aspects of a multi-level system are self-similar, you have captured something of its essence. This is part of the basis of Beer's Viable System Model – a fractally structured model of what any system needs to be viable.

Watch for
Structural similarities common at different levels of the system.

Relaxation Time Principle

Many of these systems laws and principles run counter to conventional thinking – which is what you'd expect, but this is one is fairly intuitive, at least at the conceptual level, although the significance of it is sadly often totally ignored. The **Relaxation Time Principle** states that *"a system can only stay stable if the system's relaxation time is shorter than the mean time between disturbances"*. So the relaxation time is the time necessary for the system to relax back to its stable state after it has been disturbed. If it gets disturbed again before it's had a chance to settle down, it doesn't get back to stable and if this happens repeatedly, then it may never stabilise.

A SYSTEM THAT IS REPEATEDLY SHOCKED AT SHORTER INTERVALS THAN ITS RECOVERY TIME MAY NEVER STABILISE

So far so simple, but in a lot of cases, nobody bothers to find out what the relaxation time is, and for a lot of systems, particularly organisational and social systems, the frequency at which disturbances hit is a lot more than the relaxation time. As an example of relaxation time, for anyone familiar with the Beer game popularised by Senge in the 5th discipline, this is a simple supply chain delivering beer from brewery to customer via wholesalers and distributers on a weekly cycle, the system starts off stable, receives a single disturbance and takes around 18 months to relax and re-stabilise itself. The relaxation time is way longer than people imagine. With a relatively mechanistic system like a supply chain, it's at least practicable to work out the relaxation time, but for broader organisational and social systems, calculating relaxation times is inevitably harder. Despite the difficulty we may have of getting a hold on relaxation time, the reverse isn't true, relaxation times have a hold on us and the systems we are in.

Implications
The place where this is most keenly felt is in organisational change, where stable performance gets disturbed by changes and may never stabilise if the changes hit too frequently. The obvious conclusion is to be discriminating about what to change and how often, make sure you've got a good reason for doing any changes.

More broadly, this relates to the natural rate of change of the system and in organisational systems, you can dramatically reduce the relaxation time by increasing its agility. This is closely related to the **System Survival Theorem**.

Watch for
Pattern of shocks over time - frequency x impact.
Relaxation time – how long it takes to return to within tolerances of system stability.

Scaling Stasis Principle

As systems become bigger and specifically when they become more complex, two things generally happen. First the boundary increases which, all things being equal, brings the system into contact with more of the environment and usually more complexity in the environment. Secondly, the number of interdependencies within the system increases exponentially following the **Network Power Law**. Each extension of the boundary with the environment subjects the system to more stimulus from outside and typically a higher variety of stimuli. As these stimuli ripple through the system they put more demands on the interdependencies between sub-systems.

THE MORE COMPLEX A SYSTEM IS, THE MORE CONSTRAINTS IT HAS

At the same time, the increase in the number of interdependencies within the system constrains its ability to adapt. For any part of the system, because the number of interdependencies has gone up, when you change X the number of things it's connected to is higher and each of those connections carries a 'need to coordinate' load and each of those is a potential 'need to change Y because we're changing X' burden. So the number of constraints goes up. You only need one of those constraints to be immovable and all progress stops and there can be a chain reaction of log-jammed stasis. The system finds itself beset by the need to adapt, but increasingly paralysed because of its own internal complexity.

Instead of being able to do discrete changes to adapt to pressures from the environment, any prospective change ripples through the system encountering constraint after constraint. The system design solution to this is **Root Structuration Theorem**, which limits the level of direct interdependencies and therefore reduces the level of constraint across the system. Where this doesn't get designed, the inexorable logic of it unfolds anyway, but more haphazardly, parts of the systems start to self-isolate, effectively erecting barriers to reduce interference. In the short term, isolation can help the sub-system isolating, but it still acts as a constraint to the rest of the system, just a passive constraint rather than an active one. In the longer term, isolation can lead to atrophy.

As patches of isolated system form within the system, other sub-systems restructure their connections to by-pass them, so the isolation becomes chronic. The 'live', still connected parts of the system continue to adapt to changing conditions, but the isolates tend not to and gradually lose their fit with the rest of the system.

Implications
You can see the **Scaling Stasis Principle** at work in all types of large system from IT systems to biological systems – literally 'dead wood', to organisational – metaphorical 'dead wood'.

Bureaucracy is the expression of the constraints of system interdependencies. Organisational Network Analysis often shows up 'isolates' - parts of the system or individuals that sit in complete isolation – they report no need of others and are not needed by others.

Watch for
Isolated / self-isolating parts of the system.

Conant-Ashby Theorem

Conant-Ashby Theorem is one of the cornerstones of management science. It states quite simply: *"Every good regulator of a system must be a model of that system"* and is also sometimes referred to as 'the good regulator theorem'. You might be forgiven for thinking that it only refers to regulators or formal regulatory bodies, but within the discipline of cybernetics, which is where the theorem came from, 'regulator' means anything or anyone that is trying to guide, control or direct a system. In those terms, every manager, or anyone trying to affect a system, is a regulator. **Conant-Ashby Theorem**'s relevance and applicability is very wide indeed.

THE ABILITY TO DEAL WITH ANY SITUATION DEPENDS ON HOW GOOD YOUR MODEL OF IT IS

The logic goes something like this. Since the system we're trying to manage is typically more complex than we are (in a human system, it's usually got more people in it, each with a degree of free will), we have to simplify it in order to understand it – and that is a model, a simplification that holds the key elements, relationships and dynamics of the system and ignores a lot of extraneous detail. The model is the encapsulation of our understanding of the system and we use it (consciously or not) to work out what the system is doing and what we could / should do about it.

The 'consciously or not' bit is critical here, as Einstein put it, *"Whether you can observe a thing or not depends on the theory which you use. It is the theory which decides what can be observed."* Substitute the word model for theory in that sentence and you have the essence of Conant-Ashby. The point is that we don't have a choice whether to use a model to filter our perceptions or not, we have to use a model because the world is so complex that without one we'd breakdown with sensory overload. The choice we have is whether to consciously manage the models we choose to use or allow the models we've ended up with to manage us.

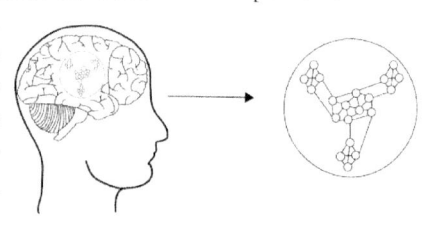

Implications

What makes Conant-Ashby so important is because of what it says about the importance of models and modelling – which is this: we use models (whether formal or tacit) to understand systems and our ability to affect any system depends on how good, how appropriate those models are. Which in turn means that modelling – building, checking and maintaining models – is not a luxury, it's absolutely essential to our understanding and to our effectiveness. Everything rests on it. If you are not actively consciously modelling and checking the validity of your models, then you're not doing Systems Thinking. More importantly, failure to build, check and maintain adequate models means that you are likely to act at random – the opposite of Conant-Ashby is March-Olsen's 'trash can' decision making. With no model or inadequate models, you intervene at random, and the results will be …. random.

Watch for

Presence of model which can explain system structure and behaviour.

Grammar of Systems

Feedback Dominance Theorem

Feedback Dominance Theorem states that *"for high gain amplifiers, the feedback dominates the output over wide variations in input."*

LOOPS WITH STRONG FEEDBACK WILL TAKE YOU WHERE THEY TAKE YOU, IRRESPECTIVE OF THE SIZE OF THE INPUT

This needs a bit of unpicking of the terminology. First feedback which is a term that has travelled from systems and cybernetics into common speech, but in the process has changed its meaning. In common speech it can mean any comment or message. In systems it's a technical term, feedback is an input to a process or system that is driven by the output from the system and which has the capability to affect the system to change that output. So feedback always has the characteristics of: a) being able to change the system or outputs and b) closure, it closes a loop between the output into the system's environment and back to the system itself. As described in the two **Principles of Circular Causality**, feedback can be positive (increasing the output feeds back to increase the output further) or negative (increasing the output feeds back to decrease the output to a norm). So that's feedback and the next term is high gain amplifier. A feedback loop can either amplify or attenuate the signal generated by the output and the gain is about how much amplification there is. Shouting at someone to be quiet in a library when they were just whispering would be a high gain in amplification, because the signal feeding back had higher capacity than the original signal.

That's the terms, now the theorem itself. The **Feedback Dominance Theorem** means that whatever the initial starting conditions, if the feedback is strong enough (high enough gain) the outcome will be the same. Take the fable of the man who did a favour for a king and as a reward asked for a grain of rice for the first square on a chess board, two for the second, four for the third and had bankrupted the treasury long before they got to the last square; because of the power of the doubling function, it doesn't make much difference if

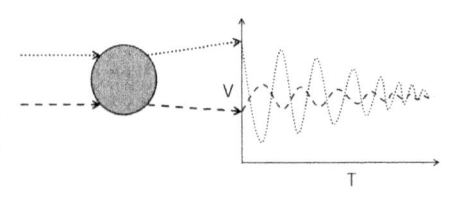

190

Grammar of Systems

you start with one grain of rice or a hundred, the effect is the same, it just takes a few more or less squares to get there. Similarly for a negative feedback system, if the power of the feedback is strong enough, it doesn't matter how off target the system is to start with, eventually it'll be brought back.

Implications
The implications of the **Feedback Dominance Theorem** are far reaching. The first is that if you do have a powerful feedback system, then if you want a different result, you need to change either the structure of the feedback loop or the gain on it. Just changing the inputs won't work for long, as the output behaviour will revert to its characteristic pattern. A good example of this is the way governments kickstarted the economy after the 2008 financial crash, but failed to change the structure or the gain on the positive feedback system that repeatedly cause crashes. The **Feedback Dominance Theorem** says that it doesn't matter how much liquidity banks start with, the feedback will once again drive inexorably towards a boom followed by a crash as they become over-exposed.

The second implication is that IF you've designed your feedback systems well, then you can wait for them to do their work and even with adverse initial conditions you can get the effect you want in time. As Beer said: *"Instead of trying to specify it in full detail, you specify it only somewhat. You then ride on the dynamics of the system in the direction you want to go."*:

Watch for
System returning to same output state or emergent properties from very different starting conditions.

"Something hit me very hard once, thinking about what one little man could do. Think of the Queen Mary — the whole ship goes by and then comes the rudder. And there's a tiny thing at the edge of the rudder called a trimtab. It's a miniature rudder. Just moving the little trim tab builds a low pressure that pulls the rudder around. Takes almost no effort at all. So I said that the little individual can be a trimtab. Society thinks it's going right by you, that it's left you altogether. But if you're doing dynamic things mentally, the fact is that you can just put your foot out like that and the whole big ship of state is going to go. So I said, call me Trimtab."

Buckminster Fuller

Grammar of Systems

Principle of Emergence

"The whole is greater than the sum of its parts" is the classic statement about the concept of systems and it is of course, a statement about the **Principle of Emergence**. Emergence is a property of a system that is not a property of the parts of the system on their own. I have the property of being able to talk, but take me apart, and none of the parts of me can talk. The **Principle of Emergence** is simultaneously commonplace and strangely elusive. Commonplace, because we live with and through emergent properties all the time – our world, our experiences are largely made up of emergent properties. Elusive because separating them out as properties of the system rather properties of parts can be tricky, but mainly because we've been trained to think reductively at parts and their properties rather than the properties of the whole. It's maybe not an accident that the chap who first named **Emergence** was (as well as a philosopher) an art critic, and you can't really understand any art form except as an emergent property.

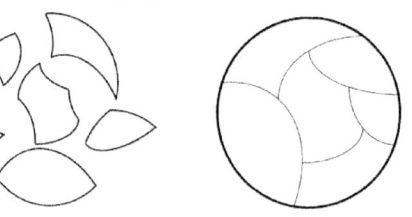

THE WHOLE IS MORE THAN THE SUM OF ITS PARTS

The **Principle of Emergence** says that systems are systems by virtue of having emergent properties. It logically follows that the point of systems as a practice is to:
- understand how a given system generates the emergent properties it does
- given a set of emergent properties, recognise the system that is generating them
- work out how to change an existing system to generate different emergents
- design systems to generate specified desired emergent properties

The emphasis on emergence means that the practice of systems tends to focus on three areas – and they are the three areas these laws and

192

principles fall into: how we identify a system and its emergent, and how systems' structure and dynamics drive emergent behaviours.

Implications
To see emergence, you have to look primarily at the system as a whole rather than the parts, hence the rejection of reductionism in systems practice.

To understand emergence, you have to look at relationships within and between systems rather than concentrating on parts of the system as things. The twin aspects of the structuring of relationships and the dynamics of those follow from this.

Part of the challenge of spotting emergence is that it can occur in systems which are separated by time and place from the system which generates it. That relational understanding helps guide where – and when – you should look for emergence.

Watch for
Effects that belong to the system that are not created by any sub-systems on their own.

Grammar of Systems – using the Laws

Using the laws – the splicing approach

As discussed in the introduction to the Grammar, if you are faced with a fairly common problem that isn't adequately dealt with using a conventional approach and which is therefore a good candidate for using systems approaches, then there's a good chance that others will also have tackled that before and that there will be a systems methodology that covers the space. If so, then for practical purposes, you can just use that. However, the world abounds with problems for which conventional approaches don't work and that don't have one of the better-known systems methodologies designed for them. In that case using the laws will always give you a different perspective on the situation and usually give you some answers.

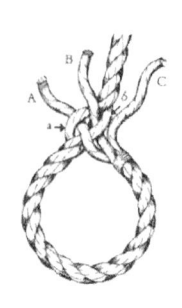

Selecting which laws to use is largely a matter of practice. You can simply take some that look like a good fit for the situation and apply those, and that does work. But the approach I'd recommend is 'splicing'.

Splicing systems principles is a four-stage process:
1. You start by picking a set of laws that look like they could be a good fit, and really only practice helps with that choice.
2. Then apply one of them, then the next. As you go, each law or principle will either tell you something useful about the situation or it won't. Save the useful ones for the next step, but reserve the discards for later.
3. Once you have a set of 'well that's interesting' observations, start to splice them together, so take what Principle A has to tell you and combine that with what Law B has to tell you and then both of those with what C has to tell you and so on. The only limit to how many you can combine is your cognitive capacity and that develops with practice. Remember that as you are doing this, what you are after is understanding how each of the Laws or Principles forms the nature of the situation you are looking at, so they are part of the situation. The splicing is really picking

Grammar of Systems – using the Laws

those apart from their essential boundedness and then recombining them into a new synthesised understanding. If you you've done steps one and two well, then the result will be a set of combined principles that fit together relatively neatly and each will have a bearing on the others, forming a coherent whole. It's common to find stray bits that don't really fit and the temptation is always to discard any untidy strands of thought, but beware of one of Churchman's 'enemies of systems thinking' here, aesthetics – an elegant solution is always seductive, but elegance doesn't always mean it's right.

4. Step four is to go back to your set of discards. Why these didn't seem relevant can be just as important, just as revealing as why the set you worked with did seem important. This is the Conan-Doyle 'dog that didn't bark' factor discussed in 'Watching the Dark' in the chapter on Uncertainties. Any law that doesn't seem relevant may tell you something because of its irrelevance – 'X doesn't appear to be at work here, therefore the situation isn't like this, which means the system is likely to be in Y state'.

Let's try that with a couple of examples and a handful of Laws and Principles in each case.

Case 1: Six systems laws and the 2008 financial crash

This was an exercise I did with a group of MBA students a couple of years after the crash. They were new to systems theory, but not to economics and some were themselves from the banking and financial sector. Using a set of these laws the students were able to generate a set of mutually consistent and coherent explanations in a short time. This set is in no way exhaustive – there are other systems laws we could have picked and those might have yielded other answers, so this doesn't purport to be a complete use of systems approaches to the problem, nor a complete answer to it, it's just an example of the laws in use and the splicing approach.

Grammar of Systems – using the Laws

Step 1 – Pick your laws

For the purposes of this exercise, I've chosen six:
- **1st Circular Causality Principle**: Given positive feedback, radically different end states are possible from the same initial conditions.
- **Adams 3rd Law**: A system composed of the lowest risk components available will be a high-risk system
- **Conant-Ashby Theorem**: Every good regulator of a system must be a model of that system.
- **Redundancy of Potential Command Principle**: In any complex decision network, the potential to act effectively is conferred by an adequate concatenation of information.
- **Feedback Dominance Theorem**: For high-gain amplifiers, the feedback dominates the output over wide variations in input.
- **Relaxation Time Principle**: System stability is possible only if the system's relaxation time is shorter than the mean time between disturbances.

Step 2 – Look at the impact of each of those in turn

1st Circular Causality Principle
The economy is built around a high-gain positive feedback mechanism - an output from part of the system feeds-back to increase the system that generated the output. In this case, money deposited with a bank gets lent out to borrowers who invest or spend it and the people they spend it with put it into .. a bank. The 'high gain amplifier' bit is that an initial deposit of £100 can through the process of lending and relending turn into £1000. In fact it's even more amplified than this because it doesn't even require an initial deposit, the process can (and does) start with the bank lending and then seeking deposits to underpin its lending. The more money is deposited, the more can be lent and the more that is deposited.

Left to its own devices, this sort of high-gain positive feedback drives exponential growth; until it hits some sort of constraint – either there is some regulatory process that can turn down the level of amplification, or the feedback loop runs out of control and crashes. A crash generally happens when the system runs out of supply. In this case, the economy

Grammar of Systems – using the Laws

first ran out of safe borrowers to lend to, so to keep it growing, loans were offered to unsafe borrowers, creating the sub-prime market. What finally ran out and precipitated the crash was a combination of confidence and the overall liquidity in the system – just too much had been lent out relative to the 'real' cash in the system.

Adams 3rd Law
We tend to assume that if we de-risk all the components in a system that will reduce the risk overall. Before the crash, each component of the financial system had been designed and the risks of each had been calculated and factored into the design. Each component, each financial instrument and product had been designed to maximise the return to the financial institution and where possible to reduce, offset or offload the risk inherent in the product. This is why there had been so much effort put into mitigating, hedging and trading the risks associated with sub-prime and other exposed loans. There were two consequences. First, what hadn't been calculated (because it wasn't any individual institution's problem) were the risks that each component posed for other components because of the risks of interdependence, and risks to the system as a whole. Secondly and more acutely, in an attempt to reduce the risk for each component, risks were sliced, diced, repackaged and sold. Naturally that only moved them up to the level of the system as a whole and made it even harder to spot what was going on.

Conant-Ashby Theorem
Conant-Ashby Theorem, also commonly referred to as the 'good regulator' theorem, means that you can't manage what you can't understand and your ability to understand how a system works depends on how good the models you have of it are. What became clear just before the crash was that the regulators didn't have a model of how all the new financial instruments worked and particularly, they didn't have a model of how they were interdependent. In terms of Conant-Ashby, this was essentially an unregulated system, one in which nobody really knew what was going on. At some stage, someone had understood how each of the elements in the system worked, but nobody understood how the whole system worked. In the UK at least, the financial regulators (including the Treasury) have always relied on non-dynamic linear models

Grammar of Systems – using the Laws

to model a dynamic system with feedback loops – this can never be 'Conant-Ashby compliant'.

Redundancy of Potential Command Principle
You can interpret Redundancy of Potential Command relatively simplistically as 'information is power', but more subtly what it states is that without an adequate set of information, it's impossible to act effectively in a complex system. Without an adequate set of information the consequences of your actions will be unpredictable. In the context of the crash, there are two major implications, the first is that in the run up to the crash, information was unevenly distributed and relative advantage went to those who had most. The second is that people trying to stabilize the system as it slid into collapse did not have an adequate set of information and so could not act effectively.

Feedback Dominance Theorem
The scariest part of the feedback dominance theorem is the bit about the '*feedback dominates the output over wide variations in input*'. What this means is that if you have the same feedback structure, then you will always get to the same endpoint no matter where you start. Given the feedback structure, the crash was pretty much inevitable. After the crash, governments and regulators worked hard to rebuild the feedback structure and restock it with fresh money so it could start up the process again. In other words, they were working to rebuild an economic structure that had just crashed and that is designed in such a way that it must crash again. In fact there have been repeated crashes in economic history, what we experienced wasn't remotely unusual. The reason the powers that be set about getting the economy back on its course is that until it crashes, the feedback generates growth and that makes people prosper and actually economists don't know how to run an economy in any other way other than continuous growth.

Relaxation Time Principle
Systems can absorb shocks if they are given enough time to recover. As shocks hit a complex system they ripple through it like ripples on a pond and the after effects can last a surprisingly long time. The relaxation time of a social economy is measured in decades, the relaxation time of a global economic system is unknown. Where a system is hit by another

shock before it has recovered from the previous one, it doesn't have chance to re-stabilise, it can stay in a state of perpetual instability and in that state it is more vulnerable. Even small shocks can have a disproportionate effect, and the impacts, whether large or small are less predictable as they can combine with the after effects of previous shocks. For the economic system, the relaxation time is unknown, but that is itself an indicator that it may be permanently unstable, subject to cycles of disruption from which it never really recovers.

Step 3 – Splice observations together

1st Circular Causality Principle + Adams 3rd Law

The positive feedback loop drove up the availability of money available for lending, or more prosaically the need for lenders to find new borrowers to lend to. Inevitably loans were made to increasingly high-risk targets and the pressure grew for each product and lender to reduce their risk and shift it to the rest of the system. At the same time as the overall system risk was growing, the components (individual lenders and products) were trying to reduce their share proportionately. But it had to go somewhere and whilst risk can be hidden from sight, not seeing didn't mean it had gone away – the risk had increased at a rate that was higher than the growth rate.

+ Conant-Ashby

Without an adequate model of how the whole system works and particularly one that models the critical variables of the dynamics of risk and growth, the effects of positive feedback and the dynamics of the growing level of risk could not be regulated effectively. In particular, it was difficult to know the point at which the instability of the positive feedback loop would hit the limits to growth. As risk got transferred from the level of individual lenders and products to the whole system more of it ended up in a regulatory blind spot. As a result, when the liquidity problems started to bite and people started to lose confidence, the chain reaction of collapse was unexpected. It had not been understood how much had been risked and how those risks had been piled one on another. What was and was not a risk was invisible to regulators as risks

Grammar of Systems – using the Laws

were disguised as assets and traded as such. That blindness in turn encouraged lenders to ramp up the displacement of risk.

+ Redundancy of Potential Command
The lack of *'an adequate concatenation of information'* compounded the problems of regulation, but didn't stop with hampering the work of regulators in preventing and then coping with the collapse. The uneven distribution of information meant (as it nearly always does) that relative advantage went to those who had most. At the core of the sub-prime market was the disguising of risk as it was sliced, diced and recombined until the level of risk was hidden from view. In the time leading up to the crash, the difference between having the information on how a complex financial instrument actually worked and not, was the difference between winning and losing. The ability of some to carry on winning in the short term whilst ratcheting up the level of risk in the long term fuelled the scale of the collapse.

Feedback Dominance Theorem + Relaxation Time Principle
In this case, Feedback Dominance doesn't splice neatly into the previous four, but it does with Relaxation Time, because these two work on a longer timescale here, more of a background to the event than the crisis itself. So this is a less than totally tidy example – aesthetics aren't everything. The pattern of boom-bust behaviour that repeats because of feedback dominance means that even from a low starting base of liquidity, the cycle will start again. That is a pattern that preceded and followed each crisis and forms part of the background rhythm of this system. Another before, during, after pattern affecting the system is Relaxation Time. Shocks to the system hit and destabilised an economic system that hadn't fully settled from the previous shock – instability feeds upon instability. And here, you can see where these two background strands affected the others – the greater the instability the more the pressure for growth driven by positive feedback and the need for 'light touch' regulation, because growth held out the promise of safety. But the promise was illusory, or at best temporary. In a Feedback Dominance way, post-crash, most of the effort seemed to go into recreating the conditions that led to the crash, because in the short term that provided growth. This has all the characteristics of addiction, but without access to alcoholics anonymous. There is no global drying out clinic for economies.

Looked at through the lens of these systems laws, the financial crash is no surprise. Together they form a picture of how and why it happened and how likely it is to happen again. They also point to how the probability of a repetition could be reduced.

Step 4 – What the discards tell us

I picked six Laws and Principles for this example for brevity's sake, but really in this case, most of the 33 were directly relevant to some degree. Many of the set around structural complexity were relevant in understanding the dynamic between the individual players in the financial system and the system as a whole. Most of the dynamic complexity set were relevant, because this was dramatically a dynamics problem and most of the set around knowing or not knowing were relevant because of the role which information and understanding – or lack of them - played in the drama.

The Complexity Instability Principle and Scaled Stasis Principle are not immediate candidates for consideration and that indicates that this probably wasn't a problem driven by overall structural complexity, beyond the two levels aspect of each individual actor's relationship to the overall system. In this case, what the discards mostly tell us is that there is a lot going on in here.

Case 2: Eight systems laws applied to fair access to renewable energy.

This was an exercise undertaken with Dr. Lesley Rowan who has a long-standing involvement with issues to do with the social impact of renewable energy. The exercise was prompted by concerns about the problems of ensuring fair access across different population groups in the light of the adoption of new smart energy technologies. This followed a report on the topic that had used a fairly conventional technology adoption model.

Grammar of Systems – using the Laws

Step 1 – Pick your laws

For the purposes of this exercise, we used:
- **Self-organised Criticality:** When the system's dynamics drive the system to collapse.
- **Homeostasis Principle:** A system will be stable if all its key variables remain within their physiological limits.
- **Power Structuration Theorem:** A system has optimal agency when its needs for agency are balanced with those of its sub-systems.
- **System Survival Theorem:** Systems fail if their environment consistently changes more than the system.
- **Viability Principle:** A system's viability depends on how well it can balance autonomy with cohesion and stability with change over time.
- **Structural Viability Theorem:** A system has optimal viability when its change rate / environmental change rate is similar to that of its sub-systems.
- **Law of Requisite Variety:** How well any system manages depends on how well it matches the variety it faces.
- **Redundancy of Potential Command Principle:** The ability to be effective in a complex situation depends on bringing together the right mix of information.

Step 2 – Look at the impact of each of those in turn

Self-organised Criticality.
The driving force behind the decarbonisation of energy supply is the criticality of the dynamics of climate change. According to the climate change models, the world's economy is locked into a self-organised criticality and unless the structure and dynamics are changed, the predictions of climate scientists are bleak. From a modelling perspective, it's worth remembering that these are models and the predictions from models and all the discipline and techniques around handling the inherent uncertainty of models are relevant here. So, in a sense, the Self-organised Criticality is the backdrop to this issue.

Grammar of Systems – using the Laws

Homeostasis Principle
Homeostasis and the collapse of homeostasis, crops up throughout this problem situation. At one end, the environmental crisis is a crisis because the homeostatic limits of the environment are being stretched to breaking point. At the other end, the homeostatic balance of society is one of the rate limiting factors in the push for change. All the other aspects of the problem: political, technological, economic have their own homeostatic constraints.

Power Structuration Theorem
It's perhaps ironic that we are applying Power Structuration Theorem to the structure of the power system. The power industry and specifically the electricity distribution network was designed to match the structure of the electricity generation industry. The economics of traditional fossil fuel generation meant large, centralised power stations and that in turn led to a centralised distribution network. Renewable energy isn't naturally centralised, it is naturally distributed – the sun shines and the wind blows everywhere. So the logic of the power structuration of the traditional system is no longer valid. The whole system could be restructured to be much more localised – with the balance shifting towards local generation, storage and distribution. A question is 'but will it, though?' Structural change doesn't necessarily follow changes in possibilities. Computers still use a qwerty keyboard that was designed specifically to slow down typing speeds so typewriter keys wouldn't jam, even though computer keyboards can't jam. Cars (horseless carriages) ended up with engines where the horses used to be, and electric cars have continued the fashion with a box where the engine / horses used to be. Will renewable energy ape a structure that is redundant and sub-optimal for its own structure of agency in power generation generating and also sub-optimal for the structure of agency of communities? More localised generation, storage and distribution could create more opportunities for communities. Currently, the pattern in the UK has been to plug new renewable generating capacity into the existing centralised distribution system and rely on smart-metering and control to manage the flow.

System Survival Theorem
There are several interdependent sub-systems in this problem space. It is a technological, environmental, economic, political and societal issue.

Each of those sub-systems is locked to each of the others and they are all moving at different rates. Those change rate differentials put stresses on the dependencies between them and a break in any of those interdependencies could mean that all of them fail. Technological change requires political economic and societal change. Each of that trio of political, societal and economic are tightly locked to one another – politicians can only lead where society is prepared to go and without societal and political backing, economic changes in the industry will stall. If the technology doesn't change fast enough, the environmental change will spiral out of control. At its heart, you can see the whole problem as a set of interlocking change rates. A lot of work has gone into measuring the rate of change of the environment. By comparison measuring the critical variable of society's change rate has not been taken seriously – greenwashing and superficial changes have proved much more attractive. Understanding differential change rates starts with modelling and the reliability of the models partly depends on the factors and variables being used. If the models being used have been transposed from a different domain, as with a typical technology adoption model, the assumptions built into the model may be wildly out. The rate and structure of technology adoption in a free market situation may be totally different to this scenario where the pressures for change will ripple through the levels of the system.

Viability Principle
The Viability Principle has two dimensions: the need to change and the balance between centralisation and autonomy. If the tension between the pace of environmental change relative to the pace of technology change is critical in thinking about this as a purely technology adoption problem, the issue of fair access sits on the autonomy / centralisation axis. As a rule of thumb, the greater the devolution and autonomy, the greater the system's capacity to respond to local needs and hence to localised issues of fair access. The tension between these two axes is that centralisation may help speed up the rate of change, but is likely to reduce fair access – which will in turn slow down technology adoption and therefore actual change in the longer run. Again, not much serious effort has gone into understanding the consequences of structural decisions around the degree of centralisation.

Structural Viability Theorem
Each element of the problem situation: environmental, technological, economic, political and societal is a layered system. Which means that none of these changes homogeneously. In each locality of community, the environmental pressures, the technology options, the political realities, economic and societal factors will be different to another locality. Each nested system level will change at a different rate to each other.

Law of Requisite Variety
As with Homeostasis, Ashby's Law crops up throughout this problem cluster – do the technological options have requisite variety? Well, not yet they don't, nobody has yet worked out where all the electricity will come from that's needed for electric vehicles unless it's nuclear, but the nuclear industry hasn't worked out how to deal with its own waste. But the Requisite Variety issue becomes particularly acute when we look at the fair access end of the problem. Different societal sub-groups: communities, age groups socio-economic groups have very different levels of variety in their ability to understand and act on the options that are theoretically open to them.

Redundancy of Potential Command Principle
The standard models of technology adoption have a major strand of the Redundancy of Potential Command Principle woven into them. Classically these models assume that different groups adopt at different rates because they have different information available to them. Specifically, it's usually not that information is hidden from any group, it is that different groups have totally different capacity to receive and understand signals and convert messages into information they can use to take decisions. In the struggle for hearts and minds in the climate debate, the accessibility and trust (is it assimilated or dismissed) of information is key.

Grammar of Systems – using the Laws

Step 3 – Splice observations together

Self-organised Criticality + Homeostasis Principle
The driving force of the climate crisis is really encapsulated in these two, the nature of the Criticality is that there is positive feedback driven growth in the socio-economic system that then hits a limit. The limit that it hits is the homeostatic parameters of the climate system. Our current existing climate is stable within certain parameters and outside of those the concern is that it will become chaotic and then possibly flip into another stable state – that state will redraw the geography of habitable space and the conditions of habitation. So that is at the driving end of this as a problem.

System Survival Theorem + Viability Principle
In response to the environmental change, the socio-economic system needs to change and needs to change at least as fast as the environment is changing. If it doesn't change fast enough it will be simply a passive recipient of the environmental change. This need for speed is compounded by the fact that the environmental change has a significant head start. That need for change is playing out in a cluster of domains (political, economic technological, societal) all moving at different speeds, so there are races within races.

+ Structural Viability Theorem + Power Structuration Theorem
Each of those domains have structural layers within them, so it's not just that they are moving relative to one another, within each one different sub-systems are moving at different rates and in different directions. Almost none of this structural dimension has been addressed in policy by governments, lobbyists or activists beyond slogans to 'think global and act local'. We are largely blind to the implications of this, but it will inevitably have a major effect on the overall change rate.

+ Law of Requisite Variety + Redundancy of Potential Command Principle
The socio-economic system's blindness to the structural and dynamic complexity of both itself and the wider problem situation mean that decision making is a lot less well informed than it could be and that in

turn means that a lot of decisions will be quite random. You can see this in a lot of superficial attempts at intervention which are aimed at making changes that deal with symptoms whilst maintaining the basic model that has got us to where we are. In other words, many well intentioned initiatives are making things systemically worse rather than better. This is true for decisions made by individuals, communities, organisations, economic sectors and governments.

Step 4 – What the discards tell us

We picked 8 of the laws for this exercise, but as with the previous one, we could have sensibly used a lot more – in fact very few of the 33 are not easily applicable in this context, which given that it involves a balance between order and chaos, shouldn't come as much of a surprise. The two Black Box Principles aren't front of the queue for attention – indicating that there is very little in this situation that can be taken as stable and reliable. The fact so many are relevant, tells us a lot about this problem's complexity, uncertainty and changeability.

Overall, the splicing together on this one is all too easy. This means there is a tendency to slip unthinkingly from one law to another without really bottoming out any of them, in which case you just end up with a tangled mess. So, holding the mental discipline of thinking through each in turn is quite important – the notes above are just notes and each law individually has a lot more to say about many aspects of this. As a problem cluster though this can be separated into parts that make it more manageable – from the environmental dynamics at one end to societal structures at the other.

Both cases show not just how the laws can be used, but also why they should be. In both cases, systems methodologies could (and should) be used but because of their focus, they can obscure almost as much as they reveal. Going back to the fundamentals I think gives a very different appreciation.

Grammar of Systems – Methodologies

What's in a methodology....

As discussed in the introduction, different systems methodologies incorporate or are built on different systems laws listed in the Grammar and emphasise different thinking patterns from the grimoire. If you have a particular allegiance to a methodology, then depending on which it is, some of the thinking patterns and Laws are likely to resonate with you and others leave you cold or bewildered in a 'that's not what I think systems thinking is!' way.

This section aims to tie some of the more common methodologies to some of the Laws and thinking patterns. It's indicative; it isn't and isn't claiming to be definitive or exhaustive, not least because I'm not about to list every systems approach, but you can do this with every approach.

System Dynamics

I'm starting with System Dynamics because that has a reasonably clear set that closely relate to it. At the heart of System Dynamics is the modelling of positive and negative feedback loops (the two **Circular Causality Principles**) and doing that to understand the emergent properties of a dynamic system (**Emergence Principle**) well enough to intervene in it

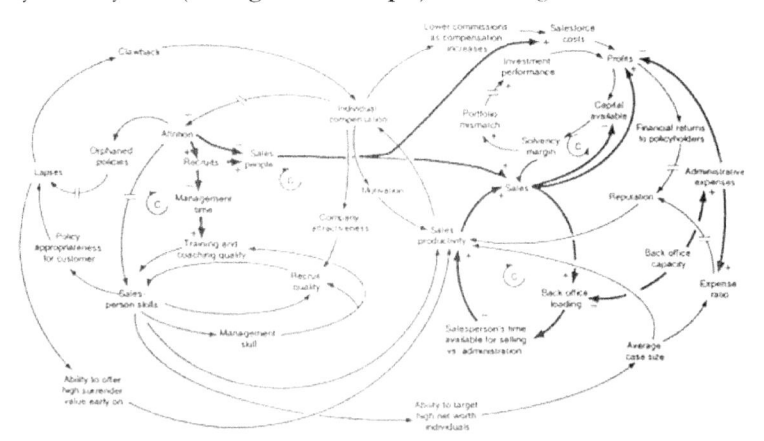

(**Conant-Ashby Theorem**). System Dynamics is interested in how systems are stable when they are (**Homeostasis Principle** and **Steady**

State Principle) and how they go unstable (**Self-organised Criticality**). One of the issues in designing an intervention using System Dynamics is that you have to change the structure or nature of the feedback loops to change the emergent properties (**Feedback Dominance Theorem**).

In terms of the thinking patterns, System Dynamics obviously majors on Dynamics and Loops, Emergence, Holism, Modelling, Relating, Dynamic Complexity and Uncertainty – which it tackles in its own rigorous way. It has much less to say about Boundaries and the structural side of complexity. Differences that make a difference it tends to handle in terms of working out which are the critical variables, relationships and thresholds in the dynamics of the system rather than for example insisting the modeller incorporates multiple perspectives.

Soft Systems Methodology

Quite a different animal and where System Dynamics is light on multiple perspectives, this is front and central in Soft Systems. The multiple perspectives are used to establish the nature of the problematic situation and to define the system that could address the problematic situation. That process of defining the nature is establishing the boundary (**Law of Calling**), and the point of the multiple perspectives is that establishing that boundary setting is done from those multiple perspectives from both inside the boundary and outside because you define the system differently from outside to inside (**Law of Crossing**). Soft Systems involves the

SOFT SYSTEMS METHODOLOGY

1. UNSTRUCTURED PROBLEM SITUATION
2. PROBLEM EXPRESSED
3. ROOT DEFINITION OF SYSTEM (S)
4. BUILD CONCEPTUAL MODELS
5. COMPARE MODELS TO REAL WORLD
6. DECIDE CHANGES SYSTEMICALLY DESIRABLE CULTURALLY FEASIBLE
7. IMPLEMENT CHANGES

REAL WORLD
SYSTEMS THINKING ABOUT REAL WORLD

explicit use of models to understand and then plan an intervention in a real-world situation (**Conant-Ashby Theorem**) and Soft Systems has a really structured set of ways to make sure that the relevant information is elicited to build those models (**Redundancy of Potential Command Principle**). Soft Systems is a learning loop model, so at the end of the process, you return to the starting position – albeit having hopefully moved things in the problematic situation – but that return to a position where you can run the process again implies a process of continuing change (**Conservation of Adaptation Principle**). Slightly more tenuously, there is a step in Soft Systems that involves building models of the system 'from first principles' and you could argue (and I would argue) that the Laws and Principles in the Grammar *are* the first principles we should be using for that.

In terms of the thinking patterns, the problematic situation Soft Systems seeks to address is an Emergent property and the methodology involves modelling a system that would address that. The Root Definition stage in Soft Systems is done at three levels of logic as per Holism. Soft Systems doesn't explicitly have ways to deal with either Organisational or Dynamic Complexity, but those are implicit in the 'build a model to...' stage and it does major on perceptual ambiguity and the complexity that comes from multiple perspectives. Naturally, those multiple perspectives provide a way to negotiate the Boundary on the basis of Differences of meaning that come with those perspectives and the nature of the Relationships between perspective holders and the system. Grappling with Uncertainty is woven through the methodology.

Viable Systems Model

If Soft Systems focuses on the knowing / unknowing set of laws and principles and System Dynamics on the Dynamic Complexity loop in the triquetra, Viable Systems majors on the Structural Complexity loop, but strays into both the other two. In one sense, the Viable System Model is a working through of **Ashby's Law** as that applies to multi-level complex adaptive systems.

It incorporates a family within the Grammar that have to do with the articulation of different aspects of complexity between levels of a system: adaptive capacity (**Structural Viability Theorem**), agency (**Power Structuration Theorem**), risk (**Adams 3rd Law**) and stability (**Steady State Principle**). And it also incorporates another family to do with the effects of complexity on stability / instability: **Complexity Instability Principle, Viability Principle, Scaled Stasis Principle, Black Box Principles** and **System Stability Principle**. It is explicitly a model of interconnected **Homeostats**, but the rest of the dynamic complexity set are part of the modelling approach you employ to use the Viable System Model, but not actually built into the model itself. Similarly, the rest of the 'knowing' set all form part of how it's used but aren't explicitly represented in the model itself.

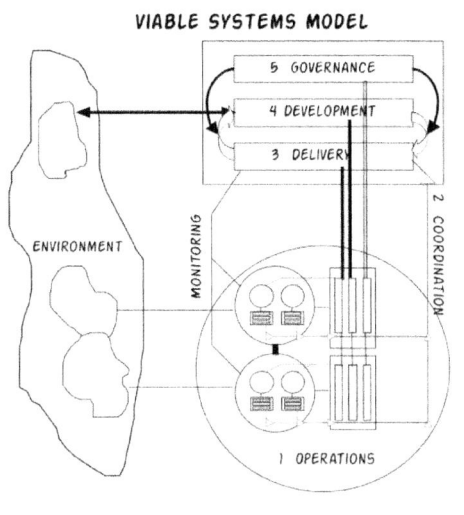

In terms of the thinking patterns, the Viable Systems Model is a set of Boundaries defined by, and defining, Differences and the Relationships, Complexity and Dynamics that bridge those Boundaries to produce Emergent properties. The model is itself multi-level and classically is done using a three level Holism. Uncertainty is a feature of the Modelling rather than the model in and of itself.

Patterns of Strategy

This is an example of designing a new systems approach directly from first principles, by using the laws and thinking patterns. The problem we sought to address was organisational strategy, where, as commented earlier, conventional approaches fail most of the time (Kaplan & Norton

Grammar of Systems – Methodologies

cite ≈ 90% failure rate, and Russ Ackoff cited 98% failure rate from one study). Henry Mintzberg had long talked about 'Emergent strategy' as what happens when 'deliberate strategy' doesn't actually happen, but he didn't explain the system that drives the emergence. And, of course, the 'emergent' in 'emergent strategy' is a systems concept.

So developing 'Patterns of Strategy' was an initiative to fill that gap by working out what the systemic drivers of emergent strategy are and developing that into a workable approach, and given that 'Emergent' is a systems concept, developing a systems approach to understand that seemed appropriate.

We started with thought patterns rather than Laws, so, Emergence, obviously (thanks to Mintzberg), and then taking Relating with Dynamics & loops, made us look at how strategic direction is driven by the dynamics of the critical relationships an organisation has. Within each relationship, Modelling the key Differences between the parties which drive the Dynamics which drives the Emergence. And in the Modelling process, the use of Holism and Boundaries specifically to clarify what is being Modelled at what level of System.

PATTERNS OF STRATEGY

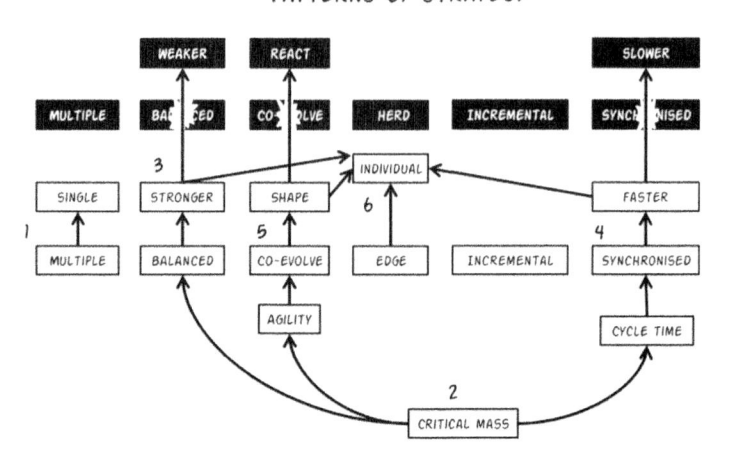

Grammar of Systems – Methodologies

Moving onto the Laws, the **Law of Reciprocity of Connections, Conservation of Adaptation Principle, Law of Calling, Law of Crossing, Law of Sufficient Complexity** and naturally the **Principle of Emergence** are all central in the approach – and were explicitly used in the development. Working out what the critical factors and variables to model (**Conant-Ashby Theorem**) to be able to understand the relational dynamics and understanding involved us using Ashby's **Law of Requisite Variety**.

In terms of systemic forces / effects we frequently see when things are strategically unstable are: **1st Circular Causality Principle, Self-Organised Criticality, Order Osmosis Principle**, and **System Survival Theorem**. And conversely, in situations that are strategically stable, we see: **2nd Circular Causality Principle, Homeostasis Principle** and **System Resonance Principle** at work. **Power Structuration Theorem** forms the basis of several of the common power-based strategies, and the **Relaxation Time Principle** features in several of the time-based strategies.

The result is a systemic approach that is totally different to conventional approaches to thinking about and doing strategy, that makes it easy to model the relational dynamics driving emergent strategy and which works.

Miscellany

This is a fairly random collection of jottings and notes on aspects of systems that aren't Laws or patterns of thinking, but which seem juicy enough to include. The only justification for the choice is that I think they're useful and I hope you might too.

Double Bind

This is just one of Gregory Bateson's models. This entered public consciousness through Heller's novel 'Catch 22' which was written around the double bind. The double bind is when you are constrained by two mutually contradictory imperatives: satisfying the conditions of one means failing on the other. Quite often they will operate at two structural levels or two levels of logic. This can happen at any scale and I encountered one major national organisation where management and regulators demanded staff in every major process worked in a way that the staff knew would cause the organisation to fail. This puts the staff in an impossible position – comply and fail, or fail to comply – either way carries risk. Bateson's point was that this sets up the conditions for schizophrenia as the person or system subject to the double bind internalises the conflict and literally splits their personality to try to cope. Organisational systems are not immune to either to this problem, or to its consequences – many organisations are schizophrenic. The classic way to deal with it is to find a position at a higher logical level that is able to transcend the paradox posed by the double bind and reconcile the opposing pressures at that level. This approach is also a feature of the 'Method of Levels' in Perceptual Control Theory.

Purpose & POSIWID

There are two very different views on 'purpose' within systems thinking. One is similar to the conventional one outside of systems: that purpose equates to intention, that it is essentially a mental or emotional construct. The wrinkle in systems is that purpose is deliberately ascribed to systems by stakeholders. The countervailing view is usually known as the POSIWID position. This states that the 'Purpose Of a System Is What It Does'. Some see this as tautological and therefore trivial – tautological it is, trivial it isn't. In this view the purpose of the system is determined by the action of the system itself, which in turn, as per **Law of Sufficient Complexity**, is a function of its structure. In other words, purpose is emergent. This is not merely some academic debate; whole disciplines fail because of ignoring POSIWID – conventional business strategy is predicated on the assumption that organisations' (systems') strategies (purposes) are about intention, whereas the evidence is very clear that in around 90% of cases its emergent – POSIWID. The reconciliation between POSIWID and the ascription view is that the system sets its own purpose by what it is and does and stakeholders then ascribe intentionality to that. It's then a question of emphasis or primacy whether you see the intentionality of individual observers as shaping the purpose of the system, or the innate purpose of the system shaping the perceptions and intentions of observers. Of course, both will be true to some extent, but the extent varies dramatically. In the field of business strategy, it's clear which way the asymmetry lies – POSIWID rules there.

Problems, messes, clusters and wicked problems.

A lot of system practice is focused on solving problems, and systems has a gradation of problem severity.

The 'problem of problems'

The whole issue of problems is tied back to the 'purpose' debate. Problems are frequently talked about as if they are intrinsic to systems in the real world, but any problem is 'just' a difference between how we think the world is and how we think it ought to be, so the idea of problem is inextricably linked to intentionality and thereby to the positioning of different stakeholders. You can then think of 'problems' as the tension between purpose as intention and POSIWID.

One by-product of this that is massively underused is that if a problem is a mismatch between how the world is and how we think it should be, that means there are two parts to any problem and two generic solutions. You can seek to change the world, or you could instead change how you think it should be. In other words, you could choose just to change your mind. Overwhelmingly, though, people assume they must be right and the world

"When we are no longer able to change a situation, we are challenged to change ourselves."

Viktor Frankl

must be wrong and changed to suit. Worth bearing in mind Einstein's comment: *"It is harder to crack a prejudice than an atom"* which maybe accounts for it. Cynicism aside, there are many occasions where changing the system is orders of magnitude harder than changing the mind of a problem owner ought to be, not least because changing the system will almost invariably involve someone else having to change their minds. It follows that a lot of problem solving is actually an exercise in shifting the burden of who has to adapt from one stakeholder to some others.

Back to the gradations of problems, there are four main ones: problems, messes, clusters and wicked.

Problems
The definition of this really boils down to 'simpler than a mess' and they are simpler not by virtue of being intrinsically easier to fix, but simpler in that they are less ambiguous, the nature of the problem is clear and largely not disputed. A pandemic is a problem – not easy to deal with, but 'conspiracy theorists' aside, the fact that it is seen as a problem isn't really debated, nor is why it's a problem – its symptoms: illness, death, economic impact etc. are all widely accepted as problematic.

Messes
Messes earn that status because whether 'X' is a problem or why it is a problem is disputed. Different stakeholders vary in their position on it and what might make X a problem for stakeholder A can be diametrically opposed to B's view, to the extent that the problem for A can be the benefit for B and vice versa. This is as common as two neighbours arguing over the height of a hedge and not surprisingly, a lot of what systems practitioners get asked to work on are messes. Part of the art in a lot of cases is moving a mess into a problem – in other words getting enough agreement to actually come to a resolution to change something and making it possible to devise and implement a technical fix. The reason messes are the norm is that different stakeholders, by definition, will have different perspectives on any system.

Problem Clusters

A problem cluster is exactly what it says, a cluster of problems – a problem that is made up of several different but interdependent problems. They are sometimes confused with messes, but the difference is that the complexity of a mess is perceptual – different stakeholders disagree on the nature of the problem, whereas with a cluster, the complexity of a cluster is structural - there are different sub-problems in the cluster. For example, the problem of deep storage of nuclear waste is simultaneously an: engineering + geological + hydro-dynamics + nuclear physics + economics + environmental + societal + political problem. And each of those affects each of the other. Which is why it's quite hard to fix. So it is a cluster, but it isn't a mess to the extent that everyone agrees it would be better if there were a solution.

Cluster problems can occasionally be 'solved' by brute force – finding a fix for one sub-problem and then forcing that through all the others, but technically, the best way to tackle them is by having an approach that matches the complexity of the problem. In other words, cluster problems demand cluster solutions (**Law of Requisite Variety**) where each problem element has a corresponding component in the development of the solution. Often they will need tackling in parallel rather than sequentially. Because problem clusters are more structurally complex, they typically have a more intricate and longer boundary than a single problem and therefore more stakeholders, so they are often messes as well as being clusters, but not always.

"For every complex problem, there is a solution which is simple, neat and invariably wrong".
H L Mencken

Wicked Problems

The amount of airtime devoted to wicked problems seems to have dramatically increased in recent years, not because the actual incidence has increased, but because it's become fashionable to claim work you are doing as wicked – it's a cheap way to claim hero status.

The classic definition by Rittel & Weber has 10 characteristics:
1. There is no definitive formulation of a wicked problem.
2. Wicked problems have no stopping rule.
3. Solutions to wicked problems are not true-or-false, but better or worse.

4. There is no immediate and no ultimate test of a solution to a wicked problem.
5. Every solution to a wicked problem is a 'one-shot operation'; because there is no opportunity to learn by trial and error, every attempt counts significantly.
6. Wicked problems do not have an enumerable (or an exhaustively describable) set of potential solutions, nor is there a well-described set of permissible operations that may be incorporated into the plan.
7. Every wicked problem is essentially unique.
8. Every wicked problem can be considered to be a symptom of another problem.
9. The existence of a discrepancy representing a wicked problem can be explained in numerous ways. The choice of explanation determines the nature of the problem's resolution.
10. The planner has no right to be wrong (i.e., planners are liable for the consequences of the actions they generate).

For me, the toughest, most critical aspect is a corollary of point 5. Every intervention has an effect and as a result, wicked problems morph every time you touch them. Where messes are defined by perceptual complexity and cluster problems are characterised by structural complexity, wicked problems always have dynamic complexity. They usually have both structural and perceptual complexity too, but the big difference is their changeability and that is down to the combination of their structural complexity and dynamics.

My personal experience is that 'tame problems' are common, but as systems practitioners we don't get asked to deal with them that often (because their solution is relatively easy). Messes and problem clusters are the norm, and genuinely wicked problems are relatively rare. I can remember only one problem where the nature of the problem shifted significantly every time we touched it, although a lot where the problem changed somewhat through time.

Last word on problems goes to Warren McCulloch's collaborator Walter Pitts – *"problems are either trivial or insoluble and an insoluble problem is trivial once it's been solved."*

Cartesian Fallacy

There's more than one Cartesian fallacy, but the one that is relevant here is the Cartesian split or the mind-body duality fallacy. Philosophers have done a comprehensive job of debunking this – in philosophy, but like a B-movie zombie it lives on long after you think you've killed it off and you can see the Cartesian fallacy thriving and proliferating in popular thinking, culture and management theory. The fallacy is that thinking and reality are separate and different types of thing. This relates straight back to the 'problem of problems' and the POSIWID debate.

The mental trap for the systems thinker here is to assume that thinking sits apart from or somehow above reality. This ignores the effects that the system has on the observer doing the thinking. It's a major problem because where you stand relative to the system does have a massive effect on what you can see, what you can think, what you can feel, so the way to cope with this is to consciously navigate your positioning whilst understanding and negotiating the effects on thought those positions have – this is the C^2 discipline. If you believe in the Cartesian split, then you assume that your thought rises peerless above the world and that what you see is somehow 'right' just because you think it. And the tricky bit is that even if you think consciously that you don't fall into the fallacy – that itself can be a consequence of the fallacy. You can think you aren't, but if you act in a way that is Cartesian in its assumptions, then you are falling into the trap. For example, if you imagine that an organisational or social system will just do what its designer or a policy maker or strategist intends, that is the Cartesian fallacy at work, and it matters because systems are not like that.

Vickers' Trap

The Vickers in question is Sir Geoffrey Vickers and his 'trap' is that: *"The nature of the trap is a function of the nature of the trapped"*. You can see this as a consequence of the **Law of Sufficient Complexity**, but for practitioners, it's worth bearing in mind when trying to unravel the significance of stakeholders and their perception of problems. And this relates back to the messiness of messes.

Korzybski's 3 Traps
The first two of these relate to the 'map is not the territory' issue that Korzybski wrote about, the third has to do with navigating uncertainty.

K 1: mistaking the map and the territory and believing that the map *is* the territory. This usually exhibits as overconfidence in the map and assuming the map is 'right' and not bothering to check the reality or ignoring evidence the map is wrong. It is very common.

K 2: mistaking the map and the territory, not being aware you're actually using a map to see the territory.

K 3: *"There are two ways to slide easily through life; to believe everything or to doubt everything. Both ways save us from thinking."* The error is a failure to maintain an appropriate level of doubt and instead to polarise thinking towards either certainty or to take an 'it's all a mystery' position.

Churchman's 4 Traps: 'Enemies of System Thinking'
'The System Approach and its Enemies' is a book by C. West Churchman and the four enemies Churchman identified are: Political thinking, Aesthetics, Morality and Religion. It's worth remembering that he was talking about 'the systems approach' rather than 'Systems Thinking' per se and what he meant was a fairly deliberate social planning approach. Nevertheless, his 4 'enemies' are worth bearing in mind for systems thinkers, since they are quite likely to slide into your thought processes and undermine it unless consciously guarded against. It's not that there is anything actually wrong with any of them, but just as it's hard to ride a bicycle and a horse at the same time, it's hard to do one of these and systems thinking at the same time.

In one sense, the question is one of primacy – which you do first, and the argument really is that for a systems thinker, if you sequence one of these before you think systems, it will inhibit your ability to think systemically, or reduce the scope of what you can see. By all means use them afterwards, and of course in a different context, they absolutely should have primacy – it would be crazy to put systems thinking before aesthetics when looking at a Turner painting. This is a bit like the holism-reductionism argument, the sequence in which you think about different facets either opens up or constrains your perception and thinking. There are few situations for most systems practitioners where you can afford not to consider the politics of the situation (obviously biological or psychological systems practice would be different) but if you consider the politics too early, then the constraints are too strong for any progress. As in Soft Systems Methodology, coming up with a 'systemically desirable solution' before checking it is also 'politically feasible' is preferable.

Churchman's account of why he first came up with the 'enemies' is: *"Then one day I was listening to a talk about the virtues of the world models which the Club of Rome had sponsored; the speaker was asking why the world's leaders had not more rapidly responded to the models' results. The answer came like a flash, "Because they're not 'in' the systems approach but rather live and decide 'outside' it."* His first point was that other people didn't accept or understand the results of systems interventions because they think using completely different paradigms that have different values. All of which is true and critically important for practitioners, whereas the argument I made above is more relevant for systems thinking itself. Churchman's second point was that: *"To me these enemies provide a powerful way of learning about the systems approach, precisely because they enable the rational mind to step outside itself and to observe itself (from the vantage point of the enemies)."* Which is a very holistic way to understand Systems Thinking – by looking at its relationship to a wider body of paradigms of which it is a part.

The four enemies then.

Politics – the 'art of the possible' and what makes things possible politically is whether people will agree or at least not disagree to the point where they prevent you from doing something. The problem of putting politics first is that in a multi stakeholder situation – i.e. the norm – there are very few unconstrained avenues. If you use systems approaches before considering political constraints, then more options may open up and stakeholders may change the constraints they impose. Also worth bearing in mind that there are systems approaches designed specifically to address political problems.

Grammar of Systems – Miscellany

Morality – there are systemic approaches to dealing with moral issues, just as there are systems approaches that deal explicitly with politics and most systems interventions will have a moral dimension as they have a political dimension. The problem with dealing with moral considerations first – rather than using them to choose between options – is that they tend to be presented as absolutes, whereas most real moral dilemmas are not simple choices between right and wrong, but between conflicting 'goods' and which would be 'the lesser of two evils'. That is much easier to do once systems options have been explored since exposing the relative 'goods' and 'evils' should form part of the practice. As Beer put it about autonomy in systems: *"The cybernetic argument for autonomy is distinct from ethical, political, or psychological arguments. It has no emotive content. It is mathematical."* But you never get to see the mathematical imperative for autonomy if you first look at it as a moral or ethical issue.

Religion – rather like morality, putting religious imperatives first tends to impose a single imperative on a complex situation. This is after all part of the appeal of religion, it brings a degree of certainty to inherently uncertain situations. For a practitioner, this 'enemy' extends beyond true religion to encompass, doctrinal positions. Many management approaches and societal movements adopt a religious model, espousing an orthodoxy, relying on 'conversion to the faith' and 'gurus', waging war between sects, excommunications etc. etc. So even in supposedly secular societies, a religious mode of thinking is common. In systems thinking, as with morality and politics taking a religious view first tends to crowd out a full exploration from a systems perspective.

Aesthetics – the other three can be a barrier to systems thinking, stopping you before you get to it, but aesthetics works in a different way, inhibiting your ability to challenge models. The astronomical model of planetary motion using platonic solids was aesthetically pleasing: elegant, coherent but it was wrong. The mental trap for the system thinker here is that once an aesthetic appeal has got hold of you, it can be really hard to shake off, not least because, by its nature, aesthetics goes straight to emotion and it's hard to replace an emotional preference just using logic or evidence. If a systems model or solution is also elegant, that's a bonus, but it shouldn't be the primary condition of acceptability.

Learning - Single Loop, Double Loop and Deutero

Systems and cybernetics have had a massive impact on learning theory and practice generally, and one that goes well beyond what we think of in terms of formalised 'learning'. These three models of learning have widespread applicability.

Single Loop Learning

Single Loop Learning is essentially a single negative feedback loop. So there is some activity – might or might not be a process – which transforms some input into a different output state. There is a comparator to assess the output against a set of values (e.g. 'it's blue and it's supposed to be green') and if the output doesn't match the comparator, there is a way to adjust the inputs or activity so that the output does match.

Note that for it to qualify as feedback, it has to be able to close the loop – to make a difference to bring the output back on track.

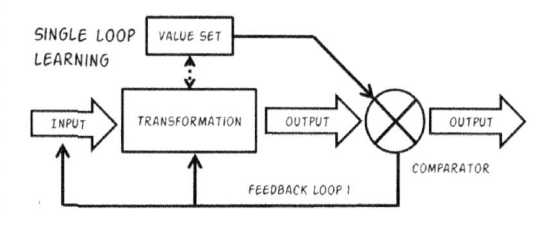

In organisational world, compliance regimes typically run on single loops. The nature of the learning is limited to *'is this what I expect? Because it ought to be'*. So what we learn is prescribed by and relative to what we already know. It is not about learning something new.

Double Loop Learning

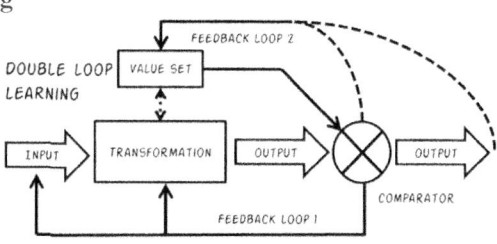

Double Loop Learning literally builds on Single Loop Learning. It takes the single loop structure and on top of that there is a second loop to adjust the value set against which the comparator evaluates the output. The informational feed for the second loop can be from the comparator, or from outside the loop, or from the system that owns the loop.

In organisational world, performance improvement regimes such as continuous improvement run on double loops.

The nature of the learning is quite different to a single loop, here the loop drives the system to learn to do new things, to achieve something more or different to what had been done before. Instead of just asking *'is this what I expect?'*, the second loop askes *'what should I be looking for from this?'*. Which is a higher order question.

Deutero Learning
Deutero Learning comes from Gregory Bateson's work with dolphins on how they learn. He observed that the dolphins didn't merely learn new tricks in training, they also learned how to learn and started to pursue learning for its own sake. Deutero Learning is the term he used, but it's also known as second order learning.

Systems Levels and Configuration
The technical language of systems deals with the nested nature of complex systems by talking about them usually as levels. A System will have a number of Sub-Systems: which are parts of the System, but confusingly are also systems in their own right. Similarly, a System will be part of one or more Meta-Systems. The relationship of a Sub-System to a System is the same as the relationship of a System to a Meta-System. All systems have a boundary (otherwise they'd be infinite in extent) and outside that boundary is the system's Environment. Recursion, fractals, embedding and nesting are all ways of describing the structuring of complex systems. Recursion and fractal mean that the different levels have a similar structure to one another.

Godel's (second) incompleteness theorem states that a logical system cannot prove its own consistency. There is a direct link to the holism argument, that the logos of any system cannot be fully understood within its own terms, but only from the system of which it is a part – its meta-system. This in turn is about the multi-level structuring of complex systems, from sub-system to system to meta-system.

Coenetic Variables

There's a much-used adage that correlation is not causality. A coenetic variable is where you have two variables that are not directly connected, but they both have a common systemic source. This means that whilst A and B are correlated – one moves when the other does – A doesn't cause B to change and B doesn't cause A to change, both are connected to C or are part of the same system that is affecting both of them. You can see this as an inevitable consequence of the **Law of Reciprocity of Connections**. The implication is that where you see correlation but no direct causation, it's often worth looking to see if there is a coenetic variable at work.

Von Foerster's 1st rule

"All other factors being equal, act so as to increase the number of choices." You can see this as a logical consequence of Ashby's law, and also as a guiding principle in thinking and practice. The rationale behind tackling Churchman's enemies is the need to 'increase the number of choices.'

James Clerk Maxwell and the Black Box

The idea of the Black Box was developed by the father of modern physics James Clerk Maxwell, who developed the first mathematical models to explain how governors work in controlling steam pressure. Before Maxwell, designing governors was a matter of trial and error and when the designers got it wrong, steam engines tended to blow up. His work was the beginning of control theory that then developed into Cybernetics.

Maxwell's idea of the Black Box was that it is a container of a *theory* used to explain some change in what is observed. It's rather like 'Maxwell's Demon', something we know is a fiction used to explain something observable. Its usage changed subtly when it was incorporated into cybernetics by Ashby and the 'conscious fiction' aspect got subsumed into a 'we don't know how this works but know it does' aspect. It's often helpful to bear in mind that it is a bit more tentative than that. There is always a hypothesis hidden in the dependability of a Black Box.

Grammar of Systems – Miscellany

Ashby Transformation

The term 'transformation' is loosely used, but in systems and cybernetics it has a technical meaning (it does also get used loosely here too). A transformation is an activity that turns an input from one state into a different state as an output of that transformation. In some approaches people talk about a process having inputs and outputs, but that doesn't have the same precision, because the focus then is on the working of the process, not on the transformation the process is there to accomplish and it's common to see processes where the desired or actual transformation is unclear to the designers or those carrying them out. Transformation defines 'work done' rather than 'process followed'. It's key in Soft Systems methodology and Viable Systems and is extremely useful in for example designing metrics – if you can define the transformation it is really easy to define the metric to measure it.

Attractors

Attractors or 'basins of attraction' or 'basins of stability' are states of relative stability that systems can 'fall into'. As systems are a) dynamic and b) subject to change all the time, the state they occupy can become unstable, at which point they may roll from one previously stable state into a new one. In organisational systems, this is sometimes very obvious when you look for it and often organisations will go through repeating patterns of state reversal, flipping back and forth between two stable states. One organisation we plotted flipping between just two strategic stances over a 200-year period. Attractors figured in early systems work, but then got somewhat side-lined. It's been much more prominent in the language of complexity theorists, but the idea is exactly the same.

Beer's Yo-yo

Systems as a discipline is and always has been multi-domain, crossing boundaries from psychology to ecology to organisational to biological, to societal to…. And to some extent, the discipline is an attempt to understand what is the same across those different domains – in what ways are the neural networks modelled by neurophysiologists Warren McCulloch and Lorente de Nó the same as computer networks explored by John von Neumann, Stafford Beer, and Warren McCulloch and in what ways are they different? The yo-yo is an approach Beer used to tackle this problem in the development of his Viable System Model, but its utility is much more general. The purpose of the yo-yo is to arrive at some laws, or principles, that are invariant between different domains.

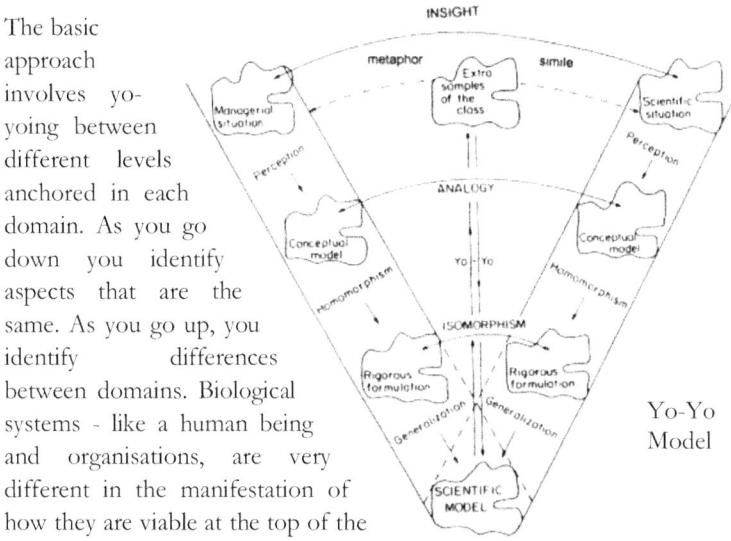

The basic approach involves yo-yoing between different levels anchored in each domain. As you go down you identify aspects that are the same. As you go up, you identify differences between domains. Biological systems - like a human being and organisations, are very different in the manifestation of how they are viable at the top of the

Yo-Yo Model

yo-yo in each domain, (e.g. the specific of what needs to be kept in homeostatic balance for each is different), but there are a number of factors in which they are identical at the bottom of the yo-yo, (e.g. the need to keep a homeostatic balance with their environment). Using the yo-yo technique requires some mental discipline, but with practice, it can be fast and powerful. One of the tricks is to not get lost in the hinterland of metaphor and analogy that lies between the top and bottom of the yo-yo.

Negative entropy

Entropy is the level of dis-order of a system, often referenced in connection with the 2nd Law of Thermodynamics, which states that in an isolated system, entropy never decreases, so if you have two connected bodies at different temperatures, their temperature difference will settle to the same homogenous temperature level. As an aside, Maxwell's Demon (mentioned above) was a thought experiment in how the 2nd law might be broken. Systems is partly looking at what happens going in the opposite direction, how it is that systems self-organise, how order emerges from disorder. In other words, how systems are neg-entropic. This doesn't mean that systems thinking contradicts the 2nd Law, merely that when you are looking at biological, social, or organisational systems, the 2nd law applies – as does the law of gravity – but it's not really any help in understanding those systems, whereas neg-entropy and self-organisation are. In some systems approaches, neg-entropy is identified with 'information' since 'information' is defined as that which creates form.

Differentials & dynamics

This is touched on in the chapter on Difference, but worth re-iterating here that the level of difference across a boundary drives dynamics. Counterintuitively, the effect of this is often so strong that it isn't spotted, because where their difference is strong, the dynamic can be so strong that the relationship is so unstable it is gone before it can really be registered. Calibrating levels of difference can be critical in practice and particularly the trend, whether the level of difference is increasing or decreasing through time.

Donella Meadows' 12 Places to Intervene

The story goes that Dana Meadows was working on the North American Free Trade Agreement and was frustrated that the debate was focused on factors that were low impact and she couldn't find a way to get the delegates to see the bigger picture or the other possibilities, so she got up and in a flash of inspiration wrote down this set of 'places to intervene'. Her original list included 9 points, later she expanded it to this 12. The list works from the lowest leverage – 12 to the highest – 1. Dana Meadows was a system dynamicist, so this comes with that perspective, but it can be useful to system thinkers and practitioners of any stripe.

1   The power to transcend paradigms
2   The mindset or paradigm that the system — its goals, structure, rules, delays, parameters — arises out of
3   The goal of the system
4   The power to add, change, evolve, or self-organize system structure
5   The rules of the system (such as incentives, punishment, constraints)

6   The structure of information flow (who does and does not have access to what kinds of information)
7   The gain around driving positive feedback loops
8   The strength of negative feedback loops, relative to the effect they are trying to correct against
9   The length of delays, relative to the rate of system changes
10 The structure of material stocks and flows (such as transport network, population age structures)
11 The size of buffers and other stabilizing stocks, relative to their flows
12 Constants, parameters, numbers (such as subsidies, taxes, standards)

Aside from Donella Meadow's original intention of pointing away from low leverage interventions, her list is useful in pointing out some places to intervene that are quite high leverage and often within your gift to change. For example, if you are outside a system boundary, you may not be able to directly work on 5 – the rules of the system, but you can quite often change 6 and make different information available, and that can affect 5 through to 2. Similarly, even positing a different paradigm from outside can open the door to actual change of paradigm and so can be an act in 1 – the ability to transcend paradigms.

Upside Down, inside out and back to front

Donella Meadows commented on an aspect of this, that often people know what the critical factors in a problem situation are, they know which lever to pull, but they almost invariably pull them the wrong way because the system works counter-intuitively. An example she used was that housing subsidies can make things worse for the very people they are intended to help. The sustainability debate is fraught with well-intentioned but totally counter-productive exhortations and initiatives that address surface phenomena, not systemic drivers.

As a broader issue within systems thinking and practice, it's common to come across situations where the accepted view has got something back to front. People are incredibly adept at reversing the logic of a situation without even noticing, so inputs are thought to be outputs and outputs treated as inputs. Not all 'Systems Thinkers are immune to this and using the logic of Ashby Transformations helps.

Inside out is similar and involves flows across boundaries, so communicating from inside a system boundary to the world outside gets reversed to become communicating from the environment into the system. I have seen this flip wreck several professional communities, where the starting intention was to have the profession talking to the world, but meetings instead become about inviting in speakers to talk to or at the community and in the process, the community is morphed from active and declarative, to passive audience and gradually dies.

Upside down comes in two variants and again is really common. Variant one is to mix up structural levels, so rather than A being a sub-system of B, the order gets reversed and B is taken as a sub-system of A. The other variant is even more common and inverts levels of logic, so a higher order proposition is taken as dependant on a lower order. For example, a 'why' and a 'how' get reversed so the how becomes the point of the why.

It is always worth checking that you've got things the right way round – which involves seeing if they make more sense if you reverse the logic / flow / communication or invert the structure.

As with trying to tell someone that they have their dress on back to front, or their coat is inside out, trying to get across to anyone that the way they are looking at a systemic situation maybe inside out or back to front is extremely delicate and has the probability of being highly embarrassing.

Autopoiesis

The concept and indeed the word itself (derived from the Greek αυτοποίεσίσ) come from the work of Humberto Maturana and Francisco Varela and means literally self-creation. Maturana and Varela were biologists and concerned with the nature of life. Autopoiesis describes a characteristic of living systems that they are structured to produce the elements that produce their structure. In other words they create themselves. So I eat food and turn that food into myself, I have processes that continuously kill off cells and construct new cells to replace them.

This is in contrast to something like a car factory which is allopoietic because the car factory doesn't make car factories, it just makes cars.

The idea migrated from biological to societal and organisational systems. It isn't automatically either good or bad - without it we die, but equally, cancer is autopoietic, it's pathological autopoiesis, but autopoiesis nevertheless. In organisations it's often used to refer to sub-systems that like a cancer grow beyond the limits of their natural function – in other words beyond the point where their cost outweighs their benefit to the wider system.

In biological systems, we know what it is that gets created – it's cells and from those organs. In organisations it's roles, so an autopoietic department grows by taking in resources and converting those into people doing tasks that create the department that takes in resources that…. It's not that the department creates people (office romances notwithstanding), but it does create roles and converts people into roles being done. Autopoiesis is often confused with self-organisation – they are not the same thing – and with Structural Coupling.

Structural Coupling

Again comes from Maturana and Varela. This is the more generally used term that is formally expressed in the **Conservation of Adaptation Principle** in the Grammar. Systems are structurally coupled to their environments in such a way that the system changes the environment structurally, and the environment changes the system structurally. Through time each changes the other to drive their evolution.

Maturana's Systems Laws

This set of Laws provides an alternative and largely complementary perspective from the work of Humberto Maturana and Ximena Dávila Yáñez. They repay further study, but if you are not familiar with the way Maturana thinks and writes, pre-reading 'Tree of Knowledge' would be a good place to start rather than diving straight in.

Any errors of interpretation in the descriptions are mine.

Grammar of Systems – Miscellany

Basic Laws
0 The possibility of knowing - All possibility of human knowing, understanding, and explaining comes through our experience of living.
1 Observing - Everything that is said is said by an observer.
2 Neither randomness nor chaos - There is no randomness in the act of living.
3 The observer and observing – There is no observing prior to the observer's reflexive distinction.
4 Recursive flow of observing - The act of reflection occurs in the operating of the observer in the conversation that distinguishes his or her own operation, and [reflection] occurs as a living process that leads to the continued conservation of recursive expansion of comprehending one's living, one's self-consciousness, and the actions at hand in the flow of living in the constantly changing present that the same recursive reflection generates, and [reflection] occurs in the act of letting go of the certainty that we know what we think we know.
5 Illusion or perception - Everything we live, we live as valid at the moment in which we live it.
6 Generation of worlds - The world we live in every moment is the realm of all the distinctions that we make.
7 Evolutionary drift - The course of evolutionary drift of living beings arises moment to moment in the flow of their living guided by their preferences.

General Systemic Laws
8 Conservation and change - Every time a set of elements begins to conserve certain relationships, it opens space for everything to change around the relationships that are conserved.
9 Structural determinism - Whenever an observer distinguishes a composite unit, the observer has distinguished a composite unit determined by its structure.
10 Simple and compound units - As observers, we distinguish simple units and composite units or systems. Systems arise in the distinction made by the observer as totalities he or she then breaks down into components
11 Components and composition - The components of a system are not components in themselves or by themselves; they are elements that

arise as components when an observer distinguishes their participation in the relationships of the composition of a system that he or she has distinguished as such.

12 Identity and change - The configuration of relationships between the components of a system that remains invariant in the flow of structural changes defines its identity.

13 Structural coupling - A system exists in the conservation of its identity with its environmental niche.

14 Domains of existence - A system exists and operates in two separate spheres of existence: in the sphere of its operating components and in the sphere of its operations as a whole in interaction with the environment.

15 Continuously changing present - A system operates in its internal dynamics at each instant according to its structural coherence at that instant.

16 Closed systems - Each time an observer distinguishes a system made entirely as a set of elements that interact with each other so that when one acts on one of them, one acts on all, we call this a closed dynamic system.

Biological Systemic Laws

17 Spontaneity of living - A living being arises when at a molecular level a set of molecules interact with each other forming a closed network of molecular productions that produces the same kinds of molecules that compose it.

18 Organisation and identity - The organisation that defines the identity of a living being is autopoietic [self-producing]. A living being lives only as long as it conserves its autopoiesis, and as long as it conserves its autopoiesis, a living being lives.

19 Adaptation - The conservation of operational congruence between organism and environment that occurs in the flow of conservation of living is the relationship of adaptation between organism and environment.

20 Structural determinism in living. Living beings as autopoietic molecular entities operate and are conserved in their operations as structurally determined entities.

21 Non-time - Everything that happens to and with systems happens in a continuously changing present in non-time.

22 What happens, happens - A living being, as a structurally determined system, does in each moment the only thing it can do in that moment according to its structural coherences of that moment.

Meta-Systemic Laws
23 History and desires - The course followed by living beings arises moment by moment defined by their desires and preferences.

24 The centre of the cosmos - Every living being in its living operates at all times as the centre of its cosmos.

25 Living beings and the environment - A living being and its environment change together in a congruent manner. If this conserves its autopoiesis and its relationship of adaptation to the environment then the being survives, but if this fails to happen the living being dies, or leaves.

26 We always do what we want - Human beings always do what we want to do, even when we say we do not want to do what we do.

27 The present - Every living being operates at each moment in the only way that it can operate in that moment according to its structural coherences in its continuously changing present.

28 Autopoiesis - Everything that occurs in the flow of living is to conserve the relationships that constitute and reconstitute the system.

29 Results and resulting -. The result of a process is not a factor in the course of the process that gives rise to it.

Last Thoughts

This has been a journey, in fact, both parts of this book have, so it's been two journeys.

A lot of what is in Part 1 are patterns of thinking that have become instinctive for me. So that involved first surfacing those patterns by checking what is actually going on and then linking that to the history of the field to ensure that these were not merely thinking quirks of my own. All of which took time and patient study.

The more formalised expressions of thinking that make up the Laws and Principles in the Grammar in Part 2 had to be hunted out. Some were very well known, like Ashby's **Law of Requisite Variety**, but some of them were unnamed so trying to track down something that nobody had bothered to name even though it was clearly used in earlier work, made the job harder. The hardest in one way were the 'new ones' formalised and useful enough for inclusion, but were these fit to stand alongside? Especially since many of them are really derivative.

For me, the journey has been its own reward. Working out which thinking patterns are genuinely systems thinking as opposed to just any old thinking has sharpened the focus and provided an extra set of thinking tools to call on. Unearthing the Laws has been worth it simply because I find them so useful.

I hope you will too.

Patrick Hoverstadt

For more information go to:
www.Fractal-consulting.com

The Fractal Organization

Building Sustainable Organizations with the Viable System Model
Patrick Hoverstadt
2007   Wiley

The world of management is in crisis - the old remedies no longer work and organizations are failing at an increasing rate. Although many talk of 'joined up thinking', few offer practical guidance on how to achieve this in organizations.

The Fractal Organization sets down the practical implications of a well-tested systemic approach to building organizations that are capable of surviving and flourishing in these turbulent times.

"An excellent read…Many organizations fail at the mercy of their own ignorance. The author has done an excellent job in making 'the science of effective organization' accessible to management." Stephen J. Brewis, Chief Scientist BT

"brilliantly serious and practical, and often entertaining too." Prof. Peter Kawalek, Manchester Business School.

"one of the most interesting, thorough and rigorous guides to management that I have ever read, … introduces new insights in every chapter Penny Marrington Senior Lecturer OU

"A great book on the theory and the practical application of the Viable System Model." Michael Frahm Deutsche Bahn

"If you read this book you will not be able to look at your, or any other, organization in the same way." Robinson Roe M.D. One Trust Apac

Patterns of Strategy

Patrick Hoverstadt & Lucy Loh
2017 Routledge

Patterns of Strategy shows how the strategic fit between organisations drives strategic direction. It is essential reading for those who wish to understand how to manoeuvre their organisation to change its strategic fit to their advantage.

The 80 'patterns' of strategy help you explore options for collaboration and competition within your strategic ecosystem. A practical and authoritative guide, you can use it to plan and navigate your strategic future.

"It is beautiful in its simplicity." David Atkinson, COO, Mindgym

"the first major new approach to strategy in a long time…. a 'must have' for strategists." Paul Barnett, CEO, Strategic Management Bureau

"a novel and very significant contribution to the strategy literature." Prof. John Brocklesby, Head of School of Management, University of Wellington

"Here, at last, is the unified field theory of strategy." Ed Straw, Director PWC Global (rtd.)

"practical in its approach, yet deep in wisdom. It is a must read… a rare combination of depth in thinking and ease of use" Prof. Jan De Visch, Flanders Business School

"a truly novel and powerful approach to working with strategy and should be required reading for, and in the toolkit of, all executives and boards of directors." Axel Kravatsky M.D. Syntegra, Vice Chair ISO Governance of Organizations

Printed in Great Britain
by Amazon